P9-AGS-207

DATE DUE

FEB 18 88

The
Explorers

·

NINETEENTH CENTURY EXPEDITIONS IN AFRICA AND THE AMERICAN WEST

·

Richard A. Van Orman

·

UNIVERSITY OF NEW MEXICO PRESS
Albuquerque

Library of Congress Cataloging in Publication Data
Van Orman, Richard A.
  The explorers : nineteenth century expeditions in
Africa and the American West.
  Bibliography: p.
  Includes index.
  1. West (U.S.)—Description and travel.   2. United
States—Exploring expeditions.   3. Explorers—West (U.S.)
—Biography—19th century.   4. Africa—Discovery and
exploration.   5. Africa—Description and travel—To 1900.
6. Explorers—Africa—Biography.   I. Title.
F591.V25   1983   978'.02   83–23413

Manufactured in the United States of America.
Library of Congress Catalog Card Number 83-23413.
International Standard Book Number 0-8263-0711-6.
First edition.

To Wade and Brenda

Contents

Illustrations

MAPS

Preface

SIGNIFICANT ADVANCES IN GEOGRAPHICAL KNOWLEDGE have occurred in only a few periods in world history. During such times, a feeling of self-confidence and pride led man to break with ancient superstitions and common cautions, aware that he was part of some larger experience. Drawn to heroic endeavors, he was compelled to bridge gaps and make discoveries.

The first period of discovery occurred with the expansion of Greece into the Mediterranean Sea in the age of Homer. Another took place during the time of Alexander's conquests in the East. The next happened in the fifteenth and sixteenth centuries when the Portuguese discovered a sea route to India and Columbus discovered America. In the eighteenth and nineteenth centuries, great geographical discoveries were made in America and Africa.

During this latter period, explorers rose to world prominence, and news of their explorations was awaited with intense interest by an expectant public. Their journals became best sellers. They were honored by geographical societies. They became national heroes. One ran for the presidency of the United States. Another was buried in Westminster Abbey.

As explorers knew few boundaries, so the student of exploration should view exploring from a broad and cross-national perspective. Great Britain and the United States were the two most active nations in nineteenth-century exploration. For these nations, foreign and domestic events served to initiate exploration. On both sides of the Atlantic, technological advances, nationalistic ardor, and revolutionary change were factors encouraging exploration.

Great Britain's and America's motivations for expansion were similar: a nationalistic need to stop other nations from acquiring land, an interest in science, and a perceived moral obligation to uplift backward peoples. Missionary fervor motivated a few explorers, such as the determined and optimistic David Livingstone, but most explored for more mundane reasons.

The result of British and American exploration was imperialism. The concept of a civilizing mission to uplift the benighted races was rationalization enough for these governments to launch their expansionistic plans. In America, this movement was euphemistically called Manifest Destiny; in Africa, it was known as the Scramble for Africa.

In this work, the emphasis has been placed on the explorer and his experience. I have used his words to capture the terrors and joys of exploration. Because of the large number of tribes involved with the explorers and my limitations in the fields of ethnology and anthropology, I have devoted less attention to the native peoples and the breakdown of their tribal cultures. The notes are set at the back of the book and take the place of a bibliography.

Sixty explorers were studied for this work, not only the most famous but also those who best represent the exploration experience. These men could be called discoverers, although many scholars would probably agree that that description should be given to those men searching for new lands in the fifteenth and sixteenth centuries. While discovery was still taking place in the nineteenth century, especially in Africa, a more accurate word for what was happening is *exploration*.

The discoverer and explorer were alike in many ways. Each possessed a passion for adventure, a need to overcome great distances and countless difficulties, and a desire for recognition. They were strangers in strange lands. But, although the explorer made discoveries, a discoverer was not necessarily an explorer. In fact, the explorer seldom went forth just to discover. A historian of American exploration, William H. Goetzmann, noted that exploration was "something more than adventure, and something more than discovery." An explorer "*seeks* discoveries." While discoveries often happened by chance, as in the case of Columbus's discovery of the New World, "exploration, by contrast, is the result of purpose or mission." Historical geographer John K. Wright noted that explorers have rarely gone out just to search for whatever they might happen to discover. "They have gone in quest of definitive objectives believed to exist on the basis of such information as could be gathered from the geographical lore of their own and earlier times."[1] Distinctions between the explorer and the discoverer were made by American historian Daniel J. Boorstin, who wrote,

The discover simply uncovers, but the explorer opens. The discoverer concludes a search; he is a finder. The explorer begins a search; he is a seeker. And he opens the way for other seekers. The discoverer is the expert at what is known to be there. The explorer is willing to take chances. He is the adventurer who risks *un*certain paths to the *un*known. Every age is inclined to give its laurels to the discoverers, those who finally arrive at the long-thought-inaccessible known destination. But posterity—the whole human community— owes its laurels to the happener-upon dark continents of the earth and of the mind. The courageous wanderer in worlds never known to be there is the explorer.[2]

I wish to thank the staff at the University of New Mexico Press, and especially my editor David V. Holtby, for their assistance. But my greatest thanks go to my wife and collaborator, Bonny, without whose help this book could not have been completed.

The
Explorers

CHAPTER ONE

The Myths

THE GREAT AGE OF DISCOVERY began in the fifteenth century, which because of economic prosperity, intellectual fermentation, and religious fervor, witnessed the greatest expansion of geographical knowledge in human history. The ships that plowed the seas were manned by Europeans who retained a youthful zest and an abiding conviction that whoever controlled the seas possessed the land.

German historian Oswald Spengler believed that the Western world possessed "a discoverer's soul," that its obstinate passion was "to *dis*-cover that which is not seen."[1] A prevalent European belief held that there was no land unknowable, nor any sea unnavigable, and that man's desire was to be, like God, everywhere.

Portugal was the first European nation to expand her geographical horizons. Because she had few natural resources and was dependent on the sea, Portugal was well placed to take the lead in exploration. The Portuguese were driven by an irresistible urge to discover, a yearning for unchartered lands and for everything unknown and dangerous.[2]

Throughout the history of discovery and exploration, the great undertakings have had their origins in the adventurous spirit of individuals. In the fifteenth century, a few outstanding men in the fields of commerce, government, and religion displayed an intense curiosity about the world and its inhabitants. These men were absorbers of information and amassers

3

of learning. Although they were often lacking in intellectual discipline and scientific training, their enduring enthusiasm for finding distant lands, along with their ability to obtain financial support, led to discovery.

The age of reconnaissance ushered in the modern period through its emphasis on empiricism and individualism and its refusal to accept ancient authority. One of the most important developments of the age was the nexus established between the new technology and the burgeoning nation-states. The emancipation of the mind was liberating men to think and to travel. The earth and sky were open to investigation. If the dark continents lured explorers, so too did the bright heavens.

Among the subjects revolutionized by this enthusiasm for man and his environment were the inner and outer worlds of anatomy and geography. The revolution in the study of anatomy was brought about through an intense desire to explore the interior of the human body. Consequently, more autopsies were performed and valuable contributions were made to the field of anatomy. Andreas Vesalius, a sixteenth-century Flemish anatomist and the acknowledged father of modern anatomy, attended executions in order to study the human body. His findings, published in 1543 and based on hundreds of autopsies, questioned some of the physiological ideas of the second-century Greek physician Galen.

Just as the Greeks had made the first important studies of the interior of the human body, so they were the first to study geography. Thales of Miletus, Eratosthenes of Cyrene, and Ptolemy of Alexandria were among the earliest geographers. What errors these men made were corrected by Copernicus's heliocentric system and the Portuguese voyages initiated by Prince Henry the Navigator.

Prince Henry, son of King John I of the House of Aviz, was the first great patron of discovery. From his geographical research institute on the southwest coast of Portugal at Cape St. Vincent, he directed Portuguese ships to the west and to the south. Between 1420 and his death forty years later, he maintained an alliance of cartographers, sailors, astronomers, and shipbuilders. Larger and improved ships were built for the extensive voyages that Henry launched. These slow but sea-worthy caravels were lateen-rigged with two or three masts. Besides supplying ships and money, Henry instructed his captains in improved methods of navigation as he sent them to discover new worlds.

At Sagres in southwestern Portugal, the prince built an astronomical observatory and library where Moorish, Jewish, German, and Italian scholars debated such questions as whether the equatorial regions were inhabitable and what was the size of the earth. Was it as Eratosthenes or as Marinus of Tyre estimated?

Henry's practical objectives of geographical discovery and increased trade, combined with his religious goal of forming a Christian coalition with the legendary priest-king Prester John, inspired the heroic Renaissance voyages of discovery. His constant dream was to find fertile lands, amass great wealth, and serve God. Influenced by his horoscope—which predicted he would do grand and exalted deeds—he sent out the first naval explorations to West Africa to determine what lay south of the dreaded Cape Bojador.[3] A prevailing superstition was that any Christian who passed the cape would be cursed by God and turned black for his insolent curiosity. In 1434, the Portuguese captain Gil Eannes rounded Bojador, urged on by Henry's maxim, "You cannot find a peril so great that the hope of reward will not be greater." But what kind of reward? A haunting contradiction developed between dream and reality when, in the following decades, hundreds of African slaves were shipped to Lisbon, even though Henry had encouraged his sailors in exploration rather than in the exploitation of the natives.

Henry looms as a giant in the age of discovery. He combined the dedication of a monk with the daring of a sailor. For the first time in history, a global policy was defined, and reconnaissance became a national goal. Henry made the search for the unknown both a science and an art; he systematized an ongoing plan for exploring and developed a grand strategy for exploration. On that windy promontory at Sagres, a new paradigm of world geography was established when Henry and a few others learned to see the earth differently. The belief up to that time, for example, had been that the best way to return to Portugal from the west coast of Africa was to sail north along the coast, but captains of Portuguese caravels recognized that it was easier to sail westward to catch the favorable south winds for their return voyage.

The impetus Henry had given to discovery continued even after his death. The famed mariners Bartholomew Dias, Christopher Columbus, Vasco da Gama, and Ferdinand Magellan continued Henry's work. But they required more than a noble spirit and firm determination: they needed the financial backing of governments and adventurous capitalists, improvements in astronomy and mapmaking, and more seaworthy and maneuverable ships outfitted with more sophisticated weapons.[4]

Aided by the technological developments of the cross-staff, astrolabe, lateen caravel, and ship-borne artillery, discoverers completed the charting of most of the continents and revealed much of the populated world. By the beginning of the eighteenth century, Europeans had founded settlements on all of the continents except Australia and Antarctica. In the process, they spread European culture over the globe, expanded geographical knowledge at an unprecedented rate, and returned with exotic tales of aborigines and their environments.

Discovery launched a revolution. Contacts were made among the world's populations, and goods and ideas as well as people were traded across the seas. The transplantation of indigenes to reservations and blacks to New World plantations were displacements that wrought havoc with the biological world and social justice and set in motion the four-hundred-year decline and fall of hundreds of native civilizations.

In response to the information brought back by the discoverers, Europeans developed new methodologies in which ancient geographical errors were corrected, cross-cultural comparisons were made, and new interpretations of man and his environment were presented.

During the age of reconnaissance, the discoverers were still men of the Middle Ages; devotedly religious, they described the new lands in biblical terms such as the lost Garden of Eden and the four rivers of paradise. These myths reveal that in ancient times heaven was said to be near earth, and one could enter paradise by finding a special tree, mountain, or river. Since those happy days, a wrenching physical separation had taken place, yet the yearning to locate paradise on earth persisted. This quest, whether undertaken by mystic or discoverer, was equivalent to a return to the beginning of time, before history, before the Fall, to what religious anthropologist Mircea Eliade referred to as the "Great Time."

The religious fervor of Columbus led him to search up the Orinoco River for the site of the earthly paradise. Prussian scientist and world traveler Alexander von Humboldt, traveling that river almost to its source in 1799, found another kind of earthly paradise when he collected sixteen hundred plants and discovered six hundred new species within a few months' time.

These world discoverers accorded an eschatological implication to geographical discovery. Columbus was among the last of the medieval travelers. Like the Venerable Bede, Columbus believed that the earth was pear-shaped and anatomically formed like a woman's breast, with the terrestrial paradise glittering at its summit. It was all so near heaven. This spiritual heir of Marco Polo was convinced on his third voyage to the New World that he had located paradise and the four rivers of the Book of Genesis that flowed from the tree of life: ". . . and Lord God planted a garden eastward in Eden." With his discovery of this holy site, the mystical Genoese navigator dreamed of outfitting an army of a hundred thousand foot soldiers and a ten-thousand-man cavalry force to recapture the Holy Sepulcher from the infidel Turk.[5] According to Columbus, this military campaign, along with the opening up of the New World by the Spanish and the conversion of the natives to Catholicism, was a prelude to the Second Coming of Christ.

The Florentine geographer Amerigo Vespucci, enthralled by the glories of the New World, imagined that he would discover the earthly paradise in South America. Upon finding an infinite variety of strange animals and plants there, the ambitious Italian wanderer was convinced that paradise was near—until he encountered a Guaraní Indian who had eaten over two hundred people.[6]

Francisco Vásquez de Coronado's costly search for the Seven Cities of Gold and Juan Ponce de León's delusive goal of finding the rejuvenating waters of the Fountain of Youth on the isle of Bimini are evidence of the influence that the religiosity of the Middle Ages and the romances of chivalry had had on the discoverers. Men have searched for the happy, hidden other world since the pristine days of Homer, relying on Old World myths in their pursuit of paradise in the West. By sailing westward, man would improve his condition. Bishop George Berkeley predicted that the future of mankind was to the west, where nature's gifts were abundant, happiness was guaranteed, and death took a holiday:

> Westward the course of empire takes its way;
> The four first Acts already past,
> A fifth shall close the Drama with the Day;
> Time's noblest offspring is the last.

If the explorer's heart was pure and he said his prayers at night, he would discover the earthly paradise. Before his ship, the *Squirrel,* slipped under the waves off the Azores, the English navigator Sir Humphrey Gilbert exclaimed, "We are as neere to heaven by sea as by land." These celestial fancies are reminiscent of the story told by Homer in *The Odyssey* in which the sea god Proteus tells King Menelaus that he is to be sent to the Elysian plain at the edge of the world where neither rain nor snow falls, nor great winds howl, "but day after day the West Wind's tuneful breeze comes in from Ocean to refresh its folk."[7]

Tales of El Dorado and Prester John were seductive legends of the age, and, no matter how outrageous, they inspired expeditions. The legend of El Dorado or the Gilded One concerned the ritual of a South American tribe, the Chibcha. Each new chief was covered with resin, powdered with gold dust, and immersed in the sacred Lake Guatavita to be purified or drown. Depending on the account, El Dorado was a king who performed this ritual annually, monthly, or weekly; in one version, the ruler was coated with gold dust and pushed into the lake every day. This legend served to strengthen the belief that fabulous riches were to be found in the New World. Among those drawn westward by this tale were the *conquistadores* Gonzalo Pizarro and Antonio de Berrío and the English explorer Sir Walter Raleigh, who searched for El Dorado in the Orinoco basin.[8]

The legend of Prester John was first mentioned in the twelfth-century chronicle of Otto of Freising and became one of the most exotic and enduring geographical myths. John was thought to be a Nestorian priest who had defeated a large Persian army and ruled over a vast, rich realm in either western Asia or northern Africa. Confusion was so great regarding the location of John's kingdom that Columbus thought he had tracked it down in Cuba.[9] The mists of geographical confusion were lifted when Ethiopia was said to be the site. His domain was described as a desert—with a difference: no poisonous scorpions, croaking frogs, or slithering snakes dwelt therein.[10] In his kingdom were harmony and unity, in contrast to the political upheavals and social discord of Europe, and through it flowed one of the four rivers that rose out of the terrestrial paradise.[11] The tale took on a deeper, religious significance when John was reported to be a descendant of one of the Three Wise Men.

In 1165, a letter appeared which was purportedly written by Prester John to Manual I, emperor of Byzantium. The missive, from the "king of kings and lord of lords," described John's great wealth and his immense emerald table at which thirty thousand people could dine. This table possessed such miraculous powers that no one seated there could become intoxicated. John boasted that his Christian land was inhabited by Amazons and contained the Fountain of Youth, precious stones, and a magnificent castle which housed his bed of sapphire.[12]

When John went to war, he was supported by a force of a hundred thousand cavalrymen and one million foot soldiers. His army was preceded by thirteen men carrying large crosses made of rubies and gold. John's personal cupbearer was both king and archbishop, and his master of horse was an abbot and king; but, even with such exalted aides, because of John's Christian humility he would not allow anyone to call him anything but Prester or Priest. For four hundred years, finding Prester John was one of the world's will-o'-the wisps.[13]

Another enduring tale was that of the Amazon women who were supposedly found in Asia Minor and at the siege of Troy. Sir John Mandeville and Marco Polo related stories of the Amazons' conquests, both military and sexual. The myth of the Amazons was of special importance in Latin America after Columbus, Juan de Grijalva, and Hernán Cortés moved the myth westward to that new world. In his *Fourth Dispatch* to Charles I, king of Spain, in 1524, Cortés wrote that he had learned from one of his captains of an island south of Panama inhabited solely by women where only the female babies were allowed to survive.

In the 1540s, Gonzalo Pizarro, youngest of the five dauntless Pizarro brothers, organized an expedition of two hundred twenty Spaniards and four thousand Indians to search for the land of the cinnamon in the lush forests east of the Andes. The Spanish conquistador Francisco de Orellana and sixty men became separated from Pizarro and traveled along a river on whose banks they encountered women who impressed them with their fighting skills. Orellana named the river the Amazon.[14]

In the kingdom of Dahomey in West Africa, the Fon tribe had a powerful army with a contingent of twenty-five hundred Amazons. In the 1860s, Richard F. Burton, the famed British explorer, traveled to Dahomey in search of the Amazons, only to discover that these women, unlike those of Greek legend, were old and ugly; "an equal number of British charwomen, armed with the British broomstick, would . . . clear them off in a very few hours."[15]

But it was reports of gold that lured men, not tales of female warriors. Europeans, who found their gold supplies decreasing, were drawn to Africa by dreams of discovering King Solomon's mines and Ophir, the wealth of the Gold Coast, and the gold mines of the Sudan, Bure, and Bambuk. Even Shakespeare's Pistol spoke of "Africa and golden joys."[16] But all too often the treasure-hunters faced the disappointment of having to accept the baser commodities of ivory, hides, and "black gold," or slaves.

Two strongly held views concerning gold served to stimulate European exploration of the African interior. One was the bullionist view that gold was a superior medium of exchange; the other was that western technology would greatly increase African mineral production.

One of the most persistent tales about Africa dealt with the golden city of Timbuktu. Located near the most northerly point of the Niger River in the prosperous empire of Songhai, the city was the terminus of important trans-Saharan commercial routes. The traders at Timbuktu served as middlemen between the merchants of North Africa and those of the western Sudan. Founded around 1200 by the fierce Tuareg as a summer encampment, Timbuktu became an important sub-Saharan metropolis. A dramatic description of the city in *The History and Description of Africa,* written by the Moorish traveler and geographer Leo Africanus and published in 1550, conjured up images of the most exciting of African cities and was a major factor in drawing explorers to Timbuktu. To be the first European to reach Timbuktu, to see its magnificent mosques and colorful markets, was a wish for which some explorers would lay down their lives. A Portuguese expedition arrived in the city in 1487, but disenchantment rather than visions of splendor greeted them. The young French explorer René Caillié, who reached the mysterious city in 1828, saw nothing but "a mass of ill-looking houses, built of earth."[17] Nevertheless, for four hundred years its supposed grandeur enticed adventurers. Alfred Tennyson succinctly captured the persistent lure of Timbuktu.

> Deep in that lion-haunted inland lies
> A mystick city, goal of high emprise.[18]

The promise of precious metals was also a spur to exploration on the American continent. In Nueva Viscaya (northern Mexico), the rich mines of Zacatecas and San Luis Potosí were discovered in the 1540s and 1550s. Tales of the Seven Cities of Gold compelled Coronado to push his *entrada de conquista* northward across the *despoblado* into the American Southwest, marching to the Indian refrain of *poco más allá.* Others searched for an *otro México,* the golden city of Manoa, and the City of the Caesars in forbidding Patagonia. Some would hear the siren call of the lake of Copala and the land of Teguayo. These legends persisted for decades, gradually decreasing in importance as the superstitions of the Middle Ages clashed with the geographical knowledge gathered during the age of enlightenment.

CHAPTER TWO

The Natives

LIKE THE LURE OF DISTANT cities, the discoverers' accounts of aborigines were to leave lasting impressions on the Western world. Naturally, the first observations of African and American natives emphasized those characteristics that clearly distinguished them from Europeans, for, as Dutch scholar Henri Baudet noted, the Europeans were in part searching for their lost past in distant lands. Baudet explained that westerners viewed the nonwestern world through their own imagination, through "images derived not from observation, experience, and perceptible reality but from a psychological urge." Their image of the native was based on their own sense of inadequacy and nostalgia.[1]

According to Rousseau, who had never visited a Sioux camp or Zulu kraal, the explorer in a sense was returning to the beginning of time, reverting to the mythical days of a lost paradise; in banishing time, he entered man's primordial state. Expecting to meet a wise and virtuous native, the explorer was not always prepared for what he did meet.

Influenced by Christopher Columbus's account of the guileless and loving Arawak, the earliest descriptions of the Native American were usually favorable. The Arawak, who occupied islands in the West Indies, were all but exterminated by the Spanish. Giovanni da Verrazano, Jacques Cartier, and Alvar Núñez Cabeza de Vaca remarked on the aid and hospitality they had received from the natives. Their favorable impres-

13

sion was closely tied to the European association of the new land with the Garden of Eden and the terrestrial paradise, and was further strengthened by the European's need for native trade and succor.

Using explorers' accounts, writers of fiction created the idealized primitive, or, in the words of the English poet John Dryden, "the noble savage."[2] Disheartened by wars, crime, and poverty in their own lands, Europeans praised "the poor Indian, whose untutored mind sees God in clouds, or hears him in the wind."[3]

In the literature of New World exploration, a common theme was that of the innocent and loving native as the antithesis of the corrupt and malevolent European. This Arcadian concept can be traced to the Golden Age of Greece, the treatise on the German tribes by the Roman historian Tacitus, and utopian idealism.

Utopianism played an important role in European literature in the seventeenth and eighteenth centuries. In 1688, English writer Aphra Behn published a philosophical novel *Oroonoko: or, The Royal Slave,* the material for which she gathered from stories that she heard while living in Surinam. A free spirit herself, Behn pictured America as a happy haven, untouched by wicked Europe, where the natives lived in a state of fetching innocence before the whites arrived and taught them how to sin. In her paean to nature, Behn mused that nature was clearly "the most harmless, inoffensive and virtuous Mistress. 'Tis she alone, if she were permitted, that better instructs the World, than all the Inventions of Man."[4]

In his satiric essay "Of Cannibals," Michel de Montaigne evoked the image of blissful Brazilian natives *fresh from the hands of the gods.*[5] The French essayist viewed their cannibalism as a peccadillo compared to their bravery in war and their devotion to family. Although they practiced polygamy, there was little jealousy among them and Montaigne found a great deal in their family life to recommend to Europeans.[6] If his praise of the natives was too lavish, he balanced it by saying, "But they don't wear pants."

Even the practical Thomas Jefferson waxed lyrical over certain characteristics of the American Indian: "They astonish you with strokes of the most sublime oratory; such as prove their reason and sentiment strong, their imagination glowing and elevated."[7] He became rhapsodic over a speech by Logan, chief of the Cayuga, considering it superior to the orations of Demosthenes and Cicero.[8]

While the image of the noble savage was being created by travelers and literati, a counterimage, that of the ignoble savage, was also presented. Unfavorable descriptions of the Native American became more and more common as the Indian was depicted as a bloodthirsty savage. Based on religious differences, racial prejudice, and the atrocities of wilderness warfare, this perception of the Indian grew during the Revolutionary War; military and moral defenses might not be strong enough to ward off the penetration of savage warriors. A student of the concept of "savagism" noted that the native was important to the British mind not for what he represented "but rather for what he showed civilized men they were not and must not be";[9] thus there was an increased emphasis on cannibalism, infanticide, and torture in literary works and explorers' accounts.

Not only were these negative images of the indigenous American based upon violent confrontations between whites and natives, but the British were quick to compare the wild Indians to the wild Irish in order to justify aggression, thus demonstrating the inclination to build relationships with the natives on naive formulas and erroneous impressions. The prevalence of these unfavorable impressions was largely predicated upon the need to deny the natives their humanity in order to rationalize the taking of their land. According to frontier logic, by being labeled both a savage and a pagan the native was disqualified from possessing land and thereby became ripe for removal and even extermination.[10]

An anatomical assault on the native was launched in page after page of travelers' accounts. Lengthy descriptions were devoted to the size of his ears and eyes, the texture of his hair, and his nakedness. A sixteenth-century friar-explorer noted that it was not enough for the Brazilian Indians "to be naked, to paint their bodies, to scratch and pluck of their harie, but also for to make themselves more disformed, they pearche their mouthes being young . . . and place a stone in it."[11]

The earliest European accounts of Africans emphasized their exotic and savage ways, making the gap between primitive and civilized peoples appear unbridgeable. The Greek historian Herodotus revealed his racial bias toward the Africans by calling them "barbarians," comparing their habits to animals', and emphasizing their strange sexual practices. He described the Libyans as "dog-headed men, headless men with eyes in their breasts."[12] A Sicilian wrote in his world history that the Ethiopians were "entirely savage and display the nature of a wild beast." Pliny the Elder, a Roman naturalist, described the Goat-pens, Satyrs, and Blemmyes, who had no heads.[13]

To these writers, the Africans were not only uncivilized but totally without redeeming virtues. They even murdered their sick and aged. Like the Indian, they were believed to be warlike, lawless, and sexually promiscuous. After reports appeared of African women cohabiting with orangutans, they were thought by some Europeans to be related to anthropoid apes. Thomas Jefferson claimed that the orangutan lusted after black women in the same way that black men desired white women.

Besides bestiality and cannibalism, the trait most commonly used to degrade the African was his color. This was especially true of the West African with his Negroid features—the eversible lips and broad nose. When comparisons were made, the physical characteristics of the Hamitic and Nilotic peoples were considered superior to those of the West Africans.[14] For Europeans, blackness carried connotations of baseness, filth, and the devil, just as whiteness connoted goodness, cleanliness, and God. Comments were made about the "rank offensive smell" of blacks. A sixteenth-century German cosmographer used race, sex, and physical appearance to degrade the people of Zanzibar. "They are all blacke and goe naked, onely covering theyr pryvie partes. . . . Theyr women are deformed by reason of theyr greate eyes, greate mouthes, and greate nosethrilles."[15] Extraordinary ideas were offered to explain Africans' dark pigmentation. Some thought blacks had been exposed to the sun too long. Others said it was due to blood fluids in their bodies. Some Europeans believed that the color of the African's skin could be traced to the biblical story of Ham, a son of Noah, who, upon seeing his father naked, was cursed by God.[16]

Montaigne cautioned the European against being tempted to give "the title of barbarism to everything that is not according to his usage" and pointed out a basic flaw in travel literature:

We need topographers to make a detailed account for us of the places where they have been. But by having this advantage over us of having seen the Holy Land, they want to have the privilege of telling us stories of new things from all the rest of the world . . . such a person may have some particular knowledge and experience of the nature of a river or of a spring, who as to other things knows no more than what everybody does. Yet to make this little fragment circulate, he will undertake to write the whole body of physics.[17]

In the eighteenth century, a new humanitarianism appeared in Europe. Predicated in part on the principle of political toleration and the demands of social justice, this new spirit produced a more favorable view of native peoples. Not only were explorers better informed and reporting more accurately, they were also more involved with native societies and cultures. Among those breaking new ground in reappraising the African was a seventeenth-century Dutch traveler who had spent time with the Hottentots in South Africa. In a letter to a European friend he stated that he was surprised that "those half-truths that are spread about our Africans should have reached even your ears." He found the Africans hospitable, truthful, and dependable, possessing "a rare nimbleness of mother wit, and having minds receptive of instruction."[18]

This new humanitarianism was seen not only in the accounts of scientists such as Anders Sparrman and François Le Vaillant, who traveled in Africa in the 1780s, but also in the more sympathetic pictures of Africans presented by explorers. Both scientist and explorer were more objective and better trained, and tended less toward hyperbole and prevarication than their earlier counterparts. A student of African exploration noted that by the eighteenth century the Europeans in Africa began to be guided "by justice, benevolence and the desire of knowledge, instead of avarice and ambition."[19] The characteristics of the African now emphasized were his freedom, bravery, and hospitality.

James Bruce, the Scottish laird-turned-explorer, recounted how he was received with civility by the royal court of Ethiopia and was even chosen to head a cavalry regiment. Another Scottish explorer, Dixon Denham, stated that, because the British knew little of the Africans, they regarded them as naked savages, but he maintained that they were religious, civilized, and kind.[20]

The youthful Scotsman Mungo Park gave up his medical practice to go exploring in Africa because he had "a passionate desire to examine into the productions of a country so little known, and to become experimentally acquainted with the modes of life and character of the natives." Park was a proponent of the unity of mankind and an amateur social anthropologist; the latter discipline was useful in his observation that the looms used by the Mandingos were similar to those used by Europeans. Even after the natives stole Park's possessions in his first African expedition he remembered their many kindnesses, for he believed that they stole because of the exotic nature of the travelers' belongings rather than from any inherent trait: "The wonder would be, not that the stranger was robbed of any part of his riches, but that any part was left for a second depredator." Park wondered whether the poorer classes of Europe would have been as considerate to a stranger in a similar situation.[21] Park's favorable attitude toward the native was strengthened when he camped near a small village and was without food and lodging for the night. A strong wind came up as darkness approached and Park resigned himself to spending the night in a tree when a native woman, noting his predicament, invited him into her home.[22]

The devotion shown Scottish missionary David Livingstone

by his African servants after his death was demonstrated by the methodical manner in which they prepared his body for shipment to England: they removed the intestines and internal organs, salted the cadaver, and set it in the sun to dry for two weeks. When it was desiccated, they washed his face with brandy, wrapped the body in calico, and put it in the bark of a tree. His servants and sixty other natives then carried the body for five months through dangerous country to the east coast of Africa for shipment home and burial in Westminster Abbey.[23]

Similarly native Americans were usually hospitable to explorers; indeed, Indians often offered white strangers food, lodging, and their women. In fact, the men of the Mandan tribe became angry when Canadian explorer Alexander Henry the Younger refused the sexual favors of their women and daughters, one of whom was nine years old.[24]

William Clark criticized the Sioux and Arikara custom of giving "handsom squars to those whome they wish to Show some acknowledgements to." He was embarrassed when two Arikara women followed the Lewis and Clark party to their camp and "pursisted in their civilities."[25] At their next camp, the explorers learned that Arikara women were "verry fond of carressing our men &c."[26] On entering Mandan country, the explorers found that Mandan women were as friendly if not as brazen as the Arikara.[27] Sexual relations were common between the men of the Lewis and Clark expedition and these "tawney damsels," and the large number of "venereal complaints" from their men prompted Lewis and Clark to bemoan native sexual promiscuity.[28]

Clark's slave York was especially popular with the Indians because of his color. A Hidatsa chief believed that York was a painted white man and tried to rub off the black. Taking advantage of his notoriety, York told the Indians that he had been as wild as a bear until tamed by Clark. An Indian at an Arikara village was so impressed with York's color that he gave his squaw to York and even guarded the entrance to his earthen lodge while York and the squaw frolicked inside. York's popularity with Indian women was such that for years his offspring were found among tribes from the Missouri River to the Pacific Ocean.[29]

Some Indian women dressed in a manner that elicited negative comments from explorers. Alexander Henry was shocked by the Chinook women's lack of modesty, as was another explorer who noted that, in a wind "or when indulging their favourite position of squatting, (the clothing) formed a miserable shield in defence of decency. . . ."[30] Describing one tribe, North West Company explorer Alexander Mackenzie commented on the clean appearance of the men and the filthiness of their women.[31] Gabriel Franchère, who clerked for John Jacob Astor's Pacific Fur Company, observed,

The Indian men go entirely naked, not concealing any part of their bodies, not even the genitals. . . . Besides the cape, women wear a kind of skirt or petticoat, made of cedar bark which they hang around their waists and which comes to the middle of their thighs. . . . With such a wretched garment they manage to hide the private parts.[32]

Explorers usually generalized in describing the natives, but they were more specific when discussing tribal differences: the Plains tribes were considered superior in appearance to those of the Pacific Coast, and an explorer for the Hudson's Bay Company pointed out disparities between the Eskimos and his party of Indians.

The slender, agile figure of the latter was strikingly contrasted with the square, rugged forms of these natives of the sea. It seemed as if . . . I had together before me descendants of the nomadic Tartar and the sea-roving Scandinavian, two of the most dissimilar and widely separate races of the ancient world.[33]

Distinctions were common between Indian tribes based on location. The climate of an area played an important role in the development of native characteristics in this geographical determinism. Philip Turnor, who was a surveyor for the Hudson's Bay Company, believed that the farther north one went, the more peaceful the Indians. Another geographical determinist, the Welsh explorer John Evans, who searched for the "white" Indians, believed that the tribes who lacked "knowledge of the whites (being yet in a state of nature) were of a softer and better character, whilst those who had frequent communications with the whites appeared to have contracted their vices without having taken any of their virtues." Alexander Ross, a Canadian fur trader and clerk, noted the baleful effects of the white man upon the Indian: as soon as the native took up the white man's ways, "like a wild animal in a cage, his lustre is gone."[34]

Explorers favored certain tribes. Lewis and Clark and Canadian fur trader Peter Skene Ogden were impressed by the courtesy and physical appearance of the Nez Perce, Shoshoni, and Flatheads, and by the aid they offered. There was also general agreement among explorers concerning those tribes they disliked. The Arikara were considered among the worst because of their attempts at extortion, attacks upon fur trappers, and loose sexual mores. American soldier-explorer John Charles Frémont was disgusted with the Digger Indians of the Great Basin: "Roots, seeds, and grass, every vegetable that affords any nourishment, and every living animal thing, insect or worm, they eat. Nearly approaching to the lower animal creation, their sole employment is to obtain food. . . ."[35] The Pathfinder assailed their "expression of countenance resembling that in a beast of prey; and all their actions are those of wild animals. Joined to the restless motion of the eye, there is a want of mind—an absence of thought—and an action wholly by impulse. . . ."[36]

A persistent image of the Indian was that he was an expert guide with an unfailing sense of direction; typical of this attitude was this description of his guide by an explorer:

He never sees a place once without instantly recognizing it on seeing it the second time, notwithstanding he may approach it from a different direction; and the very moment he takes a glance over a district of country he has never seen before, he will almost invariably point out the particular localities (if there are any such) where water can be found, where to others there seems to be nothing to indicate it.[37]

On the other hand some explorers were accompanied by incompetent native guides who on occasion deserted them or became lost. The calculation of distance was another problem for the explorers, because the natives measured it not in miles but according to the time it took to get from one place to another. Canadian explorer Simon Fraser called one of his guides "a damned blockhead,"[38] and Mackenzie described a tribe as "ignorant of the space in which they have been inhabitants of the earth. . . ."[39]

Another point of contention among explorers was whether the Indian was a peerless hunter. Alexander Henry remarked on the ability of the Ojibwa to track game by following signs that no white man could see,[40] but the governor of the Hudson's Bay Company, George Simpson, contended that Indians were terrible hunters.[41] In fact, the Indian was often a poor shot with a rifle. Fraser complained that "instead of feeding us we have been obliged to provide for them,"[42] and in his account of the Chipewyan Mackenzie wrote, "They are not remarkable for their activity as hunters."[43]

An ambivalence toward the natives is evident in the journals of Lewis and Clark. Favorable comments concerning the Shoshoni interpreter Sacajawea and the honesty of the Shoshoni were placed side by side with graphic descriptions of their eating habits: "It was indeed impossible to see these wretches ravenously feeding on the filth of animals, the blood streaming from their mouths, without deploring how nearly the condition of savages approaches that of the brute creation."[44] This duality of view stemmed partly from the long-held idea that the Indian was either a noble savage or a child of the devil. The noble savage was a free being who possessed natural skills that civilized man did not have; indeed, a criticism of civilization was inherent in this romantic image.

American explorers admired the natives' charm and their strange and exciting way of life more than did African explorers. Alexander Ross pointed to the good life enjoyed by the Indians of the Northwest, a way of life "which civilized men, wearied with care and anxious pursuits, perhaps seldom enjoy."[45] At a Sioux encampment on the Missouri River,

American explorer Jedediah Strong Smith lamented that such a life would "almost persuade a man to renounce the world, take the lodge and live the careless, Lazy life. . . ."[46] Peter Skene Ogden cut through these romantic exaggerations when he observed, "Every Indian is not a hero, nor every female a Penelope."[47]

If the white man's views of the Indian were sometimes in conflict, the explorer's image of himself had to be clear and consistent. "On all occasions," an experienced American frontiersman advised a young British explorer, "be reserved with your detachment as well as with the savages; always give to your conduct the air of importance. . . ."[48] An Indian, who was curious as to why Mackenzie was interested in finding out about the West, asked him, "Do not you white men know every thing in the world?" Mackenzie responded that indeed whites know a great deal about the world, but that there were a few gaps the natives could fill in. "Thus I fortunately preserved the impression in their minds, of the superiority of white people over themselves." Thomas Fitzpatrick, a well-known American mountain man and guide, was concerned with maintaining his dignity and believed that the best guidelines for dealing with the natives were the "rules of decorum which govern a gentleman in a civilized society. . . ."[49]

Explorers regarded their race, civilization, and religion as unquestionably superior to the native's, for the native was without technology, culture, and a work ethic. The whites believed that they were destined to open those barbarous lands to settlement and thereby uplift the natives. On Livingstone's homecoming from Africa in the 1850s, a British newspaper effused that throughout Britain there was "a thrill of exultation at the thought that, literally, the whole earth is full of our labours—that there is no region in which our industrial enterprise, our skill in arms, our benevolent eagerness to diffuse the blessings of civilization and pure and true religion, have not been displayed."[50]

Ethnocentrism was clearly evident in American and British explorers, who viewed the natives with a smug sense of self-righteousness. On the great chain of being, they placed Caucasians at the top, Orientals next, then the Indians, and on the bottom rung the Africans. They considered the Hottentots the lowest form of humankind, next to the anthropoid apes, and their language was labeled gibberish. They were never idealized as were the warlike Masai, Zulu, and Makololo.[51]

Not only were African explorers culturally biased, some were outright racist. They considered the Africans childlike because of their love of freedom and singing and dancing; they could not even control their passions. British explorer John H. Speke believed that East Africans exhibited no cultural advancement. He considered them hideously ugly and compared them to monkeys. To Speke, they were impulsive and happy children. The British traveler Richard F. Burton also considered Africans puerile. He described them as belonging "to one of those childish races which, never rising to man's estate, fall like worn-out links from the great chain of animated nature." This Renaissance man considered blacks "a futile race of barbarians, drunken and immoral; cowardly and destructive; boisterous and loquacious; indolent, greedy, and thriftless." Burton further believed that the coastal Africans were weaker and more degenerate than those of the interior and that they had picked up more vices than virtues from the Europeans and would soon die out.[52]

In the mid-nineteenth century, smallpox and syphilis were rampant in Africa. A smallpox epidemic in 1864 killed thousands of natives on the West Coast. Twenty years later, epidemics swept through the kingdom of Buganda. The Eshira tribe blamed American explorer Paul Du Chaillu for the spread of smallpox among them. Besides introducing diseases, Europeans sold alcohol to the natives which brought disruption and death, especially along the Gabon River where there were extensive trade contacts.[53]

Samuel W. Baker, who was influenced by the class and race prejudices of his father, a wealthy English businessman, said that the Africans were not only lazy but "mere apes," "contemptible dogs," and "naked brutes." He felt that their lack of a work incentive was typical of natives who lived in hot, humid climates. Believing his countrymen were *Herrenvolk*, Baker thought that the Africans had no history and were so inferior that there was no hope of civilizing them. To him, the people along the Nile River were not even bright enough to be superstitious. Their minds were "as stagnant as the morass which flows its puny world." This Victorian nabob felt that they were useful as slaves, but freed they would become a burden to society; the black would become "a plotter and intriguer, imbued with a deadly hatred to the white man. . . ." Baker further believed that evidence of African inferiority lay in the fact that Asians had domesticated the elephant and Africans had not.

Baker asserted that, because the Africans loved music, the safest way to explore "would be to play the cornet, if possible without ceasing, which would insure a safe passage. A London organ-grinder would march through Central Africa followed by an admiring and enthusiastic crowd, who, if his tunes were lively, would form a dancing escort of the most untiring material." Baker's constant dread—reminiscent of white fears in the American South—was that his young mistress might fall into the hands of the "savages." One chief raised Baker's anger to the boiling point when he suggested that Baker's mistress remain with him while Baker went exploring. Baker became so enraged by what he took to be a sexual innuendo that he drew his gun and pointed it at the insolent native. Clearly and succinctly Baker told the chief that, if he made that suggestion again, he would kill him. That ended the matter once and for all.[54]

Even the tolerant Livingstone, who sought to avoid fights with the Africans, became enraged when he contemplated rape: "Our blood boils at the very thought of our wives, daughters, or sisters being touched—we, as men with human feelings, would unhesitatingly fight to the death, with all the fury in our power."[55]

Favorable comments were likewise made about Africans, especially concerning their fighting abilities and appearance. Besides praising the Waheke and M'henge tribes of East Africa, explorer Joseph Thomson admired the independence and toughness of the Masai; but toward other Africans such as the Berbers of Morocco he showed disdain. Generally, weak tribes were held in contempt while strong tribes were admired. Anglo-American explorer Henry M. Stanley compared the warlike Masai favorably with the Comanche and Apache. Burton liked the Fon of Dahomey because of their light complexion and fine features; to him, they were almost European in appearance. Baker and the British explorer-administrator Harry H. Johnston felt that most Africans were indolent and childlike, but they were both taken with the Galla tribe. The bellicose Wataveta and Wankonde were admired by Thomson and Johnston because of the Arcadian state in which they lived.[56]

Believing that through God's love the world was progressing toward a golden age, Livingstone was certain that the African, although childlike, was capable of being elevated culturally through religion and trade, as were the poor in Britain. He optimistically believed that trade would be important to the African because it soon "demolishes that sense of isolation which heathenism engenders, and makes the tribes feel themselves mutually dependent. . . ."[57] Thus, through his exploring and being "a fellow worker with God," he hoped to discover a highway into Central Africa by which traders, missionaries, and colonists would travel, spreading Christianity and civilization through trade.

To redeem the Africans, Livingstone organized the costly and ill-fated Zambezi expedition in the 1850s which was supposed to intertwine the twin pioneers of civilization—Christianity and commerce—in the Zambezi Basin. To one of the members of the expedition, Livingstone expressed his belief that the Anglo-American race was the hope for the world's future:

We come among them as members of a superior race and servants of a Government that desires to elevate the more degraded portions of the human family. We are adherents of a benign holy religion and may by consistent conduct and wise patient efforts become the harbingers of peace to a hitherto distracted and trodden down race.

Livingstone believed that he could improve the condition of the African and the poor in Britain by supporting a plan for the immigration of thousands of poverty-stricken people from the British Isles to Central Africa.

In the 1850s Burton noted that the cry from England concerning Africa was "Cotton, Civilization, and Christianity," spurring Englishmen to the center of tropical Africa as well as to the distant corners of the globe. Joseph Thomson remarked that those three words became magical incantations, giving the Western world rights and privileges under which almost every kind of destruction and disruption could be carried out.[58]

The connection between exploration and capitalism became increasingly obvious. Commercial geographical societies were established in many European countries to further the West's economic opportunities in Africa. Explorers in Africa became agents for commercial companies, sent out more to sign trade agreements with the natives than to discover rivers.

Like their American counterparts, British explorers found native men less repugnant than the women. Indeed, Livingstone found African males handsome: "Many of the men have as beautiful heads as one could find in an assembly of Europeans." He never saw a beautiful African woman but did find some who had "fine, small, well-formed features," even though they filed their teeth, which made their smiles resemble those of crocodiles.[59] Two means of strengthening an African peace were marrying a woman of another tribe and drinking human blood; Livingstone would have preferred the latter. He believed that beauty came with civilization as ugliness came with exposure to the elements.[60]

These negative views of native women were given credence in Britain through the published works of the explorers. Burton, recalling a Spanish proverb—"English women should be seen at the window, the French woman on the promenade, and the Spanish woman everywhere"—added that African women "should be seen nowhere, or in the dark." He described the black's facial angle as "quasigorillahood" and maintained that Africans would not eat ape because of its physical resemblance to them. Scottish explorer Hugh Clapperton believed that women were the same the world over in one respect: government could check the evil ways of human nature, "but it is beyond the power even of African despotism to silence a woman's tongue: in sickness and in health, and at every stage, we have been obliged to endure their eternal loquacity and noise."[61]

The arrival of the white man was always an exciting event in Africa, and the natives brought friends and family to see and touch him. But they often wondered why the white stranger was always searching for a lake or river. The chief of the Latooka tribe asked Baker, "Suppose you get to the great lakes, what will you do with it? What will be the good of it? If you find that the large river does flow from it, what then?" Not all were pleased to see these white-skinned apparitions; native children became upset and sometimes even hysterical. On entering towns where whites were seldom seen, Livingstone noted, "If we met a child coming quietly and unsuspectingly toward us, the moment he raised his eyes, and saw the men in 'bags,' he would take to his heels in an agony of terror, such as we might feel if we met a live Egyptian mummy at the door of the British Museum." Even dogs and chickens fled from the white man.[62]

Mungo Park had a number of interesting experiences with Africans. The prosperous and peaceful people of Bondu were struck by his whiteness and the prominence of his nose. They believed that both features were factitious, that the whiteness of his skin had been produced by repeated dippings in milk when he was a child and that his nose had been squeezed into its unusual shape. At Benoum, a party of curious Moslem women came to Park's tent to find out if he had been circumcised as was the custom for Moslem males. Park refused to have all eyes on him, but he agreed to let the most attractive woman in the tribe observe that particular part of his anatomy and report back to the others.[63]

Like American explorers, those in Africa often had difficulty obtaining accurate information from the natives. Park called the Mandingo knowledge of geography "puerile." Livingstone bemoaned the fact that some Africans lacked geographical knowledge.[64] These explorers probably did not know about the African admonition never to tell anyone, especially a stranger, more than half of what you know. To the natives, this type of deception was not the lie it was considered to be by the European. The concept of time, as well as distance, was often the cause of misunderstanding. Whereas the westerner was concerned with the precise measurement of miles, days, and hours, the native was concerned with seasonal time and a leisurely pace.

In that Victorian age, the explorer viewed the African as suffering from excessive sexual freedom caused by the humid climate, nudity, and lack of self-control.[65] Burton believed that chastity was difficult to preserve in the tropics.[66] With his abiding interest in eroticism, Burton maintained that in humid lands the sexual needs of women exceeded those of men, creating an "unbridled licentiousness."[67] Nudity was considered sinful by the explorers; to them, the transformation of comely young native girls into tired old hags with shriveled breasts was a clear illustration of what bodily freedom had done.[68] Speke noted that Somali women were pretty when young but, after bearing children, their beauty faded: "They swell about the waist and have that large development behind, which, in polite language, is called steatopygia."

Nineteenth-century middle-class morality kept discussion of sex to a minimum, however, and this conspiracy of silence led to a phenomenon that was closely associated with the Victorian Age—prudery. If there was secrecy concerning normal sexual relations, then interracial sex was taboo. In any case, Livingstone could not believe that any European could be enticed sexually by an African woman. Yet Speke shared a hut with a Buganda woman named Meri and fathered her child. John Shaw, a member of Stanley's expedition to find Livingstone, was more interested in African women than in finding the "lost" doctor. And William B. Baikie, a West African explorer, had a black mistress and fathered numerous children.[69]

Burton enjoyed upsetting Victorian mores with his shocking statements and erotic publications. Livingstone, who hated Burton for his criticism of missionaries and his independent lifestyle, wrote that Burton's actions in Africa were deplorable and could not be told "without disgust—systematically wicked, impure and untruthful."[70] Livingstone was hinting at Burton's supposed sexual affairs with African women.

Sexual temptation was often a concern for African explorers. In Masailand, Joseph Thomson was presented with a young Masai woman by her husband, who wanted Thomson to conceive a child with her. Although he considered Masai women good looking, in the best Victorian tradition Thomson demurred. The Masai warrior persisted, so Thomson gave the woman a concoction of water mixed with fruit salts and explained that this is how the British did it. The skeptical Masai thought it was a strange way to impregnate a woman, but accepted Thomson's explanation.[71]

In a town near the Niger River, a wealthy widow named Zuma fell in love with Richard Lander. Encouraged by Lander's companion, Hugh Clapperton, to follow her heart, the widow intensified her advances toward Lander. Lander was delighted to accept provisions from this large lady, but weak from exploring, he was fearful "that, from the warmth and energy of Zuma's embraces, I shall actually be pressed to death between her monstrous arms!" When Lander refused her, she turned her attention to Clapperton, with no more success.[72]

Livingstone felt that most of the criticism of the African was based upon *bogiephobia,* or fear of black skin.[73] He warned that travelers had recently gotten "too much into the novel-writer's habit of turning up the whites of our eyes, and holding up our paws, as pious people are all thought to do, whenever we meet with any trait not exactly 'Europe fashion.' "[74] Livingstone's liberal views were attacked. As summarized by Christine Bolt in *Victorian Attitudes to Race,* some said his appeal was to "Nigger Worshippers, missionary exporters, and other Exeter Hallitarians." He was criticized for possessing a "poor naked mind bedaubed with the chalk and red ochre of Scotch theology, and with a threadbare, tattered waistcloth of education hanging around him."

Although Livingstone admired a number of Africans, including the Makololo chief, Sebitoane, he feared being contaminated by the sins of the Africans and felt a need to separate himself from the natives. Stanley described Livingstone as a doctor attempting to cure a sickness "without remaining longer in the filth than is necessary to his work."[75] Stanley wrote about Livingstone's isolation that he had lived too long in a world "out of which he seldom awoke except to attend to the immediate, practical necessities . . . so that wherever he might be, or by whatsoever he was surrounded, his own world always possessed more attractions to his cultural mind than were yielded by external circumstances."[76]

British explorers considered it bad form to socialize with the natives. It was important to present a facade of power and superiority so that the Africans could not detect weakness or emotion in the whites. Thomson believed that the natives should never see him being carried by his servants, no matter how far he had to travel or how sick he was. Stanley reflected on this image when, ill with fever, he continued on to Lake Tanganyika. He later admitted it was a foolish thing to do, but he believed that whites should never go back on their word and that his reputation with the natives would have been tarnished had he stayed behind or delayed the march due to illness.[77]

One must be aloof and maintain a "stiff upper lip." Samuel Baker and Harry Johnston dressed formally for dinner each night in the African bush; and Stanley and Livingstone made it a point to shave and wash everyday. The epitome of British reserve was Stanley's classic understatement on finding Livingstone at Ujiji, "Doctor Livingstone, I presume?"[78]

Among the many things explorers discovered was a native character, and they created stereotypes around that character which had a significant and lasting influence on the Western world. As more explorers were sent out, information about native tribes became increasingly available. Explorers altered some of the stereotypes, but the prevailing view of basic native traits remained. On the negative side were the loose sexual mores, superstitions, violent behavior, and laziness (especially among the males). Torture, scalping, and cannibalism were graphically depicted in explorers' accounts. On the positive side were native hospitality, bravery, nobility of character, and love of family. These traits were often superseded by the negative ones, however, and in any case were never comparable to the superior traits of the whites.

Distinctions were made between males and females (usually to the advantage of the males), between those tribes that were influenced by whites and those that were not, and between coastal and interior tribes. Intertribal comparisons were made, with explorers from various European nations favoring different tribes.

Explorers were generally critical of tribal culture. Some of their criticism stemmed from encounters with the natives, but many of their prejudices were formed before they left home. Western prejudices toward native peoples antedated nineteenth-century exploration by at least three hundred years, and explorers were no different from other people in being influenced by prevailing racial views.

CHAPTER THREE

The Land

THROUGHOUT THE AGES, geographical images as much as facts have been spurs to discovery. The Norwegian arctic explorer Fridtjof Nansen believed that "great illusions have always played an important part in the history of mankind"; and John K. Wright, intellectual historian and geographer, asserted that "throughout the history of geography erroneous notions have exerted a powerful fascination over men's minds and mistaken concepts have been hardly less influential than those finally found to be correct."[1]

John L. Allen, a historical geographer, noted that "no exploratory venture begins without objectives based on the imagined nature and the content of the lands to be explored." He felt that the conduct and thinking of explorers were usually influenced less by facts than by suppositions. The geographical objectives of explorers were based on both inference and fact; this led explorers to think that they knew more about a region than they actually did. Optimistic by nature, explorers believed that their information was better than it was. They tended to extend what they knew about one area to regions partially or totally unknown to them. This led to disagreements with native guides over travel routes, which sometimes caused the expeditions to break down. Because the movement from known to unknown areas was usually gradual, explorers often did not recognize when the region of real knowledge became the region of perceived knowledge.[2]

Explorers used their imaginations on expeditions, and, as searches for the Seven Cities of Gold and Prester John attest, those imaginations were fertile. Explorers would search for a place as originally described, and their inability to use more recent, accurate data, coupled with their refusal to change their ways of thinking, often caused failure. There was a tendency to push aside unpopular facts that did not fit into the established image. American explorer John Ledyard recognized that "to be traveling is to be in error." Exploration is a process of discarding geographical folklore and developing a truer picture of the land while traveling through zones of information. The successful explorer moved from small dreams to large realities, supplanting his own preconceived images with geographical facts.[3]

More than any other continent, Africa evoked a sense of gloom and mystery in which dragons, winged horses, and camelopards abounded. Disease and death were the twin fates of those who entered that forbidding land. In describing Africa, a British traveler referred to lines from a poem by the Scottish poet James Thomson:

> A boundless deep immensity of shade,
> Here, lofty trees, to ancient song unknown,
> The noble sons of potent heat, and floods
> Prone rushing from the clouds, rear high in heaven
> Their thorny stems, and broad around them throw
> Meridian gloom.[4]

The horrors of the savage African interior were recorded by a Scottish geographer:

This region, to the ancient world, inspired always emotions of wonder and curiosity, mingled with terror. It was the region of mystery, of poetry, of superstitious awe. The wild and strange aspect of man and nature, the immense tracts abandoned to wild beasts, the still more immeasurable deserts of sand beyond, and the destruction which had overwhelmed most of those who attempted to penetrate.[5]

To another geographer, even the rays of the sun added to the frightening picture:

The barrenness in several places, the brutality and savageness of the natives and the ferocity of the innumerable wild beasts in most of its countries evince that the rays of the sun are here so fervid and powerful as to dry and burn up the animal creation, so that the first is rendered futile and the latter furious.[6]

Geographers were not alone in creating dark and often false images of Africa; poets also exaggerated its dangers. The "rattling terrors of the vengeful snake" in an unknown land "where crouching tigers wait their hapless prey,/ And savage men more murderous still than they"—as pictured in the poems of Oliver Goldsmith, William Blake, and James Thomson—reflected the prevalent misinformation concerning both Africa and America.[7]

No matter how the land was depicted, man has always been fascinated by the abominable. Moreover, exploring is also a journey into the inner *terra incognita,* a special psychological landscape in which man confronts the most dreaded unknown, himself.

English cartographer James Rennell pointed out significant geographical differences between Africa and North America as a reason for Europe's ignorance of the African interior.

Africa stands alone in a geographical view! Penetrated by no inland seas, like . . . Hudson's Bay; nor overspread with extensive lakes, like those of North America; nor having, in common with the other continents, rivers running from the centre to the extremities: but, on the contrary, its regions separated from each other by the least practicable of all boundaries, arid deserts of such formidable extent, as to threaten those who traverse them, with the most horrible of all deaths, that arising from thirst![8]

In the 1770s, a writer for the *Encyclopaedia Britannica* remarked that, although the African continent had been unknown for centuries, "its situation is more favorable than either Europe or Asia for maintaining an intercourse with other nations."[9] The landscape of Africa was generally less awe-inspiring and dangerous to the explorers than were the Amazon jungle, the Rocky Mountains, or the Australian outback. The Sahara Desert joined as well as separated, natural harbors were found along the African coast, and some African rivers could be navigated for considerable distances. Ancient trade routes linked large parts of the African continent. Explorers encountered a dense native population in Africa, whereas in America they could travel for days and see no one. In 1820, soldier-explorer Stephen H. Long traveled for five weeks without seeing an Indian; Lewis and Clark explored for over two months and never met a native.

Trade routes and the dense population would seem to have made Africa an easier land to explore than North America. This was not the case, however, because the danger of disease in Africa was more than enough to offset any geographical advantages it possessed. This was the most significant difference between African and American exploration and the major deterrent to exploring Africa where death from disease was so common that it produced a mordant fatalism: "It was quite customary of a morning to ask 'how many died last night'?"[10] "Deadly, a Golotha, a Jehannum [sic]," warned Richard Burton, sent to study mortality rates in West Africa.[11]

Henry Stanley described the land as "Fatal Africa." Samuel Baker noted with anger, "The luxuries of the country as usual—malaria, marshes, mosquitoes, misery, far as the eye can reach, vast treeless marshes perfectly lifeless."[12] The malarious West African coast gained the title "the White Man's Grave," and British sailors sang the ditty, "Beware and take care of the Bight of Benin. There's one comes out for forty go in."

Malaria, dysentery, and yellow fever were among the deadly diseases from which African explorers suffered, along with sleeping sickness, yaws, bilharziasis, and guinea worm. Little was known about African diseases in the eighteenth century, but with each expedition new information was gathered. Further medical knowledge about the continent was obtained in the late 1700s when the English naval surgeon James Lind published his work on tropical diseases, *Diseases of Hot Climates*. Lind recommended cinchona bark for treatment of malaria; for those who suffered from more than one attack of fever, he suggested regular doses of the Peruvian bark mixed with wine.[13]

Fever was the major cause of death for whites. The *Anopheles gambiae* and *Anopheles funestus* mosquitoes, which carry the protozoan parasites that cause malaria, were responsible for the high death rate. Philip D. Curtin, a historian of African epidemiology, estimated that African diseases killed perhaps half of the Europeans sent to work at the slave trading factories in the late eighteenth century.[14]

A clear link between fevers and climate was thought to exist, and a hot, humid climate was credited with relaxing fibers in the body, making the blood thinner, and causing fevers. Swamps, rains, and humidity were associated with death and disease in dozens of medical books and journals. Like the stereotypical view of the native, these generalizations about Africa's climate were usually erroneous. It was maintained, for example, that the interior was healthier than the coast and that people who lived in a tropical climate were more likely to have violent tempers and hot passions.[15]

Another hindrance to African explorers was the hostile native who was apprehensive of white penetration. Several tribes feared that whites might cause a rerouting of trade which would disrupt their business connections and interfere with the lucrative slave trade.

Africans believed that the British intended to conquer their land as they had India, and Hugh Clapperton, who was sent to Africa to trace the course of the Niger River, was suspected by the zealous caliph of Sokoto of being a British spy. Arab merchants were fearful that British trade would compete with their economic dominance,[16] and Moslem hatred of infidels was a source of difficulty. Native hostility had been overcome by force and persuasion in other areas of the world, and would be in Africa as well.

A few tribes looked forward to the appearance of the white man. Three chiefs, the king of Bambuk, Sekeletu of Kololo, and Mutesa I, kabaka of Buganda, were pleased by his arrival because it would open trade, especially in weapons, and bring about political alliances with the whites. Treaties with the British—for guns, ammunition, and support—greatly aided certain tribes in their wars. Generally, explorers demonstrated that diplomacy rather than force was the best way to open up the interior. Until that happened, however, the main reason for the lack of European involvement with Africa was simply that there was no cause strong enough to induce Europeans to expend their time, money, and lives on this hostile land.

The Portuguese sailing down the West Coast of Africa were the first Europeans to make contact with the natives (the discoveries later made by Park, Stanley, and Livingstone were often rediscoveries of things the Portuguese had known.) Soon French, Dutch, and British merchants would follow. These three nations were primarily involved with the area between the Niger Delta and the Senegal River, forcing the Portuguese to concentrate their efforts to the south. Through treaty arrangements with the native chiefs, the Dutch, French, and British opened factories along the coast for trading in slaves and tropical products.

In the seventeenth century, the Dutch captured a number of bases from the Portuguese, as they had already done in the Far East. By that time the French were concentrated on the Senegal River. In the 1630s, King Louis XIII gave monopoly rights to merchant companies to construct forts at the mouth of the river; one built on the island of St. Louis in the Senegal twenty years later became the French headquarters. But it was not until 1697, with the arrival of André Brue, the director of a new French trading company, that important upstream expeditions began. Brue was a dynamic leader who established forts and developed a French colony along the upper Senegal. Two decades later he was succeeded by Sieur Compagnon, who explored Bambuk at the confluence of the Senegal and Falemé rivers. But in a short time hostile natives forced the French to retreat.[17]

In the 1620s, English merchants and adventurers penetrated West Africa along the Gambia River, and supercargoes George Thompson and Richard Jobson were among the first Englishmen to enter the region in search of gold. Thompson had been sent by London merchants to explore the upper reaches of the Gambia, but in 1619 he and most of his men were killed by natives. Jobson arrived on the Gambia a year later and traveled hundreds of miles upriver seeking gold. He found none, but returned home with vivid stories of the natives he encountered along the river, some of whom he compared to European Gypsies. Others, probably of the Ubangi tribe, hid from the white men. "The reason why these people will not be seene is for that they are naturally borne with their lower lippe of the greatnesse it turns againe and covers the greater part of their bosome. . . ." Sixty years later, Cornelius Hodges, an enterprising sea captain working for the Royal African Company, traveled farther inland than had Jobson. On reaching the gold fields of Bambuk, Hodges learned that famine had forced the closing of the mines.[18]

By 1800 there had been a number of African explorations, but the interior still remained largely *terra incognita*. The meanderings of the three great rivers—the Nile, Niger, and Congo—remained geographical blanks. The sources and directions of these flowing highways were the major questions of African exploration, the key to unlocking the secrets of the continent. Unlike the Mississippi and Missouri, these important African rivers often turned into series of dangerous rapids. They held ancient mysteries that had attracted geographers and explorers for hundreds of years.

The greatest African quest was the search for the source of the Nile. The Latin poet Lucan had written:

> Yet still no views have urged my ardour more
> Than Nile's remotest mountains to explore.

African explorer Harry Johnston called the Nile Quest "the greatest geographical secret after the discovery of America."[19]

What was the source of the Nile? Egyptians believed that it started with the tears of the goddess Isis: Herodotus was told by an Egyptian scribe that the Nile flowed out of a bottomless cave between two conical mountains named Crophi and Mophi. The river was linked with gold and fabulous wealth. In Genesis, it was associated with Pharaoh's dream of seven kine. Indeed, Egypt was known as the "gift of the Nile." Ambivalence played a part in the mystery of the Nile; it was near yet far, known yet unknown, seen yet hidden. Using information gathered from a Greek merchant, Ptolemy placed the source of the Nile in two lakes fed by the Mountains of the Moon. His theory was close to the truth.[20]

Augustus Caesar began the historic search when he sent an expedition to find the source of the White Nile. Later, Nero dispatched centurions to the Nile, but they were stopped by the sudd, the impenetrable swamp. Much of the early explorers' emphasis, as seen in James Bruce's exploration, was placed upon the Blue Nile, which flows out of Lake Tana in Ethiopia; but it was the parent stream, the White Nile, that held the key to the "secret of [the] Nile's cradle."[21]

Some associated the Nile with the Niger; a few believed that it flowed across Africa from the Atlantic into the Indian Ocean. Other popular views were that the Nile flowed out of India, that it began in the Red Sea, and that it rose in the Comr Mountains. The source of the Nile was even linked to the legend of Prester John: the river was said to flow from a great cavern at whose entrance he had constructed two great towers and a large fence. A related story was that whoever looked into the cave and heard its music would never want to leave.[22]

The source of the Nile was not discovered until the 1850s. In 1856, the same year that Livingstone began his ill-fated Zambezi expedition, John Speke and Richard Burton explored Central Africa. They were sent by the Royal Geographical Society to find the "solution of that great geographical problem, the determination of the sources of the White Nile." The two men had been together a year earlier on the Somaliland expedition, which ended disastrously when Somalis attacked the party and almost killed Speke.

In February, 1858, Burton and Speke discovered Lake Tanganyika, the second largest lake in Africa. On their return, they halted at Tabora, where they heard about a large lake to the north. Leaving Burton behind at Tabora, the self-confident Speke struck out on a "flying trip" to investigate. On July 30, 1858, he first saw Africa's largest lake, which he named Victoria Nyanza or Lake Victoria: "I no longer felt any doubt that the lake at my feet gave birth to that interesting river." Unable to explore the lake further, Speke nevertheless believed that it was the true source of the Nile. Upon his return to camp, Speke told Burton of his discovery, but Burton refused to accept Speke's claim and a serious argument ensued. A question of geographical discovery was turned into a personal feud. Plagued by jealousy and self-doubt, Burton turned his frustration and anger on Speke. He complained that—although he had taught Speke "archery day by day—when his arm waxed strong; 'twas me he shot." When Speke boasted of his discovery on his return to England in 1859, Burton continued his attack by remarking that Speke conversed in broken English "as if he had forgotten his vernacular in the presence of strange tongues."[23]

In addition to Burton, a number of British geographers did not accept Speke's claim of discovery. Some continued to believe that the Nile originated in the snow-capped mountains of Kilimanjaro and Kenya that had been discovered by German missionaries in the late 1840s. Others argued that the secret was to be found in the recently discovered Lake Tanganyika. In this dispute, not only was Speke attacked as a discoverer and geographer, but his character was assailed as well. In self-defense he launched a second expedition to Africa in the early 1860s with his friend James A. Grant, whom he had met in India when both served in the British Army. The two men shared a love of hunting and an interest in the study of natural history and, like Lewis and Clark, they were opposites who got along well. Speke was reckless and impulsive; Grant was cautious and patient. When the loyal Grant became incapacitated with an ulcerated leg, Speke set out on his second "flying trip." On July 28, 1862, he saw the historic spot where the Victoria Nile flowed northward out of Lake Victoria. He cabled Sir Roderick Murchison, president of the Royal Geographical Society, that "the Nile is settled."

Many more now supported Speke's discovery but some, like Burton, continued to question his assertions. The British Association scheduled a debate between Speke and Burton for September 16, 1864, on the question of the source of the Nile, but on September 15 Speke died of a gunshot wound suffered while hunting. In the years following his death, Speke's claim of discovering the source of the Nile was both attacked and defended. Not until Verney L. Cameron's and Stanley's expeditions in the 1870s was that claim finally substantiated.

The Niger had been to Englishmen of the early nineteenth century what the Nile became to the mid-Victorians. No river had baffled Europeans for a longer period of time than had the Niger. From the days of Herodotus on, there had been confusion about its source, the direction of its flow, and indeed its very existence.[24] The Arab geographers al-Idrīsī and Leo Africanus speculated that the Niger flowed from east to west; Pliny the Elder, Herodotus, and Ptolemy believed that it flowed from west to east. Pliny thought that the river flowed into the Nile; Ptolemy theorized that it had no outlet to the sea.[25] Others maintained either that the river ended in a great inland sea or that the Niger and the Congo were the same river. Searches for the mouth of the Niger opened West Africa to European exploration. It was difficult to obtain reliable information about the Niger because its course was erratic and it went by several different names. Furthermore, reaching the river from the north involved crossing the dreaded Sahara Desert, while the inland route from the West Coast subjected one to the risk of deadly fevers.

With the founding of the African Association in 1788, a new attempt was made to solve the riddle of the Niger. The association was established primarily to support African exploration and promote British trade and authority in West Africa. John Ledyard, who had sailed with Captain James Cook, was one of the first explorers sent out by the African Association to search for the Niger, but Ledyard died in Cairo in 1789 before he could begin his southward trek. Simon Lucas and Daniel Houghton were also employed in this quest, but failed to discover the source of the Niger. Lucas returned after crossing a hundred miles of desert; Houghton was killed by Moors. The association then dispatched Mungo Park to find the Niger. On July 20, 1795, Park saw the "majestic Niger, glittering to the morning sun, as broad as the Thames at Westminster, and flowing slowly *to the eastward.*" His was one of the great discoveries in eighteenth-century exploration. Other expeditions were sent to the Niger, but most contributed little to the geographical knowledge of the region. A Scottish geographer theorized that the Niger flowed into the Gulf of Guinea, not into the Nile. This view was proven correct when, in the 1830s, Richard and John Lander sailed down the Niger to its delta and out into the gulf.

In the 1480s, the Portuguese sent Diogo Cão, a navigator of humble origins, to reinforce their claims to the West Coast of Africa. Cão entered the mouth of the Congo River in 1482 and erected a *padrão* or stone column on its north bank to mark his discovery. When Gaspar Bocarro made one of the first explorations into the interior for the Portuguese in 1616, the lower Congo and the upper areas of the Zambezi were revealed. The natives called the river *nzere,* "the river that swallows all rivers." In the eighteenth century it would become known as the Congo, named for the Bakongo people who lived along its banks. Because of the river's treacherous rapids, as late as 1800 only one hundred miles of its three-thousand-mile course had been seen by Europeans.[26]

The most accepted notion of the river's source was that it flowed out of a great lake in Central Africa, a lake fed by the rivers flowing from the Mountains of the Moon, from which the Nile was also thought to flow. In 1816, James K. Tuckey, a captain in the Royal Navy, traced the Congo's lower course upstream as far as Isanghila, where his progress was checked by the rapids. Not until the mid-1870s, when Stanley successfully navigated the Congo, were its secrets uncovered. And with his discovery the "romance" of African river exploration ended.

There were a number of reasons for European ignorance of the African interior; besides disease and hostile natives, the difficult terrain was a major hindrance to explorers. The arid wastes of the Sahara, unnavigable rivers, and deadly swamps turned back many explorers. But none of these obstacles was so overwhelming as to permanently halt exploration or stop geographers from drawing their maps. Cartographers abhor a vacuum, and blank spaces on a map are an embarrassment. Indeed, when Tuckey was sent to the Congo, his instructions from John Barrow, second secretary of the Admiralty, stated that "a river of such magnitude . . . not . . . known with any degree of certainty . . . is incompatible with the present advanced state of geographical science." A Scottish geographer wrote that Africa "is still humbling to that pride of knowledge, which Europe very justly indulges with regard to the other quarters of the globe." This geographical reproach was partially resolved by mapmakers who chose to fill blank spaces with drawings of animals, a practice borne out by Jonathan Swift's popular ditty:

> Geographers, in *Afric*-maps
> With Savage-Pictures fill their Gaps;
> And o'er unhabitable Downs
> Place Elephants for want of Towns.[27]

Because maps were based largely upon the imagination of geographers, even well-known areas were often misplaced. By the age of enlightenment, however, important advances in mapmaking appeared. This was especially true of the African maps by the French geographers Guillaume DeLisle and J. B. Bourguignon d'Anville. D'Anville's 1727 map of Africa was the first truly scientific map of the continent and would later be used by British geographers. Free from much misleading exaggeration, d'Anville's maps were among the most complete of his time.

James Rennell was the leading English geographer of the eighteenth century. Born in 1742, he served in the British Navy in the East Indies during the Seven Years' War and, when the war was over, joined the East India Company. In 1764, he was named surveyor-general of Bengal by Robert Clive, the governor of the East India Company. During his seven years in India, he made the first important geographical survey of that country—the *Bengal Atlas*—for which he was called the "father of Indian geography." When Rennell returned to London in the 1770s, he was named a fellow of the

Royal Society. Through his scholarly work on Herodotus, he became interested in African geography. He was made the first honorary member of the African Association and became its geographical advisor. Rennell wrote accounts of association explorers and drew maps of their expeditions. In his passion for complete maps, Rennell was said to believe that "the blanks on the map were eyesores."[28]

Like Africa, the North American wilderness was described in formidable terms. The view was of the wonder of it all, the enchantment, the spiritual uplift, accompanied by an overuse of superlatives. As one literary historian expressed it, at the center of the narrative of discovery appeared "the ravished observer, fixed in awe, scanning the New World scene, noting its colors and shapes, recording its plenitude and its sensual richness."[29]

Compared to forbidding Africa, America was generally perceived as a vast, green world, a paradise, a utopia. Exploring along the Carolina coast in the 1580s, the English captain Arthur Barlowe found the natives "gentle, loving and faithfull" and the land amazingly fruitful; "the earth bringeth forth all things in abundance, as in the first creation, without toil or labor."[30] The fertile lands of Virginia and New England prompted Captain John Smith to speculate that a three-day work week was more than sufficient for any settler to raise abundant crops. Here all men could have "shoes on their feet, cloaths on their backs and beef in their bellies." The lure of economic abundance was commonly used in promotional literature. But the paradox was that all of the talk about a land of plenty was not an unmixed invocation of happiness, for this Eden could create luxury leading to spiritual degeneration.[31]

Even the animals were exotic in this verdant land. One writer told of creatures wounded by hunters that healed themselves by rubbing against certain trees from which flowed a magic elixir.[32] Countless explorers were struck by the profusion of animal life. Describing the Piedmont, a seventeenth-century English explorer, John Lederer, noted that "these thickets harbour all sorts of beasts of prey, as wolves, panthers, leopards, lions, etc. (which are neither so large nor so fierce as those of Asia and Africa)." The vast animal herds on the high plains captured the imaginations of Lewis and Clark. "Buffaloe deer Elk and Antilopes were seen feeding in every direction as far as the eye of the observer could reach." Lewis noted that the pronghorn antelope resembled the "Gazella of Africa," for, just as the Mississippi River was compared to the Nile and the "Great American Desert" to the Sahara, American animals were sometimes compared to those of Africa.[33]

American explorers were amazed by the size of the buffalo herds. In 1804 Lewis and Clark counted over three thousand head along the Missouri River. On their return trip down the White River, they recorded, "we discovered more than we had ever seen before at one time; and if it be not impossible to calculate, the moving multitude, which darkened the whole plains, we are convinced that twenty thousand would be no exaggerated number."[34] American soldier-explorer Zebulon Montgomery Pike, on his expedition in 1806, was impressed by the number of buffalo grazing along the Arkansas River.

Disease was much less a factor in American than in African exploration. Although malaria came to the upper Mississippi valley after 1800 and reached epidemic levels after 1820, by 1870 it was on the decline. In the 1830s and 1840s, cholera was another cause for concern, but few American explorers were stricken with these diseases and none died of them.

If disease did not spread fear in America as it did in Africa, there was more than an occasional hint of danger and death, as seen in the language of Daniel Boone describing the western land: "The aspect of these cliffs is so wild and horrid, that it is impossible to behold them without terror." But to Boone, nature was more often a series of wonders and a fount of pleasure, as he noted while tracking in the wilderness: "The diversity and beauties of nature I met with in this charming season, expelled every gloomy and vexatious thought."[35]

Boone's narrative of the destruction of that natural life includes a haunting ambivalence. To some, it represented the beginning tragedy of America's fall from grace:

Here, where the hand of violence shed the blood of the innocent; where the horrid yells of savages, and the groans of the distressed, sounded in our ears, we now hear the praises and adorations of our Creator; where wretched wigwams stood, the miserable abodes of savages, we behold the foundations of cities laid, that, in all probability, will rival the glory of the greatest upon earth.[36]

George Catlin, the famous portraitist of Indians, described the North American landscape in the 1830s as

a place where the mind could think volumes; but the tongue must be silent that would *speak,* and the hand palsied that would *write.* A place where a Divine would confess that he never had fancied Paradise—where the painter's palette would lose its beautiful tints—the blood-stirring notes of eloquence would die in their utterance—and even the soft tones of sweet music would scarcely preserve a spark to light the soul again that had passed this sweet delirium.[37]

In F. Scott Fitzgerald's *The Great Gatsby,* Nick Carraway captured that mystical feeling when he marveled, "For a transitory enchanted moment man must have held his breath in the presence of this continent . . . face to face for the last time in history with something commensurate to his capacity for wonder."[38]

In America, the words *continent* and *continental*—the latter affixed to the army, the association, and congress—were in popular use at the time of the American Revolution in describing magnitude. This concept of bigness was expressed by Thomas Paine, who boasted that the American cause was "not the affair of a city, a county, a province, or a kingdom; but of a continent—of at least one eighth part of the habitable globe." Paine mused, "There is something very absurd, in supposing a continent to be perpetually governed by an island. In no instance hath nature made the satellite larger than its primary planet. . . ." In a letter to his wife, Abigail, in 1775, John Adams wrote, "The continent is really in earnest, in defending the country."[39]

In America as in Africa, the story of exploration involved imperial rivalries, scientific curiosity, and the search for wealth, all of which opened the West to exploration. British, French, and Spanish explorers pushed into the vast unknown, looking for the river or strait called the River of the West that would lead to the Pacific Ocean.

The history of exploration is studded with *idées fixes,* a term John Wright defined as "an idea (whether true or false, helpful or misleading) that has 'set' like concrete and is no longer amenable to change in the light of factual evidence or rational thought."[40] The *idée fixe* in African exploration was discovering the source of the Nile; in America it was finding the Northwest Passage. That image compelled explorers from John Cabot to John Charles Frémont to search for a water route that would lead to the golden shores of Cathay. Evolving from Verrazano's Sea to the Strait of Anian and finally to the San Buenaventura River, the location of this elusive route retreated before explorers until it was tracked by Frémont to the Great Basin, where the mythical river evaporated in that desert of interior drainage.

As Spaniards moved up the coast of California in the eighteenth century, the Russians sailed down from Russia America (Alaska), and soon ships from Spain, France, Russia, and Britain rode the waves in the bays and inlets along the Pacific Coast.[41] A number of important Spanish scientific expeditions sailed along the coast in the late eighteenth century, one of the most significant of which was commanded by Italian-born Alejandro Malaspina, who had many of the same objectives as did Captain James Cook on his third expedition. One of these was to discover a strait (to Malaspina it was known as the Strait of Ferrer Maldonado) which would be a passage to the Atlantic, a reversal of the Northwest Passage concept. Finding this strait would allow Spain to recapture some of her lost glory. Because of the British predominance in the area and Spain's involvement in European wars, however, Spain was forced to pull out of the northern Pacific Coast area by the late eighteenth century, and she gained little from her well-organized and costly exploring expeditions.

Spain's push northward from New Mexico took place in the mid-eighteenth century. A prize of 3,000 pesos was offered to the first Spanish subject to reach the South Sea via the Missouri River. One of the first important exploring expeditions was led by Juan de Rivera from New Mexico to the Gunnison River in 1765. The Domínguez-Escalante Expedition of 1776, headed by two Franciscan friars, was the first to make a journey into the Colorado Plateau area and the Great Basin. There they searched for the San Buenaventura. Although Escalante's journal and the maps drawn by the military leader of the expedition, Bernardo Miera y Pacheco, were comprehensive, two geographical errors helped perpetuate the myth of the San Buenaventura. The first was their mistaken belief that Utah Lake and the Great Salt Lake were the same body of water, known as Lake Timpanogos, and that from there a navigable river flowed westward; the second error was moving the Green River westward on the map and identifying it with the Great Basin, believing it to be the San Buenaventura. Instead of recognizing the main fork of the Colorado, they thought that they were at another watershed.[42]

Francisan fathers Pedro Font and Francisco Garcés, who explored the Southwest in the 1770s, believed in the Sea of the West, and their views, along with those of Escalante and Miera, were incorporated in a map of Spanish North America published in 1785. Until Frémont solved its riddles in the 1840s, this vast area of the American continent was the last important region unknown to geographers.

In the 1600s, French explorers moved westward and southward from the Great Lakes. LaSalle opened the way to the west in the 1680s; after his murder in Texas in 1687, others followed. In 1719 Bénard de la Harpe traveled along the Red River of Texas in hopes of reaching the Pacific; finding no River of the West, he brought back reports of precious stones and unicorns. A few years earlier, a French patrol under Juchereau de Saint-Denis had moved into Texas to compete with the Spanish for that frontier. The Frenchmen were captured by Spanish soldiers, taken to Mexico City, and later escorted back to French territory.[43]

The great adventurer Étienne Véniard, Sieur de Bourgmond, was sent by the French government to ascend the Missouri River to the Platte River in 1714 to make treaties with the Indians. Bourgmond was well qualified for this task because, after deserting his command at Detroit, he had lived with the Indians of the Missouri valley for over a decade. In the early 1720s, he constructed Fort d'Orleans three hundred miles upriver at the mouth of the Grand River. Bourgmond was not only the first explorer of the Missouri, he also opened up French trade along the Arkansas and Platte rivers. His trading skill won over a number of Indian tribes such as the Kansas, Iowa, and Comanche. But French plans for further exploration ended with the Natchez and Fox Indian wars in the late 1720s, which led to the abandonment of Fort d'Orleans.[44]

Following the route laid out by Bourgmond, the brothers Pierre and Paul Mallet believed that the Missouri River would be an excellent route to the Spanish settlements. In 1739 they set out with six others from the Illinois country. When told by Pawnee Indians that the route they were following was the wrong one, they moved to the Platte River; guided by an Indian, they left the river's north fork, pushed southward until they reach a Spanish mission near Taos, New Mexico, and continued on to Santa Fe, thereby becoming the first white men to cross the plains between the Missouri River and New Mexico.[45]

In New France, the image of the River of the West evolved from several concepts. The earliest was the belief that one could find a connection to that river along the western shore of Hudson's Bay. The next was that the River or Sea of the West meandered south and not west. It was also believed that the river would be discovered west of Lake Superior or in the upper Mississippi valley. Much of this conjecture led to questionable journeys and disappearing rivers, all linked to fabulous Indian kingdoms. Explorers were enticed by tales of a nation of dwarfs, golden sand near a river of red water, and a mountain called the "Dwelling of the Spirit" whose rocks sparkled day and night. These stories and even accounts of Prester John appeared in the fascinating works of the French soldier Baron de Lahontan and the Franciscan cleric and explorer Louis Hennepin.

Another French cleric, Father Bobé, searched for the Sea of the West along Lake Superior. In 1688 a French trader, Jacques de Noyon, moved farther west where natives told him of a nearby sea. Sieur de la Noue built a fort on Lake Superior in 1689, with financial support from the royal court. New posts were opened by the French in the Sioux country which aided the expansion of the western fur trade. In the early 1720s, Father Pierre-François-Xavier Charlevoix made a trip to the Mississippi River to find out about the sea. Based on this Jesuit scholar's recommendations, other Jesuits entered the West. They were interested in the search for the western sea, not only because of their interest in saving souls but especially because of their love of learning. It was said of the Jesuits that their "desire for fresh geographical knowledge was an adornment to their character and an honour to their time."[46]

In the 1730s, the search for the river involved the omnipresent Pierre Gaultier de Varennes, Sieur de La Vérendrye. A soldier and fur trader, La Vérendrye was ordered by the governor of Canada in 1727 to establish a string of forts from Lake Superior westward to counterbalance the British threat from Hudson's Bay. In his plans to develop French claims to the West, he also began a search for the western sea. La Vérendrye and his sons and nephew sought that sea in four voyages between 1731 and 1743 and, after a decade of searching, believed that the River of the West would not be found west of Lake Superior.

One of La Vérendrye's biographers wrote that he was a failure as a discoverer because of his "significant incuriosity" when, in 1738, only a short distance from the Missouri River—the supposed River of the West—he refused to view it. Perhaps he realized that the Missouri would not take him to the western sea. But, with little support from the French government, he did manage to extend the frontiers of New France to Manitoba, keep the Indians loyal to the French king, and build a number of posts west of the Great Lakes. The elder La Vérendrye wrote of "the zeal by which I have always been animated for the King's service and especially for the discovery" of that sea. "Money . . . was moreover always a secondary consideration with me."[47] But it could have been that La Vérendrye was more interested in a sea of beaver than in the sea of the west.

La Vérendrye was told by Indians that the river was located in Mandan country, and another misconception was created. The Mandans were a tribe of town dwellers, proficient in the arts and crafts. Because of their cultural concentration and their light skin and fine features, they were thought to be, at various times, the white Indians, the lost tribe of Israel, and descendants of Phoenician traders, Viking explorers, and Welsh lords.[48]

The story was told by British writers such as Walter Raleigh and Richard Hakluyt that America was discovered in 1170 by Madoc, son of a Welsh lord. A tribe of Welsh Indians in the West was supposed to be descended from him and other colonists from Wales. These stories became more prevalent in the late eighteenth century. One man even applied to the African Association for support in finding the tribe of Welsh Indians. In the 1790s, an experienced fur trader, James Mackay, and his assistant, John Evans, ascended the Missouri River to trade and search for the tribe. Evans, a young Welshman, lived with the Mandans for six months. On his return to St. Louis, he wrote that the Welsh Indians did not exist, but the legend continued for another forty years.[49]

Growing out of the River of the West theory was the concept of a river emanating from the Rocky Mountains and flowing to the Pacific. Connected to this concept was the belief in a pyramidal height-of-land in the West. This division of waters myth, which endured from the early 1700s (when Charlevoix and La Vérendrye searched for it) until the mid-nineteenth century, involved the belief that in the interior highland area was a drainage system from which rivers flowed like spokes of a wheel radiating from the hub; if the sources of these rivers adjoined, once one located that area one could sail to the seas contiguous to North America, traveling solely by water. Four rivers were thought to flow from the pyramid: the River of the West to the Pacific, the St. Lawrence to the Atlantic, the Mississippi to the Gulf of Mexico, and the Colorado to the Gulf of California. The location of this land formation was as elusive as the River of the West until 1845 when Frémont, with a realistic view of the Continental Divide, demonstrated that it did not exist. Nevertheless, the height-of-land concept did play an important role in the perception, or misperception, of the American West.[50]

Just as there was some agreement about the existence of a pyramidal height-of-land, there was disagreement about the western mountains, called the Shining, Stony, and Rocky Mountains. Some believed they ran from Canada to Mexico; others said that they ended around the 48th parallel. They were either the grandest in the world or mere hills that offered no barrier to westward expansion. It was common in the nineteenth century to describe mountains as sublime and majestic because great heights were often associated with gods and heaven.

Some of the greatest British explorers—James Cook, Alexander Mackenzie, and George Vancouver—searched for the River of the West; after Cook discovered the Hawaiian Islands in 1777, he sailed along the northwest coast of North America in search of the river. At the time of his death in 1779, Cook was still searching for the elusive passage.[51]

Most of these explorers had neither the time nor the experience to make important generalizations or significant statements about the landscape. Alexander Mackenzie, who was born in Scotland in 1764 and entered the fur trade of western Canada in 1785, remarked that he did not have "the science of the naturalist . . . I could not stop to dig into the earth, over whose surface I was compelled to pass with rapid steps; nor could I turn aside to collect the plants . . . when my thoughts were anxiously employed in making provision for the day that was passing over me." Mackenzie, haunted by a belief in the mythical river, made the first transcontinental crossing north of the Spanish possessions between 1792 and 1793.[52]

During the same period, Captain George Vancouver, who had sailed with Cook on two voyages, launched an expedition to the Pacific Coast for the purpose of obtaining "information [about] any water-communication which may tend, in any considerable degree, to facilitate an intercourse, for the purposes of commerce, between the north-west coast, and the country upon the opposite side of the continent."[53] Between 1800 and 1812, Canadian fur trader and explorer David Thompson traveled along the Columbia River from its source to its mouth and demonstrated the relationship of the rivers in the central Canadian plains to the Missouri. But, except for these great Canadian explorers, the opening of the new fur trading regions was usually an end in itself for Canadian fur traders.

From an early age, Thomas Jefferson had been fascinated with the idea of a passage to India. When he became President, he sent Lewis and Clark out to discover this geographical link. He instructed them that one of their main objectives was to locate "the direct water communication from sea to sea formed by the bed of the Missouri & perhaps the Oregon."[54]

To celebrate the return of Lewis and Clark, the American poet Joel Barlow conjoined African and American river explorations in a patriotic poem entitled, "On the Discoveries of Captain Lewis."

> Let the Nile cloak his head in the clouds, and defy
> The researches of science and time;
> Let the Niger escape the keen traveller's eye,
> By plunging, or changing his clime.
>
> Columbus! not so shall thy boundless domain
> Defraud thy brave sons of their right:
> Streams, midlands and shorelands illude us in vain,
> We shall drag their dark regions to light.[55]

While Republicans viewed Jefferson's versatility and curiosity as signs of greatness, his Federalist opponents made fun of his geographical preoccupations, especially his belief in the existence of a mountain of salt and a giant mammoth in the West. John Quincy Adams poked fun at Jefferson's protégé Meriwether Lewis in a doggerel verse entitled "The Discoveries of Captain Lewis."

He never with a Mammoth met,
However you may wonder;
Nor even with a Mammoth's bone,
Above the ground or under.

His father, John Adams, continued the partisan attack on American exploration: "There is so much Rhodomontade of Travellers in our Wilderness which have proved in the end to be mere delusions, that I give little attention to them. The Country is explored and thinly planted much too fast. . . ."[56]

One of the most persistent misperceptions of the American West, and one for which explorers were largely responsible, was that a large part of the West was a treeless plain unsuited for any kind of agriculture, a barren waste forever uninhabitable. From the days of Cabeza de Vaca to the nineteenth century, the term "desert" was used to describe large parts of the West. This word connoted not only sterility and treelessness but also an unoccupied land. In the 1790s three explorers, Pedro Vial, James Mackay, and Jean Baptiste Truteau, conjured up a desert in their descriptions of the West. Mackay, who was sent out by the Upper Missouri Fur Company in 1795, described the "great desert of drifting sand without trees, soil, rocks, water, or animals of any kind. . . ." Truteau, approaching the foothills of the Rockies, noted sterile prairies with scarcely any grass.[57]

There were reports of the existence of a Great Desert not only from Spanish and French travelers but from Americans such as Henry Marie Brackenridge, Patrick Gass, and Lewis and Clark. Pike's journal of his 1806–1807 expedition to the West, published four years after his return, further contributed to the image of a Great Desert; his initial optimism about the West had changed: "In that vast country of which we speak, we find the soil generally dry and sandy." Pike believed that "these vast plains of the western hemisphere, may become in time equally celebrated as the sandy desarts of Africa."[58] He saw a positive political aspect to this awful aridity: "From these immense prairies may arise one great advantage to the United States, viz: The restriction of our population to some certain limits, and thereby a continuation of the union."[59]

Other explorers offered similarly bleak views of the West. In the summer of 1817, Major Stephen H. Long of the United State Corps of Topographical Engineers was sent on an exploring expedition from Belle Fontaine, Missouri, up the Mississippi to the falls of the St. Anthony. The objectives of his first expedition were to chart the course of the upper Mississippi, "to exhibit the general topography of the shores, and to designate such sites as were suitable for military purposes."[60] Later that same year he was sent to select a site for a fort in Arkansas and to explore the region along the Arkansas River. No other American explorer of that period traveled more miles, commanded more expeditions (five), or brought back more scientific information than Long.

Two years later, Long commanded America's first systematic scientific expedition. Paralleling Jefferson's broad instructions to Lewis and Clark, Secretary of War John C. Calhoun ordered Long to obtain complete and accurate information about the upper Missouri valley. Five scientists went along on the expedition, including Titian Peale and Thomas Say. As was the case with the Lewis and Clark expedition, the American Philosophical Society furnished Long's party with a list of questions to ask the Indians. Long ordered a steamboat built for this Yellowstone Expedition. Resembling a huge sea monster, the *Western Engineer* was designed to frighten the natives. At the prow was the head of a black serpent emitting steam from its gaping mouth. Unfortunately, muddy water clogged the boilers, and Long's experimental attempt to explore the West by steamer failed.

On his next expedition, in 1820, Long and his party traveled along the Platte River to the Rocky Mountains searching for the source of the Red River. As evidenced by the emphasis of these journeys, the United States government was demonstrating the need to include scientists on western expeditions, and three of the scientists from the Yellowstone Expedition again accompanied Long. Unfortunately, Long failed to find the source of the Red, but on the return trip he delineated a strip of land six hundred miles wide, beginning in Texas and continuing to the Canadian border, which bore "a manifest resemblance to the deserts of Siberia."[61] Long continued, "It is almost wholly unfit for cultivation, and of course uninhabitable by a people depending upon agriculture for their subsistence."[62]

Long and his chronicler, Edwin James, supported what had already been written about desert conditions in the West. Their chief contribution lay in the fact that they gave the concept scientific credence and named it "the Great American Desert." These views left a lasting imprint on the American image of the Great Plains and took nearly fifty years to refute, although how inhibitive to westward migration this stereotype was is difficult to say.

Until the beginning of the Civil War, the appellation Great American Desert appeared on a number of maps in school textbooks as the label for the area that stretched from the 100th meridian to the Rocky Mountains. Before this view became popular in the 1840s, geographers had compared parts of the American West to the Sahara and other African deserts. The image of the Great American Desert persisted until the late nineteenth century, when it was replaced by another image, that of the West as an agrarian utopia or "Garden of the World."[63]

French explorers were among the first to contribute to the belief that the West was a garden of temperate climate, fertile soil, and scenic beauty. "No better soil can be found, either for corn, for vines, or for any other fruit whatever," than that of the Mississippi valley, wrote a French explorer.[64] LaSalle, Lahontan, and Hennepin added to the garden theory, and a French traveler boasted that the soil of Louisiana was similar to Egypt's after the Nile overflowed its banks.[65]

Jefferson also believed that the West was a garden. He sent Lewis and Clark on a three-thousand-mile journey partly in order to support scientifically his view that the West was suitable for settlement by farmers. As Lewis and Clark moved up the Missouri, they described "rich plains and prairies" that possessed all of the attributes for agricultural development, even though they both had believed earlier in the desert concept.[66] In the 1840s, Frémont thought that the plains were barren and sterile, but influenced by his father-in-law, Senator Thomas Hart Benton of Missouri, he later became excited about the area's agricultural possibilities. Frémont "saw visions" of the Kansas River valley as "a beautiful and wooded country of great fertility of soil, well adapted to settlement and cultivation." To this he added the region of the upper Arkansas River valley which was well suited to farming, "well watered and fertile."[67]

William Gilpin was one of the men who traveled with Frémont to the Columbia River in 1843. Influenced by the writings of Alexander von Humboldt, this western entrepreneur was a propagandist for the pastoral image. Through books and articles, Gilpin promoted his geopolitical theories, including his belief in an isothermal zodiac located in a region near the 40th parallel. Gilpin believed that, just as great European civilizations had risen in the past, the greatest of all civilizations would arise in America in the area he designated the Great Plains.[68]

Canadian explorers drew similar desert-garden polarities. Mackenzie held that neither the soil nor the climate of the West could be considered "sufficiently genial to bring the fruits of the earth to maturity."[69] In the 1850s, Captain John Palliser, who was a great admirer of Livingstone, became the leader of a Canadian exploring party. Like the African explorer Samuel Baker, Palliser had only been interested in hunting early in his career, but he soon graduated to exploring. Palliser sparked a bitter debate when he used the words "central desert" to describe the plains close to the Canadian-American border. This was the Canadian version of the Great American Desert and is known as "Palliser's Triangle." Just as Americans envisaged benefits deriving from the Great American Desert (e.g., the prevention of a too-rapid migration westward), so Canadians hoped the concept of their desert would keep Americans from pushing across the 49th parallel. Palliser also used the term "fertile belt" to describe an area farther north, around the Assiniboine and Saskatchewan rivers, which he believed was capable of supporting settlement.[70]

Professor Henry Youle Hind of Trinity College, Toronto, who led expeditions in 1857 and 1858, also believed in the desert theory. Although he placed the arid region farther west than had Palliser, he too, felt that the area was not "fitted for permanent habitations of civilized man." Like Palliser, Hind believed that the lack of trees created the major difficulty for agricultural settlement.[71]

Some years after Palliser's report was published, another college professor, John Macoun, presented a strong rebuttal to Palliser's "desert concept." Like the overstatements on the garden versus desert debate in the United States, Macoun's account exaggerated the verdancy of the southern Canadian plains.[72] Although Macoun in 1879 followed a route which barely touched the "arid belt" that Palliser had visited two decades earlier, he asserted that "the so-called arid country was one of unsurpassed fertility, and that it was literally the 'Garden' of the whole country. . . ."[73]

Trapped in images from the past, the explorers trudged ahead through numerous encounters with danger and death. They brooded over the loss of worlds to explore as the virgin land receded before them. But some of their views were remarkably correct, and disregard of them would later lead to agricultural collapse, as the disastrous droughts in the United States and Canada in the 1930s were sadly to demonstrate.

At the beginning of the nineteenth century, geographical images of Africa and America were based largely on myth and error. Tales of unicorns, golden cities, and Prester John prevailed. New pieces added to the geographical puzzles were slowly accepted. But as more expeditions were sent out, clearer images began to emerge, and the increased information brought back by explorers eroded and replaced the older concepts.

In gathering this information, explorers were the foremost problem solvers of the time. From the sudden glory of the Mungo Park and Lewis and Clark expeditions at the dawn of the century to the major exploring expeditions of Frémont and Livingstone at mid-century, they revealed the unmapped regions of Africa and America.

CHAPTER FOUR

The Enlightenment
and Exploration

THE AGE OF SCIENTIFIC EXPLORATION dawned with the Enlightenment. Explorers and philosophers were the heroes of that period, the foremost citizens of a volatile age, and among the first great personalities on the world stage. In 1780, the Neapolitan writer Gaetano Filangieri published his radical treatise on political science, *La Scienza della Legislazione.* He designated the philosopher a "citizen of all places and ages" who had the entire world "for his country and earth itself for his school."[1] In portraying the citizen of the world, he could have been describing the explorer. Both explorer and philosopher chose the entire world for their domain. They were guided by the polestar of reason and propelled by a boundless curiosity. A student of the European Enlightenment called the coalition of philosophers "a family."[2] Explorers, too, were a family; while the family of philosophers was formulating new political systems, laws, and concepts of human behavior, the family of explorers was searching for uncharted worlds. The philosophers and explorers were certain that they would discover the answers to ancient questions about man and his world.

People of the eighteenth century had an abiding interest in the unknown. The energy used to overcome the influences of the past instilled in men of the Enlightenment a sense of independent force and grand design. Never before had man experienced such an all-encompassing desire to correct social wrongs. Never had there been such a fermentation of minds demanding new answers to old questions. A historian of eighteenth-century science noted that the age's moral and intellectual strengths "were harnessed to the chariot of human progress as they had never been harnessed to it before."[3] A "recovery of nerve" instilled in scientists and explorers a self-confidence that led to informed and bold ventures at home and abroad.[4]

Boldness was a major ingredient in that secular age which produced Voltaire, Cook, and Jefferson. Men of the Enlightenment greeted new worlds with excitement and the courage of their convictions. A trust in themselves and in their strength to break the geographical barriers of ancestral fears and terrifying superstitions inspired them to take risks, to court danger. It was not by happenstance that the motto of the age was Kant's *Sapere aude*—"Dare to know."[5]

Eighteenth-century England witnessed significant advances in the arts and sciences.[6] It was the dawning of the Industrial Revolution and the age of Samuel Johnson, Joseph Banks, and James Cook, men who inhaled energy and brilliance with the island fog. The last decades of the century were a period of amazing activity undertaken by dynamic explorers, brave soldiers, and able administrators. Australia was settled, Canada was conquered, and the Indian Empire was founded. England's greatness lay in the brave acts of enterprising men around the world. England's victory over France in the Seven Years' War "had enlarged without exhausting the national spirit," and England was now the greatest power in the world. Yet she was still unfulfilled.[7] James Bruce lauded her indomitable spirit which, elevated "by a long and glorious war, very naturally at the return of peace received itself into a spirit of adventure and enquiry."[8]

Englishmen of the eighteenth century witnessed the spread of knowledge to more areas of the globe than ever before, and they believed that mankind would be vastly improved by this permeation. The circulation of ideas was greatly facilitated by new technology, such as the improvements in the printing press that increased the production of all sorts of reading matter. Newspapers proliferated, as did magazines and reviews such as

Gentlemen's Magazine, The London Magazine, and *The Rambler.* The popularity of these periodicals demonstrated the reading public's growing interest in ideas. Along with the rise of libraries, these publications spread information within England and satisfied a need for instructional reading material.[9]

The learned journals of the eighteenth century helped to create an international cultural life. From the days of the earliest journal, France's *Journal des Scavans,* which first appeared in 1665, their purpose was to offer information concerning happenings in the expanding European republic of letters. These publications represented a revolution in the flow of scholarly information that crossed language barriers and national frontiers. the first significant scholarly magazine in England was *The History of the Works of the Learned,* first published in 1699. Other English periodicals were *Memoirs of Literature* and *The Present State of the Republick of Letters.*[10]

Over sixty newspapers were published in America between 1719 and 1783, and by the mid-eighteenth century nearly every colony had at least one. In 1790, nearly a hundred newspapers were printed in the United States. They carried local news and advertisements and excerpts from the works of William Cowper and Goldsmith and Cook's *Voyages.*[11] In that same period, a number of American magazines began publication, including William Bradford's *American Magazine* and Benjamin Franklin's *General Magazine.* Although they were short-lived, they reflected America's growing intellectual interests. It was Franklin who, in 1731, founded the first subscription library. By the end of the century, libraries had spread across the handful of states.

In 1771, the American Philosophical Society began publishing its *Transactions,* and the American Academy of Arts and Sciences issued its *Memoirs* in 1785. But the only American periodical approximating a scientific magazine was the *Medical Repository,* first issued in 1798 by Dr. Samuel Latham Mitchill. Its editors noted that for too long a time it had been accepted that Americans would obtain their scientific information from abroad but that, recently, "a more correct opinion has prevailed among them . . . to turn their backs to the east, and direct their views to the inviting and productive regions of the interior of America."[12] In America, books and magazines might sell, but almanacs were guaranteed to. Many homes had only two books—the King James version of the Bible and the farmer's almanac. Almanacs presented the common man with scientific information and provided calendars and reports on the tides and phases of the moon. Franklin's *Poor Richard's Almanack* made the world of science interesting and understandable to the average American. These many publications were evidence of the growing cultural and scientific sophistication developing in America.[13]

During this time, writers and philosophers were gathering information from around the world in order to better understand the human race and find the answers to man's quest for a "General Plan." While philosophers were delving into the beginnings of human history in order to discover the origins of man, explorers were searching out native peoples, who were considered the progenitors of modern man, and assembling facts in order to fill the gaps in geographical knowledge.

Exploration expanded the horizons of knowledge. Exploring is in part an act of comparing one culture or area with another, and the information from the explorers' journals permitted intellectuals to develop new disquisitions on political sociology and cultural anthropology. The influence of explorers' accounts can be seen in the works of Hobbes, Locke, and Rousseau, men steeped in the literature of exploration. That Hobbes had read about the bellicose Indians of North America can be seen in his *Leviathan*. The writings of Locke and Rousseau were influenced by the accounts of more peaceful tribes which they had read in the journals of the explorers.

Cultural relativism was a new method of study in Europe and America and it owed its conceptualization to the exploration experience. Explorers revealed that the world was much larger, more exciting, and more diverse than was previously thought; they demonstrated that "the range of possible beliefs, customs, institutions, and defensible human behavior was enormous." This grand diversity caused Montesquieu to exclaim, "The true is not always probable."[14] The interest in different cultures prompted Rousseau to encourage the estab-lishment of scientific societies for the purpose of outfitting expeditions to study primitive peoples. There was a need to collect, to kill, to stuff; the more exotic, the better. Mummies, fetuses in alcohol, the bones of prehistoric animals, and fet-ishes were considered prized possessions.

Through this gathering of scientific information, the West could impose its order over a world it did not understand. Facts would lead to a larger coherence and newer vision. It was the age of the collector. Through the art of collecting, the mind would be opened and the gaze broadened to include the widest possible range of experience. To the scientific explorer, everything was important: collect the obvious and the trivial. An inventory of the earth was being taken. In London, both public and private repositories such as the British Museum and Sir Ashton Lever's museum were opened in the mid-eigh-teenth century to display the collections brought back by ex-plorers. In the early 1790s, Charles Willson Peale founded the world's first popular museum of natural science and art in Philadelphia. Many of its most valuable items came from ex-plorers. Meriwether Lewis presented the museum with a Sho-shoni peace pipe, Indian weapons, and costumes. In 1808, Zebulon Pike caught two grizzly bear cubs for the museum's zoo. Presumed to be. tame, they soon revealed their fierce disposition when one bear ripped off the arm of an inquisitive monkey. The bear escaped and had to be shot by Peale, who also killed its mate.[15]

The greatest scientific collector of that period was Carolus Linnaeus, professor of natural history and medicine at the University of Uppsala, who made Sweden the kingdom of botany. Since his youth, when he traveled to Lapland, Lin-naeus had been a scientific explorer. He later explored the world through the eyes of his friends and students. In 1753, Linnaeus published *Species Plantarum.* Based on his and others' researches, this work established the binomial nomenclature of genus and species. Linnaeus was a superb scientist, and his impressive character influenced his students and others. Im-bued with Linnaeus's intellectual curiosity, his students scattered throughout the world to observe and collect. One of them, Peter Kalm, came to the United States in 1748. After traveling through America for nearly four years, he returned to Sweden with a collection of American plants. Anders Sparrman and Carl Thunberg, also students of Linnaeus, traveled to Africa, and, along with Kalm, they helped to make botanical exploration fashionable in the late eighteenth century.

Before Linnaeus, botany was a confusion of unclassified facts. He gave the science coherence and unity and brought classification and the scientific method to the field. Instead of remaining the preserve of the gardener, it became the prerogative of the botanist and the scientific-minded amateur. Botany was a new science for a new age. A similar transformation was seen in the explorer, who advanced from being poorly to being scientifically trained.

As discussed in Chapter 1, exploration had a profound effect on the literary world. Using explorers' journals, writers created an image of the "noble savage." British explorers James Cook and Mungo Park played a part in creating, respectively, the "noble Polynesian" and the "noble African," just as American explorers Jonathan Carver, Robert Rogers, and William Bartram had helped create the "noble Indian." Reports about natives were brought back and translated into an Arcadian literature that became fashionable in England and the United States in the eighteenth century. Among the more popular works were Aphra Behn's *Oroonoko: or, The Royal Slave,* John Bicknell's *The Dying Negro,* and Philip Freneau's *The Dying Indian.*

The cult of the primitive made one of its most striking appearances in Diderot's *Supplément au Voyage de Bougainville,* published in 1772. This brief polemic was based upon the travels of the French explorer Louis-Antoine de Bougainville, who circumnavigated the globe between 1767 and 1769. In the work, Diderot contrasted the sexual mores of the Tahitians with the less natural practices of people in the Western world.[16]

James Cook represented an especially significant development in European literature, which one scholar has named the

"Cook-syndrome." Two major images that emerged from his travels were those of the explorer-scientist-hero-traveler and the happy-native-utopia. Cook's voyages fired the imagination of the European. Over one hundred editions and impressions were made of the journals of Cook and his companions between 1770 and 1800. His accounts fueled an interest in the exotic and primitive as he offered Europe a great deal of information about the non-European world and its strange inhabitants. One of his biographers wrote that the discoveries of Cook "opened new scenes for a poetical fancy to range in. . . ."[17]

Quaker botanist William Bartram believed that the American Indian was a noble savage. On his scientific expedition to Florida, he was well received by the Seminoles, whom he described as "well-tutored and civil" and "free from want or desires." To Bartram, Indians were people of morality and "certainly stand in no need of European civilization."[18]

The rise in the popularity of travel literature in the eighteenth century was basic in laying the foundation for the great interest in exploration. From the time of Hakluyt and Purchas in the seventeenth century, England had been the leader in its publication. Even though many of the facts in these works were erroneous, fascinating information about distant worlds emerged which challenged previously held beliefs and prejudices and was valuable in encouraging exploration.

Shakespeare's *Othello* and *Henry the Fourth,* Samuel Johnson's *The History of Rasselas: Prince of Abyssinia,* and William Blake's *The Little Black Boy* were some of the significant works that dealt with Africa. Hack writers also used Africa as the setting for such works as *The Guinea Voyage, The Princess of Zanfara,* and *The Wrongs of Africa.* In the late eighteenth century, a number of popular books on Africa were written by Africans residing in London. Two favorites were the *Autobiography* of Olaudah Equiano and the *Letters* of Ignatius Sancho, both of which appeared in the 1780s.

An earlier fascination with distant lands is evidenced by the establishment of chairs in Arabic studies at Cambridge and Oxford universities in the seventeenth century. Histories of the

Arabs and translations of Arabic works increased interest in Oriental studies in the eighteenth century, as did exotic stories about China. China was a new world with an ancient heritage; a great deal could be learned from her, and Chinese art, furniture, architecture, and goldfish became the rage in London.[19]

During this inquiring age, studies were made of Egypt and Ethiopia. Englishmen had long been fascinated with the pyramids, and the work of Richard Pococke, an English clergyman, heightened interest in Egyptology. In 1768, James Bruce embarked upon an expedition to discover the source of the Nile. (see Chapter 2.) He spent four harrowing years in Ethiopia and, in 1790–1791, published his six-volume work, *Travels to Discover the Source of the Nile*. This daring Scotsman has been called the first great explorer of Africa in the modern age and his work "the epic of African travel."[20]

An Italian proverb maintains, "Long voyages, great lies," and, because travel writers were inclined to exaggerate, their critics sometimes charged them with dishonesty. On Bruce's return from Ethiopia, the tales he told were stranger than fiction. One of his fantastic stories concerned the favorite repast of the Ethiopians, blood-drenched meat cut from a live cow. Samuel Johnson, who was an authority on Ethiopia, having translated Father Lobo's *Voyage to Abyssinia* and published *Rasselas: Prince of Abyssinia*, doubted the veracity of Bruce's stories. The English writer Horace Walpole told humorous stories about "Abyssinian Bruce" and the "live beef." One concerned Bruce's being asked at a dinner party if the Ethiopians had musical instruments. "Yes," he responded, "the lyre," whereupon one guest whispered to another, "I am sure there is one less since he came out of the country." On another occasion, when Bruce overheard someone belittling his raw beef story, he left the room and returned with a strip of raw meat. "You will eat that, sir, or fight me." Bruce's physical presence (he was over six feet tall) convinced the critic to eat the meat along with his words.[21]

Bruce was not the only explorer to be made the butt of jokes. After Stanley found Livingstone, his famous greeting was parodied in a play called *King Carrot* and in a musical spectacle titled *Africa* featuring the American song writing team of Harrigan and Hart. Stanley's honesty was attacked when the story circulated in Britain that Livingstone had rescued Stanley. In the 1890s, a takeoff on Stanley's *In Darkest Africa* was published under the title *In Darkest England and the Way Out.*[22]

Although nineteenth-century governments sponsored exploring expeditions, exploration in the late seventeenth and early eighteenth centuries was supported by private companies and scientific societies, and the adventurer was more buccaneer than explorer. William Dampier was one of the few adventurers who made significant contributions to exploration. He was a pirate, circumnavigator, hydrographer, and captain in the British Navy. In 1697, he published his *A New Voyage Round the World,* with several editions appearing during the next two years. With the success of this book, Dampier became a London celebrity who dined with the greats of English society and was lionized by members of the prestigious Royal Society. Cook praised him and the British government consulted him. In the passion for science that he brought to exploration, Dampier was a precursor of Joseph Banks. Dampier's works, like Cook's *Journals,* had an effect on English literature, as the works of Daniel Defoe and Jonathan Swift reveal.

Besides Dampier's narrative, among the most significant British travel accounts were the collections of the voyages and travels of Thomas Astley, Awnsham Churchill, and John Harris. These multivolume works in numerous editions aroused a deep interest in strange peoples and foreign lands.[23] Notwithstanding Samuel Johnson's observation that "those whose lot it is to ramble can seldom write, and those who know how to write very seldom ramble," these volumes were popular in England. Similar in structure and encyclopedic in tone, these accounts offered the reader a plethora of facts on exotic peoples and places.[24] Johnson described this type of work in his comments on a book of travels: "A great part of his book seems to contain very unimportant accounts of his passage from one place where he saw little, to another where he saw no more."[25]

The period around 1720 was especially remarkable for the amount and quality of travel literature produced. In 1719, Daniel Defoe brought out *The Further Adventures of Robinson Crusoe,* and in the next year he published *The Life, Adventures, and Pyracies of the Famous Captain Singleton.* A few years later, Jonathan Swift produced *Gulliver's Travels.*

Robinson Crusoe is one of the great adventure stories in world literature. Based on the life of Alexander Selkirk, who lived for four years on the island of Juan Fernandez before his rescue, the book became a best seller. Defoe's story had what the British public admired: an exotic journey, stirring discoveries, reverence for God, and the Christian ethic of disobedience-punishment-repentence-deliverance. On that "dismal unfortunate" island Crusoe was in control, and the noble savage Friday was his obedient servant in that incipient capitalist world. The master of all he surveyed, Crusoe was to experience for a short time a power comparable to the worldly power of the Englishman in the eighteenth and nineteenth centuries. Like the successful explorer, Crusoe overcame incredible odds by mastering himself and coping with his environment; he invented new ways of doing things in order to survive. Also like the explorer, Crusoe had to escape his past to discover himself and deal with new worlds. In Crusoe, Defoe presented the essential qualities of the great explorer: ingenuity and an ability to survive and prevail.

But some aspects of the adventurer's story were neglected by Defoe and others: the effects of years of isolation, the feelings of guilt in breaking family ties, and the unending solitude. The literature tended to reduce such abnormal situations to normality. Selkirk's peculiar way of life after his return to civilization—living like a hermit and sleeping in a cave—was lost to the reading public.[26] The nightmare of Mungo Park's capture by an African king continued to haunt his dreams long after his return from Africa, and the terror of that memory stayed with him for months.[27]

Defoe recognized the vicarious thrills which exploration literature could bring to middle-class Englishmen. In his novel *The Life, Adventures and Pyracies of the Famous Captain Singleton,*

Defoe wrote about a Lockean man who journeyed from a state of nature, as represented by Africa, to a state of maturity and deliverance. The young picaresque hero, Bob Singleton, explorer and pirate, completed a bloody trek across Africa from the East Coast to the Gulf of Guinea, giving credence to Samuel Johnson's remark, "I do not much wish well to discovery for I am always afraid they will end in conquest and robbery." By his juxtaposition of fact and imagination, Defoe added a touch of frightening reality to his story and confirmed the eighteenth-century concept of Africa when he described it as "the most barren, desolate, desert, and inhospitable country in the world."[28]

Travel literature changed in the nineteenth century. Before that time, the aims of the writer were to be informative, impersonal, and clear; to state the facts simply and leave himself out of the narrative; but, above all, to be objective. This prosaic impersonality was displaced in the romantic age by a subjective and personal tone, often humorous, sometimes even lyrical and poetic. Facts were still essential, but there was now more emphasis on feeling and atmosphere. The travel writer was interested in evoking word pictures in place of the earlier concern with detail. The emphasis was on a wider spectrum of information. Richard Burton described this change by noting that the public in earlier times had accepted the "dry details" of exploration and had been satisfied with latitudes, longitudes, and elevations. But those days were past, and the traveler

is expected to survey and observe, to record meteorology and trigonometry, to shoot and stuff birds and beasts, to collect geological specimens and theories, to gather political and commercial information . . . , to advance the infant study of anthropology; to keep accounts, to sketch, to indite a copious, legible journal . . . and to forward long reports which shall prevent the Royal Geographical Society napping through its evenings.[29]

Burton was convinced that African travel literature had all the necessary ingredients for attracting the public: far-off places, savage tribes, and violent splendor. Through all the difficulties and suffering, the white explorer revealed his natural dignity and European superiority. Burton also pointed to the "smiling recollections" of the authors as they noted the differences between their pleasant repose, as they began their writing, and the dangers and hardships about which they wrote.[30]

In an independent and expanding America of the late eighteenth century, dozens of histories, geographies, atlases, and works of fiction were published emphasizing the greatness of America and the need for exploration. Thomas Jefferson's *Notes on the State of Virginia*, written in response to a French diplomat's request for information on that state, was an intellectual exploration of America by the nation's greatest advocate of exploration.

Jonathan Carver's *Travels Through the Interior Parts of North America*, published in 1778 and inscribed to Joseph Banks, was a great success on both sides of the Atlantic. A second edition appeared in 1779, as did an Irish edition. By 1786, the book had gone through German, Dutch, and French editions as well. Over the years there would be numerous reissues. Carver, who was born in Massachusetts and fought in the French and Indian War, was sent by Major Robert Rogers to map the rivers of Wisconsin and Minnesota, note the various Indian nations, and look for the Northwest Passage. Starting out from Michilimackinac in the fall of 1776, Carver traveled west to Prairie du Chien, then to the Falls of St. Anthony. By the summer of 1767, his party had reached Grand Portage on Lake Superior; Carver was forced to return to Michilimackinac, however, because of a lack of supplies. Between 1778 and 1838, *Travels Through the Interior Parts*, which told the story of that expedition, went through thirty editions, and Carver became, after Daniel Boone, the best-known explorer in eighteenth-century America.[31] Carver's work has been called "probably the most widely read book of American authorship written in the eighteenth century." It was popular not only because of its mixture of fact and fancy but because it represented the essence of American exploration: individualism, bravery, and national expansion.[32] Carver's favorable descriptions of the Indians were used by European writers such as Chateaubriand in *Voyage en Amerique* and Schiller in "Indian Death-Dirge."

State histories played a role in interesting Americans in exploration. One of the most famous was John Filson's *The Discovery, Settlement and Present State of Kentucke,* a philosophical real estate tract published in 1784 and translated into French and German. In the section entitled "Adventures of Col. Daniel Boon," Filson created the first archetypical American explorer. It became a literary sensation and was known as "Filson's Boone." Despite its stilted language and numerous errors in historical accuracy, Filson's story of Boone entering the Kentucky wilderness interested thousands of readers and created the first and foremost frontier hero. Although he did little actual exploring, Boone has been considered the essential explorer, from his blazing of the Wilderness Road to his death on the Missouri River. Because of Filson's pamphlet and the dramatic litany of other writers, Boone was transformed from a stolid, illiterate cuckold into the American Adam, innocent, confident, and free. A friend of Filson's, Gilbert Imlay, who moved to Europe in the 1780s, spread tales there of Boone's heroic encounters. Shortly afterward, Lord Byron extolled the dramatic life of Boone in his epic *Don Juan:*

> Of the great names which in our faces stare,
> The General Boon, back-woodsman of Kentucky,
> Was happiest amongst mortals anywhere.[33]

Boone was lauded as the American Moses, the American Ulysses, and the Achilles of the West, and was celebrated in Timothy Flint's biography, which went through fourteen editions between 1833 and 1868. In 1813, Daniel Bryan published *The Mountain Muse, Comprising the Adventures of Daniel Boone,* which included the lines:

> Of objects, which are link'd to the grand theme
> O'er all the mazzy complicated chain
> That with sublime sensation swell the soul;
> Boone now in all its forceful influence felt.[34]

James Fenimore Cooper acknowledged his use of Boone as a model in drawing the character of Natty Bumppo for *The*

Leatherstocking Tales. American writers such as James Hall, Robert Montgomery Bird, and William Gilmore Simms also used Boone as a model in their works. John J. Audubon, Thomas Sully, and George C. Bingham, among others, drew portraits of Boone.[35]

The Revolutionary War and the consequent advancement westward marked the beginning of America's age of exploration. The well-publicized exploits of Boone in Kentucky, the victories of George Rogers Clark in the West, and the post-war westward migrations encouraged a vision of a grand, ever-expanding America and bestirred Americans into supporting exploration.

Even the staid George Washington was excited by the possibilities when in 1783 he mentioned to a French friend that he would not be "contented 'till I have explored the Western Country, and traversed those lines (or great part of them) which have given bounds to a New Empire." The American explorer John Ledyard affirmed that the American Revolution "invites to a thorough discovery of the continent. . . ."[36]

Americans wanted to learn about their country's geography and natural resources. There was a growing sentiment among them that they should make their own discoveries rather than rely upon Europeans to do it for them. Edwin James, who was with Stephen Long's 1820 expedition to the West, believed that it was time that Americans "no longer be indebted to the men of foreign countries, for a knowledge of any of the products of our soil, or for our opinions of science."[37]

American scientists depended less on European ideas and experiments during the 1780s and 1790s. The Reverend Gotthilf Muhlenberg began his great study of American plants, and Benjamin Smith Barton, Manasseh Cutler, Caspar Wistar, and Benjamin Waterhouse produced significant works in the field of natural history, collecting plants, shrubs, and trees in the South and West.[38]

Peace brought a renewed vision of the "rising Grandeur of America." American exploration in part came out of the patriotic need to round out the country created by the Treaty of Paris of 1783. A prominent London physician, John Coakley

Lettsom, patron of American science and a member of the African Association, reminded Dr. Benjamin Rush that "the season of peace is the harvest of science" when natural history should be studied with a new emphasis.[39]

The War of American Independence also stimulated a new interest in American geography. Since so much of America was unknown, geographical information held a special appeal for Americans. The Reverend Jedidiah Morse was America's most celebrated geographer, and *Geography Made Easy* and *American Universal Geography* were his most important works. The father of American geography, Morse believed that, as a result of the Treaty of Paris, Americans were free of Great Britain and no longer had "to look up to her for a description of our own country."[40] Dr. Rush urged a few years later that, since "we occupy a new country," America's main concern "should be to explore and apply its resources, all of which press us to enterprize and haste."[41]

American intellectuals and European visitors to America like Johann David Schöpf, a German physician, and André Michaux, a French botanist, believed that further exploration would unlock the secrets of nature or, as Benjamin Franklin said, "increase the Power of Man over Matter, and multiply the Conveniences or Pleasures of Life."[42] The Marquis de Chastellux, French soldier and philosopher, had faith in America's capability to "render herself illustrious by the sciences, as well as by her arms and her government." He felt that "the extent of her empire offers for her observations a large portion of heaven and earth. What observations may not be made from Penobscot to Savannah? From the lakes to the sea?"[43]

The Reverend Manasseh Cutler, who believed that research in natural history was in its infancy in America, sought funding for the American Academy of Arts and Sciences by declaring that

discoveries and discriptions of the natural productions of the Country merit particular attention, as they may be improved for advancing our internal wealth and resources—an object of the highest importance at this happy period, in which independence and peace is so gloriously established.[44]

One of the most significant events in the field of natural history in America at this time was the publication in 1791 of William Bartram's *Travels Through North and South Carolina.* . . . The book came out during the period when a large amount of scientific work was being published. In 1785 Bartram's cousin, Humphry Marshall, finished his treatise on American trees and shrubs, *Arbustrum Americanum,* which has been considered the first thoroughly American study of botany. Because of Linnaeus's influence on American scientists, botany became their favorite science. Caught up in the need for exploration, Marshall wanted to send out a western expedition "to make Observations etc. upon the Natural productions and Curiosities of those Regions."[45]

Scientific and philosophical societies were an important spur to exploration. The Royal Society of London from its founding in 1660 was interested in the natural sciences and exploration. By 1770, the society had sponsored more than forty scientific expeditions. Other nations were sending out similar explorations. Russia sent the Danish explorer Vitus Bering on two voyages to the Arctic between 1725 and 1742. And Carsten Niebuhr, another Dane, explored Yemen in the 1760s, accompanied by artists, a surveyor, a zoologist, and a botanist. At the same time, the French sent an expedition to Peru and Ecuador, to measure the arcs of the meridian.

In the 1760s, the Royal Society encouraged the British government to dispatch scientific expeditions to the Pacific to observe the transit of Venus. No other scientific enterprise of the period so excited the intellectual world as the two astronomical observations of the transit in 1761 and 1769. Scientists in the late eighteenth century were obsessed with the information that would be gained because, on the basis of the resulting calculations, the distance between the earth and the sun could be determined. In order to be scientifically accurate, these sightings had to be taken from different points around the globe. Consequently there was a need to call upon several nations to establish observer teams to detect the solar parallax, and this effort resulted in the first important international scientific cooperation.[46]

Captain James Cook was appointed commander of the expedition to investigate the second transit of Venus.[47] No explorer solved more geographical problems than did this man from the Yorkshire village of Marton-in-Cleveland. A historian of naval exploration declared that Cook was "so singularly fitted by training and temperament for the tasks he was called on to perform, as to suggest a conspiracy of fate."[48] A recent biographer wrote that Cook was a "genius of the matter of fact"; for him, there was always "the possibility of something more. . . ."[49]

Born in 1728 and raised in an environment that developed toughness and stamina, Cook went to sea at the age of eighteen. When he enlisted in the British Navy in 1755, tensions were once again increasing between Britain and France. Cook saw service in Canada during the Seven Years' War and was present at the British capture of Louisbourg. After the war, he was ordered to chart the St. Lawrence River and survey the coasts of Newfoundland and Labrador. Although he became an excellent marine surveyor and navigator, it was his friendships with the Earl of Sandwich and Joseph Banks that helped Cook get his first command.[50]

The Admiralty appointed Cook commander of the four hundred-ton bark *Endeavour* in 1769 and sent him to Tahiti to observe the transit. In secret orders he was instructed to search for the Southern Continent; his search disproved the existence of the continent. (Sometimes proving something did not exist was as valuable as proving that it did.) Between that voyage and his violent death a decade later, Cook discovered eastern Australia, islands in Melanesia, and the Hawaiian Islands. He sailed along the coast of New Zealand, searched for the Northwest Passage, and supported Vitus Bering's discoveries in the Arctic. Cook improved the science of cartography, aided the field of navigation, and reduced the number of cases of scurvy on his vessels by supplying his men with fresh food rich in vitamin C. He possessed a clear and methodical mind and was the personification of the great explorer in his capacity to lead, his ability to grow intellectually, and his professionalism.

Cook's success was based upon more than these characteristics, however; he had the good fortune to work with intelligent British officials, to be blessed with good ships and equipment, and to be served by competent and loyal officers and men, some of whom, such as William Bligh, George Vancouver, and John Ledyard, became famous in their own right. Moreover, Cook was accompanied on his voyages by scientists the caliber of Joseph Banks and Daniel Solander, and his expeditions came at a critical time in the history of exploration when the explorer-scientist was making his first significant appearance.

Cook was as important to the age of exploration as Columbus and Magellan had been to the age of discovery. Through Cook's voyages and the explorations of others, most of the seas had been explored by 1800. Indeed, in the late eighteenth century, they were better mapped than the land. To Europeans the known world was largely a series of coastlines and harbors connected by seaborne trade.

Within two decades of Cook's death, the great explorations would be by land. Geographer James Rennell noted that

the Voyages of the late Captain Cook have so far afforded gratification, that nothing worthy of research by Sea, the Poles themselves excepted, remains to be examined; but by Land, the objects of discovery are still so vast, as to include at least a third of the habitable surface of the earth: for much of Asia, a still larger proportion of America, and almost the whole of Africa, are unvisited and unknown.[51]

With Cook's three voyages between 1768 and 1780, the Age of Exploration began. But factors other than the magnificent achievements of the noble Cook contributed to the new age. Scientific and technological advancements in transportation and communication were essential to the furtherance of exploration.

By the eighteenth century the most fundamental technical advances to aid exploration were improved ship design, especially innovations in the steering gear and rig; an improved magnetic compass which appeared around 1750; advanced horologic and surveying instruments; new and improved navigational instruments, such as John Hadley's sea octant and John Harrison's marine chronometer, which gave navigation a new precision; and the development of cartography, especially in France under Guillaume DeLisle and J. B. Bourguignon d'Anville. These Frenchmen set high standards with their maps of Africa and America. Later, James Rennell would use their African maps as models in drawing his own.[52] "The Science of Geography," noted a British geographer in 1787, "is now become the most fashionable as well as the most rational Amusement of the present polite and enlightened Age."[53]

In America, mapmaking became almost fashionable. A historian of the American mind believed that "the science that, next to agriculture, probably lay closest to the vital core of the American experience was geography."[54] A number of accurate maps were drawn in the middle of the eighteenth century. Two of these were published in 1755: Dr. John Mitchell's *Map of the British and French Dominions* and Lewis Evans's *General Map of the Middle British Colonies in America*. The Evans map was so popular that it went through eighteen editions before 1800.[55]

Britain began to "promote knowledge" of Africa after the loss of her thirteen American colonies. American independence had increased Britain's need for raw materials and new markets and, by the 1770s, British exports to Africa had risen to £866,000. Liverpool slave dealers, London merchants, and Jamaican planters had close economic ties to Africa. Africa's strategic importance was clearly demonstrated in Britain's naval battles with the French off the West Coast of Africa.[56] By the late eighteenth century, Horace Walpole told a friend that Africa was "coming into fashion."[57]

Burton considered that the heroic age of African exploration was the period in which Park and Bruce explored Africa, but he also believed that the prestige and excitement of the exploration of Africa diminished as the public became glutted with African adventure stories. Burton thought that the travels of Livingstone and Paul Du Chaillu had created a renewed interest in African exploration which was important in preparing the groundwork for the great Scramble for Africa in the late nineteenth century.[58]

Scholarly associations performed valuable services in encouraging exploration in the eighteenth and nineteenth centuries. Twelve wealthy Britishers with a scientific bent founded the Association for Promoting the Discovery of the Interior Parts of Africa on June 9, 1788, at St. Albans Tavern in London. The African Association, as it was called, was the first learned society to encourage the systematic exploration of Africa for humanitarian, scientific, and, especially, commercial reasons.[59] Two men were the heart and soul of the society: Quaker merchant Henry Beaufoy, who was elected the association's first secretary, and its first treasurer, Joseph Banks. The association stated that its reasons for sending out explorers were the study of nature, the lure of the unknown and, most of all, "the advantages to which a better acquaintance with the inland regions of Africa may lead, the first in importance is the extension of commerce and the encouragement of the manufactures of Great Britain." The association hoped to see England's fabrics traded to over one hundred million Africans; members could well believe that few trading areas in the world could be found that would yield as much profit.[60]

Until its merger with the Royal Geographical Society in 1831, the African Association sent out a number of explorers, including Simon Lucas, Daniel Houghton, Mungo Park, Frederick Hornemann, and J. L. Burckhardt, most of whom made important contributions to the geographical knowledge of Africa. The association was especially curious about certain areas of the African interior—the Sahara, the region between the Senegal and Gambia rivers, and the Niger River valley—and, through the association's efforts, explorers made expeditions to these regions. The journals of these explorers revealed to Europeans that Africans were not savages with tails and other deformities but able, educable, and in possession of numerous skills. The botanical collections that these explorers brought back produced new information about the flora and fauna of the continent. Most important of all were the ideas that the association developed regarding the commercial possibilities of Africa's interior.[61]

Men of the Enlightenment were well aware of the terrors of the African slave trade, and some attempted to stop it. In so doing, they launched one of the most effective propaganda campaigns of the period. Their speeches, pamphlets, news-papers, and books allowed Englishmen to become better in-formed about Africa than they had ever been. The struggles to end the slave trade and the continued exploration of the interior proceeded concurrently. In 1788, William Wilber-force offered the first resolution in the House of Commons to abolish the slave trade. Two decades later, Wilberforce and other British abolitionists organized the African Institute in order to support humanitarian concerns and encourage re-search on Africa. Paradoxically, in the parliamentary debates over the abolition of the slave trade emphasis was placed on British trade and its positive effects on African society. These ideas were incorporated into the rationalizations for creating British trusteeships in Africa in the late nineteenth century.[62]

The urban center of American scientific life was Philadel-phia, and Philadelphia's intellectual center was the American Philosophical Society. Founded by Benjamin Franklin first in 1743 and for a second time in 1769, the society was one of the few national institutions in existence at that time. Because of its active members and their cosmopolitan concerns, a deep interest in exploration developed, as seen in the preparations for observing the transit of Venus in the 1760s and the sup-port given by the society to the Lewis and Clark expedition. In America, which had the unique distinction of being born be-fore it was explored, the scientist, philosopher, and politician often spoke with one voice of the need to explore.[63]

Franklin viewed the American Philosophical Society as a means to "cultivate the finer arts and improve the common stock of knowledge."[64] Patterned after the Royal Society of London, the American Philosophical Society became increas-ingly involved with scientific exploration that worked toward "the improvement of their country, and advancement of its interests and prosperity."[65] Scientific exploration served to foster intercolonial cooperation. A minister from New Hampshire, Jeremy Belknap, hoped that a thorough, systematic exploration could be undertaken under the leadership of the American Philosophical Society. "Why may not a *Republic of Letters*," he wrote, "be realized in America as well as a Republican Government?"[66] Besides Franklin, among its most distinguished members were Jefferson, Benjamin Smith Barton, Manasseh Cutler, and John and William Bartram, all closely associated with the beginnings of American scientific exploration. Jefferson served as the society's president for eighteen years, and Joseph Banks was one of its most distinguished foreign members.

Increasingly, explorers shared an international partnership of ideas and techniques. The transit of Venus in 1769 was the basis for future international cooperative efforts. This scientific ecumenicalism was seldom touched by wars or diplomatic disputes; indeed, during the Revolutionary War, Franklin intervened to prevent American vessels from impeding Cook's third expedition, which Franklin called

an undertaking truly laudable in itself, as the Increase of Geographical Knowledge facilitates and Communication between distant Nations, in the Exchange of useful Products and Manufactures, and the Extension of Arts, whereby the common Enjoyments of human Life are multiply'd and augmented, and Science of other kinds increased to the benefit of Mankind in general.[67]

The percolation of ideas influenced exploration during the Enlightenment. Explorers were better trained and more humane in their relationships with natives than their predecessors because of the new emphasis on science and humanitarianism. The ideas of that age both initiated exploration and created a new type of explorer.

The scientific world encouraged explorers to explore, and the explorers in turn became more scientifically minded. The influence of ideas challenged explorers to greater enterprise—and what could be more challenging than to reveal the mysteries of Africa and America?

CHAPTER FIVE

The Patrons

THOMAS JEFFERSON, WHO NEVER got farther west than the Warm Springs Valley of Virginia, was the preeminent patron of American exploration. Although the Lewis and Clark expedition was his only major exploratory success, Jefferson's value to American exploration lay in his encouragement of western exploring expeditions and his establishment of the precedent of government sponsorship of exploration.

The West held such a strong fascination for Jefferson that he even built his home, Monticello, facing west. Jefferson inherited his interest in exploration from his father, Peter, who had been a mapmaker and surveyor. In 1746, three years after his son's birth, Peter Jefferson took part in the Fairfax Line expedition to the headwaters of the Potomac River.[1] Five years later, with Joshua Fry, he completed the first map of Virginia to be made from actual surveys.

Thomas Jefferson devoted a great deal of attention to the West in his *Notes on the State of Virginia*. He wrote not only about the Potomac and James rivers but the Ohio and Missouri as well. One of his biographers remarked that Jefferson began "with Virginia but proceeded by irresistible impulse into the vastness of the West."[2] Jefferson's vision was grand; no other president became as involved with exploration as he, and his interest in the unknown areas of the country made him the most significant figure in the opening of the West. His most important biographer noted, "In few things that he did as President was he more in character than as a patron of exploration. . . ."[3]

Jefferson first attempted to send an expedition to the American West in the 1780s when he was a member of the Continental Congress. This initial proposal came about partly because he suspected that the British were attempting to explore and colonize the West. Jefferson asked his friend George Rogers Clark to head this western expedition. Unlike the Lewis and Clark expedition, Jefferson's proposal to Clark was not well planned. In any case, Clark was deeply in debt and, not willing to take on further obligations, declined the offer.[4] Clark did suggest to Jefferson, however, that too large a party would frighten the Indians, and he recommended that only three or four men be sent "at a very Trifling Expence."[5]

When Jefferson was American minister to France in 1785, he met that romantic Yankee John Ledyard, who he described as "a man of genius, of some science, and of fearless courage and enterprise." Historian Bernard De Voto described Ledyard as "part genius and part moongazer."[6] Ledyard was born in 1751 in Groton, Connecticut. His father was a sea captain in the West Indies trade. After his father's death in 1762, Ledyard, the eldest of six children, had a disruptive childhood, living first with his grandfather and then with his uncle. In 1772, with the intention of becoming an Indian missionary, he entered Dartmouth College, but left after one year. Two years later he sailed to England where he joined the Royal Marines. Ledyard subsequently met Captain Cook, who agreed to take him on his third voyage in 1776.[7]

After Cook's death in the Hawaiian Islands in 1779, Ledyard returned to England. From there he traveled to Connecticut, where in 1783 he published the journal of Cook's last expedition. Back in Europe, Ledyard soon numbered among his friends Joseph Banks, Jefferson, Lafayette, and John Paul Jones.[8]

While visiting the fur-rich Pacific Northwest with Cook, Ledyard learned of the economic feasibility of the sea otter trade with China. When he returned to England, he failed to obtain financing for a trading company, but to pursue his dream of establishing a trading post in the West he agreed to Jefferson's proposal to explore the American West. Jefferson and Ledyard concocted a mad scheme: Ledyard would walk across Russia, take a ship to Nootka Sound, proceed across North America, and end up in Virginia, protected only by his winning ways and two dogs. This eccentric Connecticut Yankee was confident that neither oceans nor mountains would impede his "passage to glory." With his heart "on fire," Ledyard believed that he would succeed in that monumental undertaking and thereby become the first man to circumambulate the globe. He traveled into Russia without first obtaining a passport from Catherine II, empress of Russia, however, and was arrested by her police in Siberia. After Ledyard was released from custody at the Polish-Russian frontier, he complained in the understatement of the age that "the royal dame has taken me out of my way." Ledyard's next idea was to penetrate the West from Kentucky. But before this expedition could begin he was persuaded by Joseph Banks and the African Association to explore the Niger River. While in Cairo preparing "to see what he can do with that continent," he died suddenly.[9]

But interest in western exploration continued. The United States War Department sent out Lieutenant John Armstrong in 1790 to secretly explore the Missouri River. Armstrong had traveled only a few miles above St. Louis when he was stopped by hostile Indians.[10] Three years later, Jefferson, then secretary of state, supported French botanist André Michaux's proposal for a western expedition. Michaux had been sent to America in 1785 by the French king, Louis XVI, to ascertain whether American trees could be grown in French soil in order to supply lumber for his country's naval construction program. Jefferson explained to Michaux that the main goal of his expedition was "to find the shortest and most convenient route of communication between the U.S. and the Pacific ocean." Michaux's scientific expedition to the Pacific was to be sponsored by the American Philosophical Society, and a number of distinguished Americans were to subscribe to this scientific undertaking. However, because of Michaux's connection to the western intrigues of the French minister to the United States, Edmond Charles Genet, President Washington asked the French government to recall Genet, and the expedition was aborted.[11]

There was a ten-year interruption in Jefferson's plans for a western expedition. In 1801, he became president. A year earlier, Spain had retroceded Louisiana to France, and, to meet this significant geopolitical change, Jefferson prepared to launch a military reconnaissance of the West. Its main task was to learn about foreign influence in the upper Louisiana country and then continue on to the Pacific. At this time in London, Alexander Mackenzie published his *Voyages,* in which he encouraged Britain to search for a land route to the Pacific. This work further convinced Jefferson of the need to dispatch Lewis and Clark.

Jefferson was interested in determining how the United States might counter foreign penetration and in finding out whether the West was suitable for American farmers. To his secretary of the treasury, Albert Gallatin, "the great object" was to learn "whether from its extent and fertility that country was susceptible of a large population in the same manner as the corresponding tract on the Ohio."

In a secret message to Congress in January, 1803, Jefferson proposed sending an expedition to the Pacific. He declared that its aim was to advance geographical knowledge "for the purpose of extending the external commerce of the U.S.," and he requested from Congress an initial $2,500.[12] Thus was born the famous Lewis and Clark expedition, whereby Jefferson hoped to solve the centuries-old question of the Northwest Passage, answer military questions, and develop trade along the Missouri.

The plan for the explorers was to map the water route up the Missouri to the Columbia. Jefferson suggested that this route could offer cheap and fast transportation between the Pacific and the Mississippi. From the latter, goods could be shipped to the Atlantic by way of the Illinois or Wabash rivers or the Great Lakes and Hudson River.[13] Jefferson wrote his friend and private secretary, Meriwether Lewis,

The object of your mission is to explore the Missouri river, & such principal stream of it, as, by it's course and communication with the waters of the Pacific ocean, whether Columbia, Oregan, Colorado or any other river may offer the most direct & practicable water communication across this continent for the purposes of commerce.[14]

When the American minister to France, Robert Livingston, signed the Louisiana Purchase treaty with the French government for the acquisition of all of Louisiana in June 1803, the military reasons for the expedition became less significant. Jefferson now emphasized the scientific and diplomatic aspects of the undertaking. After the treaty signing in Paris, geographical information about its newly acquired territory was even more important to the United States government. Furthermore, peace treaties were to be signed with western Indian tribes that then resided on American soil.[15]

Lewis and Clark got along famously, unlike a number of African explorers such as Burton and Speke and Livingstone and some of the members of his Zambezi expedition. The two explorers "agreed and worked together with a mutuality unknown elsewhere in the history of exploration and rare in any kind of human association."[16]

Few others performed their missions as well or returned from such long and dangerous treks with so minimal a loss of life as did Lewis and Clark. Only one man died, and probably even the facilities of an eastern hospital would not have saved him. The greatest logistical problems of the expedition were a defective chronometer, which made most of the observations inaccurate, and the failure of the boat the *Experiment,* which Lewis designed and had built at the Harper's Ferry Arsenal. The expedition was forced to abandon the boat when cracks appeared in the hull. In the requisite skills for exploring, Lewis and Clark complemented each other: Clark had frontier and negotiating skills, and Lewis had some training in the sciences.

The expedition's success can be further attributed to the intelligent preparation that went into it. Lewis took cram courses in various scientific subjects in the spring of 1803 while he was in Philadelphia and Lancaster purchasing scientific equipment for the expedition. Philadelphia physician and anatomist Caspar Wistar taught him about fossils, and from Robert Patterson, professor of mathematics at the University of Pennsylvania, he learned the use of the sextant and chronometer. He discussed medicine with Dr. Benjamin Rush, who gave Lewis a list of questions to ask the Indians.[17]

Because of the high caliber of its leaders and the thoroughness of their preparation, the Lewis and Clark party returned with more useful information than any other American expedition before or since. Among the facts uncovered were that there was no short water route to the Pacific, that travel to the West Coast was more difficult than had been thought, and that the West was rich in flora and fauna.

Although most explorers are perceived as loners, there were a number of successful partnerships besides Lewis and Clark's. The most famous among African explorers were Speke and Grant's and Stanley and Livingstone's. Compatible personalities and common interests were basic ingredients in Lewis and Clark's partnership. Their only difference of opinion seemed to be over dog meat and salt; Lewis like these comestibles and Clark did not.[18]

After the French ceded Louisiana to the United States, Jefferson became interested in sending expeditions to explore the rivers of the Southwest, especially the Arkansas and Red. This was part of his grand plan to explore the Louisiana Purchase territory and open up the area to settlement. William Dunbar, a scientist who lived in Mississippi, and Dr. George Hunter of Philadelphia were selected to lead an expedition. A product of the Scottish Renaissance, Dunbar was born in Scotland in 1749, graduated from King's College, Aberdeen, and moved to London. He traveled to the United States in the 1770s because of poor health. Settling in Natchez, he became distinguished as a surveyor, botanist, zoologist, and mathematician. This Renaissance man of the American Southwest was also a member of the American Philosophical Society.

Jefferson's plan was for Dunbar and Hunter to lead their party up the Red River to its head, cross to the headwaters of the Arkansas, and return home by that river. For this exploration, Congress appropriated $3,000. Setting out from Dunbar's Mississippi plantation in October, 1804, the party of seventeen traveled to the mouth of the Red and then upriver to the Ouachita. They reached the headwaters of the Ouachita in early December, but, due to problems with the Osage Indians and threats from the Spanish patrols, they began their homeward voyage on January 8, 1805. Their reports and a map drawn by Nicholas King based on Dunbar's notes were the first well-informed views of the southern reaches of the Louisiana Territory, even though they alluded to unicorns and crops produced without rain.[19]

Jefferson was encouraged enough by this expedition to send out another. Because Dunbar and Hunter were unwilling to make a second journey, he chose surveyor Thomas Freeman to lead the next Red River expedition. The Freeman party comprised twenty–four men, including a botanist, when it set out in April, 1806, but six hundred thirty miles above the mouth of the Red River a large Spanish force halted the expedition.[20]

In contrast to the success of the Lewis and Clark exploration, these two expeditions to the Southwest accomplished little. Dunbar and Hunter had done a credible job of exploring the Red River and drew up the first scientific report on the hot springs of Arkansas, but the fact that Freeman was turned back by the Spanish damaged the American government's reputation with the Indians. Jefferson understood the difficulties scientists faced in the West: "These expeditions are so laborious and hazardous, that men of science, used to the temperature and inactivity of their closet, cannot be induced to undertake them."[21]

The next expedition to the Southwest was led by Lieutenant Zebulon M. Pike and initiated by the rogue general James Wilkinson with Jefferson's approval. The New Jersey-born Pike had had an undistinguished record as an army paymaster until selected for this assignment by Wilkinson. Leaving St. Louis in the summer of 1805, Pike's first expedition was an ascension of the Mississippi River to explore its headwaters, collect facts about the animals and population, purchase sites for military forts, and invite Indians to visit St. Louis. A severe winter allowed the expedition of twenty men to progress only as far as Cass Lake. Very few Indians came back to St. Louis with the party in April, but the expedition did succeed in furnishing the first significant maps and reports of the upper Mississippi.

Pike was next ordered to escort a group of Osage Indians to their village in southwestern Missouri, to continue westward into Nebraska and make peace with the Kansas and Pawnee tribes, and to discover the source of the Red River. A number of questions have been raised about this expedition because of the fact that it was organized by Wilkinson, who was in the pay of the Spanish government and had earlier advised the Spanish to arrest Lewis and Clark.

Starting out in the summer of 1806, Pike's force was made up of troops, among them Wilkinson's son, and civilians. Moving across the plains of Kansas, the party explored the Arkansas, and Pike ordered the younger Wilkinson and some of the men to descend the river. The rest continued westward up the Arkansas to the Rockies. On a cold day in November, four members of the fifteen-man party, including Pike, attempted to climb a snow-covered peak which Pike called Grand Peak and which was later named for him. They failed, and hunger and cold plagued their steps as the men crossed the Sangre de Cristo Mountains in search of the Red River and arrived at the Rio Grande, which Pike thought was the Red. In early 1807, the party built a small stockade on the Conejos, an effluent of the Rio Grande, where before long a Spanish patrol arrested Pike and his men for trespassing on Spanish territory. The devious Wilkinson allegedly had alerted the Spanish to the American reconnaissance. Pike and his party were taken to Santa Fe and through northern Mexico; Pike was finally released by the Spanish at Natchitoches in June, 1807.[22]

In all probability, Pike had been lost and was delighted to be captured, for the Spanish authorities gave him a grand tour of the Southwest, the same area about which he had been seeking information. Nevertheless, Pike's expedition proved to be more successful as espionage than as exploration.[23]

Another strong supporter of western exploration was John C. Calhoun, who served as President James Monroe's secretary of war from 1817 to 1825. Calhoun sent out four military-exploratory teams in 1820: one party was sent to the confluence of the St. Peters and Mississippi rivers; the governor of Michigan Territory, Lewis Cass, explored the south shore of Lake Superior for copper deposits; Jedidiah Morse was sent to Mackinac Island and Green Bay to study Indians; and, finally, Major Stephen Long explored the plains. This last expedition grew out of the Yellowstone expedition of 1819, organized by Calhoun to build military fortifications in the upper Missouri valley to counter British advances.[24]

Thomas Hart Benton, United States senator from Missouri, was another strong advocate of western exploration. Benton visited Jefferson at Monticello in 1824, and his daughter, Jessie, believed that this visit was a symbolic laying on of hands for her father. With Jefferson's death in 1826, Benton donned the mantle of American exploration. In his autobiography, *Thirty Years' View,* Benton wrote that Jefferson's hope when he sent out Lewis and Clark was to open trade with Asia. Benton envisioned the Missouri and Columbia rivers as links to Asian commerce.[25]

Benton was obsessed with the idea of a passage to India. He believed that the American rivers had the potential to become "what the Euphrates, the Oxus, the Phasis, and the Cyrus were to the ancient Romans, lines of communication with eastern Asia and channels for that rich commerce which, for forty centuries, had created so much wealth and power wherever it has flowed."[26] Benton repeatedly compared the soil of the West with the rich soil of Egypt. His interest in western exploration can be seen in his strong support of the exploring expeditions of his son-in-law John Charles Frémont, who served in the Topographical Corps. In 1842 Benton pushed through the United States Senate an act authorizing Frémont to map a road to South Pass.

Some years later, Benton was unsuccessful in convincing Secretary of War Jefferson Davis to send out an expedition to explore the West along the central route for a proposed railroad, but he convinced his friend Edward F. Beale to explore the central plains for that purpose. A few months later, Benton claimed that Beale found the central route to be "good for roads and settlements, and inviting the hand of the farmer to improve it."[27] Because of his political influence and his interest in western commerce, Benton became one of exploration's most valuable supporters.

The American government sent out exploratory expeditions until the 1870s. Stephen Long made five expeditions between 1817 and 1823, and Frémont and Charles Wilkes undertook explorations in the 1830s and 1840s. In the 1850s, the great railroad surveys were launched by the government to determine the best route for a Pacific railroad. These surveys were an initial attempt at a systematic and thorough reconnaissance of the West along specific lines of latitude. In that same decade, naval lieutenant William Lewis Herndon explored the Amazon River. The Pacific Ocean was explored by expeditions under naval officers Matthew C. Perry and Cadwalader Ringgold. By mid-century, explorers sailed to the Arctic in hopes of finding the Open Polar Sea. At that time there were even two American naval expeditions to Africa. The Society for the Exploration of Central Africa was established in New York City in 1856. After the Civil War, the United States Geological Surveys were begun under the leadership of Clarence King, Ferdinand V. Hayden, George M. Wheeler, and John Wesley Powell who, along with dozens of geologists, topographers, and a host of scientists, completed the exploration of America. Powell visited the last unexplored regions of the West in the 1860s—the canyons of the Colorado and the Plateau Province of Arizona and Utah. One of the last expeditions was undertaken in 1871 by Powell's brother-in-law, Almon Thompson, who located the last-discovered river in America, the Escalante. With that discovery, Wheeler wrote, "The day of the path-finder has sensibly ended."

If Jefferson was the founding father of American exploration, Sir Joseph Banks was British exploration's patron saint. A British explorer told Banks, "It is with real pleasure & satisfaction that I look up to you as the common Center of we discoverers."[28] Banks was born in London in the same year as Jefferson, 1743, and at the age of eighteen he inherited a fortune from his father. When he matriculated at Oxford, he was so taken with the study of botany that he hired a private tutor to instruct him in the intricacies of that science. Banks's friend, Swedish botanist Carolus Linnaeus, was a major influence on him. Banks's love of botany took him to Newfoundland and Labrador where he began the collecting that was to become the basis for his great herbarium. George III appointed Banks director of the Royal Botanical Gardens at Kew in 1772, and Banks made Kew a scientific mecca for botanists and established botanical gardens in India, Australia, and Africa.[29] As had Linnaeus, Banks initiated botanical expeditions to Africa in the 1770s and 1780s, and he made the study of botany part of Britain's imperialist scheme.

Many of the best scientific minds of the western world came to Bank's splendid home in Soho Square to study his collection of plants, fishes, and insects. His library of natural history was considered the largest in the world. In 1766, at the age of twenty-three, Banks was elected to the Royal Society. Twelve years later he became president, a position he retained for nearly fifty years. He knew the leading scientists of the time and, through his interest, supported dozens of scientific projects. Believing that the sciences were "never at war," he presented Benjamin Franklin with the Royal Society's gold medal for his protection of Cook's ships during the Revolutionary War. Banks's commitment to science never wavered; during Britain's war with France, he helped protect the collections of French scientists. As a symbol of scientific camaraderie, he allowed French explorer Jean-François de La Pérouse to use Cook's dipping needle.[30]

Banks sailed with Cook in 1768 on the world's first scientific expedition, and with his own money outfitted the *Endeavour* with scientific equipment. He brought back one hundred new genera and one thousand new species. His travels with Cook brought him worldwide recognition and demonstrated that he was an excellent scientific explorer. Banks's explorations and Linnaeus's books made botanical exploration fashionable. One English satirist wrote:

> Lord, that's Sir Joseph Banks,
> How grand his look
> Who sailed all round the world with Captain Cook.[31]

Banks did not sail with Cook on his second and third voyages, but he remained active in supporting other explorers such as Matthew Flinders, who explored the Australian coast and circumnavigated that continent and Tasmania in 1803. Banks sent out Captain William Bligh on the famous H.M.S. *Bounty* in the late 1780s to transport breadfruit trees from Tahiti to Jamaica.

Banks was a founder and, for many years, treasurer of the African Association, the society involved with the opening of Africa to scientific exploration. In May, 1799, to celebrate Mungo Park's return, Banks delivered a lengthy address to the association in which he called on the British government to launch expeditions to penetrate the African interior. Banks was an early proponent of British imperialism, asserting that

by Mr. Park's means (we have) opened a Gate into the Interior of Africa into which it is easy for every nation to enter and to extend its Commerce and Discovery. . . . As increased Riches still increase the wants of the Possessors, and Our Manufacturers are able to supply them, is not this prospect, of at once attaching to this country the whole of the Interior Trade now possessed by the Moors, with the chance of incalculable future increase, worth some exertion and some expense to a Trading Nation?

Banks continued, "If this Country delays much longer to possess themselves of the Treasures laid open to them by the exertions of this Association, some Rival Nation will take possession. . . ." He also believed that British control of Africa would mean a happier life for the natives: slavery would be abolished and British culture and Christianity would overwhelm the pagan.[32]

Banks resigned as treasurer of the association in 1804 but remained on its committees until his death in 1820. Most of the explorers sent to Africa by the association went on Banks's recommendation. A friend of Banks believed that no one more "deserved the name of philosopher than he whose life was devoted to the love of wisdom, whose rich reward was the delight of the study, whose more noble ambition left to others the gratification of recording their progress in books." He was called "the Father of research, the laborious advocate of enquiry, and the friend of the adventurous traveller."[33] Banks unleashed a chain of scientific events that was to lead to the British colonization of much of Africa.

Early in the nineteenth century, John Barrow, second secretary of the Admiralty for almost forty years, initiated voyages to further knowledge of geography and navigation. Among these were Arctic expeditions, most notably those of William Parry and John Ross. Barrow organized the Congo expedition of 1816 and, for many years afterward, kept up his interest in African exploration by writing books and articles on the subject. Barrow helped establish the Royal Geographical Society and served as its third president.

Roderick Murchison was the great patron of British exploration in the mid-nineteenth century. Born in Scotland in 1792, the son of a man who had made his fortune in India, Murchison served in the Napoleonic Wars. He was later honored for his geographical studies of Europe. Murchison investigated the rock strata in Wales and England in the 1830s and, as a result of his studies, established the Silurian period as a new geologic system. He was elected president of the Royal Geographical Society in 1843, a position he held off and on for sixteen years.

The society was founded in 1830, and its objective was to promote trade and scientific knowledge. It held "African Nights" in which explorers reported on their expeditions. The society's royal medal, which it bestowed upon explorers, marked the ultimate in recognition. Among those who received the medal were Livingstone, Burton, Speke, Grant, and Frémont. Sir Bartle Frere, president of the society from 1873 to 1877, remarked that it always supported the "practical views of public policy," and that exploration was the "pioneer of progress." Armchair geographers associated with the Royal Geographical Society performed a service by gathering information and writing books on Africa. With their pens, W. D. Cooley, James M'Queen, and Charles Beke stimulated interest in Africa. Cooley also organized African expeditions.[34]

A student of Victorian exploration called Murchison "the presiding genius of the great years of African exploration." One of his greatest honors came when Samuel Baker named the great falls on the Nile after him. Murchison was called by a student of exploration a "latter-day Sir Joseph Banks." His home in Belgrave Square, like Banks's house in Soho, was a gathering place for scientists, explorers, and politicians. In 1865, Murchison wrote of exploration, "Oh for the good days of adventure, of Raleigh and Drake. . . ."[35]

When Livingstone returned to England in 1856, after fifteen years in Africa, Murchison suggested that he write the story of his travels. *Missionary Travels and Researches in South Africa* was published in 1857 and dedicated to Murchison, whom Livingstone called, "the best friend I ever had."[36] Murchison contacted Livingstone in 1865 and recommended that he explore Lake Tanganyika in order to locate "the watershed or watersheds of South Africa"—in other words, to discover the source of the Nile. Livingstone agreed, and the Royal Geographical Society provided £3,000 for his journey. The British government gave him £500 and a consulship to help with expenses. More government funds would later be spent on this expedition and, after Livingstone's death, on his funeral, which was the largest since the Duke of Wellington's in 1852. The total cost of Livingstone's expedition was over £6,000. The Royal Geographical Society also paid a large part of the cost of Verney Cameron's expedition of 1873–1875, during which Cameron became the first man to cross the African continent from east to west.[37]

Murchison encouraged Lord Clarendon, British foreign secretary, to support Burton's expedition in 1856 with a £1,000 government grant. John Speke was sent to Africa in 1860 by

Murchison and the Royal Geographical Society to obtain information about the interior of East Africa. The Society directed Speke to travel around Lake Victoria, find the head of the White Nile, and follow it north to Gondokoro. Through Murchison's influence, the government gave Speke £2,500 and the Admiralty was prevailed upon to allow Speke and his second-in-command, James Grant, to travel to Zanzibar aboard a British warship.[38]

From the days of Prince Henry the Navigator to those of Thomas Hart Benton and Roderick Murchison, patrons were vital to exploration. Although they seldom participated, they performed a number of important functions. They organized societies to encourage exploration; they raised money for expeditions and selected the men to lead them; and, either through their direct involvement in governmental affairs or their influence with high-ranking governmental officials, the patrons played notable roles in the preparation, promotion, and launching of African and American expeditions.

CHAPTER SIX

The Literature
of Exploration

FROM THE SIXTEENTH CENTURY ON, exploration inspired a vast amount of literature. So it is no surprise that exploration literature flourished in Europe and America in the eighteenth and nineteenth centuries because of public curiosity about travel in distant lands. The reader of exploration literature entered a world where everyday life was displaced by a new reality: the story of how the traveler experienced a reawakening, an awareness of the world and his fellow man, and how he was changed by this.

Although there were many interesting aspects of exploration, the reading public was especially fascinated by the lives of the natives. Nicholas Biddle, who was the first editor of the Lewis and Clark journals, wrote to William Clark in 1810 about their forthcoming publication:

If you have any information as to any system of signs by which you are able to communicate with the Indians, or which enables different tribes to converse together I should like to have it. To you who understand all these things so well, they do not perhaps appear curious because they are familiar. But in our towns, and in Europe too where we know nothing of Indians every little matter is a subject that excites curiosity.[1]

Richard Burton recognized that, although the British public had read many books on Africa, still

The theme has remoteness and obscurity of place, difference of custom, marvellousness of hearsay; events passing strange yet credible; sometimes barbaric splendour, generally luxuriance of nature, savage life, personal danger and suffering always borne (in books) with patience, dignity, and even enthusiasm.[2]

Alexander von Humboldt stated that, for those who traveled only by their fireplace,

The objects with which we are acquainted only by the animated narratives of travellers, have a particular charm; imagination wanders with the delight over which is vague and undefined; and the pleasures of which we are deprived, seem possessed of a fascinating power compared to which all we daily feel in the narrow circle of sedentary life appears insipid.[3]

Books on African exploration were popular in America, just as those on American exploration were popular in Europe. The American Geographical Society was founded in New York City in 1852 and became the center of American interest in African exploration. Meetings on Africa were an important activity of the society, and on December 13, 1875, the society held an evening on Africa to tell its members about Stanley's explorations.

Practically everyone who explored wrote a book about his or her experiences. At least eight members of the Lewis and Clark expedition wrote accounts of it. Indeed, Patrick Gass's journal of the Lewis and Clark expedition, *A Journal of the Voyages and Travels of a Corps of Discovery,* published in 1807, scooped Lewis and Clark's. Although Gass made little money from the book, his editor and ghost writer, David M'Keehan, did quite well financially because it was the first account by a participant of the expedition to come off the press, the price was only $1 a copy, and excitement over the expedition was still high. The journal went through seven editions in as many years. Three European editions were published, in Paris, London, and Weimar; three more were published in Philadelphia by the well-known publisher and bookseller Mathew Carey.[4]

The first two counterfeit editions of the Lewis and Clark expedition appeared in 1809, and even they sold well. One of them carried the somewhat substantial title of *The Travels of Capts. Lewis & Clarke, by order of the Government of the United States, performed in the years 1804, 1805, & 1806, being upwards of three thousands miles, from St. Louis, by the way of the Missouri, and Columbia Rivers, to the Pacifick Ocean: Containing an Account of the Indian Tribes, who inhabit the Western part of the Continent unexplored, and unknown before. With copious delineations of the manners, customs, religion, &c., of the Indians. Compiled from various authentic sources, and Documents. To which is subjoined, A Summary of the Statistical View of the Indian Nations, from the Official Communication of Meriwether Lewis. Embellished with a Map of the Country inhabited by the Western Tribes of Indians, and Five Engravings of Indian Chiefs.*[5]

Two apocryphal editions were translated into German. Even after the official account was published, a counterfeit edition appeared as late as 1840.[6] The apocryphal editions must have sold well since there were a number of them. When the authentic account appeared in 1814, however, its sales were poor, perhaps because of the many books already written on the expedition and because it had been eight years since Lewis and Clark's return to St. Louis, a considerable lapse of time in the publishing trade.[7] Jedediah Smith, the great American explorer and fur trader, carried a copy of Lewis and Clark's journals with him on his many explorations.[8]

An American who was excited by the 1814 edition was Hall Jackson Kelley, an indefatigable promoter of Oregon. In the 1830s, Kelley became an enthusiastic propagandist for that area's exploration and settlement. Through his publications, especially his *Geographical Sketch of That Part of North America Called Oregon*, published in 1830, the East became interested in the Pacific Northwest, and much opposition to America's expansion into Oregon was overcome.[9]

No American explorer captured the public's imagination as did the Pathfinder, John Charles Frémont. Because of his daring exploits, a popular romantic image was created that led to his nomination by the Republican Party for the presidency of the United States in 1856. Frémont lost to the Democratic candidate, James Buchanan, in a close election.

Except for Washington Irving's *Astoria* and *The Adventures of Captain Bonneville,* little of literary merit was written on western exploration in the nineteenth century. The volumes by Pike, Long, and others made for dull reading. With the help of his talented wife, Jessie, however, Frémont succeeded in combining scientific accuracy with literary polish.[10]

Tens of thousands of Frémont's reports were distributed to the American people; there were six American and two British editions.[11] His description of the expedition of 1843–1844, which included excellent maps by the German-born cartographer Charles Preuss, became a popular work. It was a large and thorough report, "a classic of exploring literature." Its influence was felt by a number of Americans; some set out to the West "guided only by the light of Frémont's *Travels.*"[12] Humboldt lauded Frémont, who had patterned his exploration on Humboldt's by combining the objectives of the naturalist with the skills of the mapmaker.

Frémont's works were popular in Britain as well. And when a moving panorama of Frémont's western expeditions was presented in England in the 1850s, three hundred thousand people viewed it in its six-month run, even though, at twenty-five thousand feet in length, it took two hours to turn.[13]

As a result of Frémont's favorable account of the Great Salt Lake, Brigham Young moved the Mormons to that area in the late 1840s. One of the most popular western guidebooks, Joseph E. Ware's *The Emigrants' Guide to California,* published in 1849, was largely based upon Frémont's journals.[14] Allan Nevins, a biographer of Frémont, wrote that, after Lewis and Clark, no one else "was half, nay one-tenth as widely read or eagerly quoted; none exerted half as much influence on the westward exodus."[15]

Frémont's luck ran out in his later years. His autobiography, *Memoirs of My Life: A Retrospect of Fifty Years,* was overpriced and full of boring detail. It was a financial failure. Frémont's health was damaged as a consequence, and he died in 1890, three years after the memoirs were published.[16]

Charles Wilkes, who led a worldwide naval exploration between 1838 and 1842, published in five volumes *The Narrative of the United States Exploring Expedition* in 1845. Although the work contained an inordinate number of pages, twenty-five hundred, the first two editions of 1,250 copies were quickly sold out at $10 a set, and three more printings were made in 1845. A grand total of sixteen editions was issued, the final one appearing in 1858.[17] In his *Autobiography,* Mark Twain noted the effect of Wilkes's expedition on Americans in the 1840s:

The name of Wilkes, the explorer, was in everybody's mouth. . . . What a noise it made, and how wonderful the glory! Wilkes had discovered a new world and was another Columbus. Wilkes was a marvel in another way, for he had gone wandering about the globe in his ships and had looked with his own eyes upon its furthest corners, its dreamlands—names and places which existed rather as shadows and rumors than as realities.[18]

British interest in Africa was growing by the beginning of the nineteenth century, as can be seen in the popularity of John Leyden's and John Pinkerton's works on African exploration. Mungo Park's *Travels* was the first great publishing success by an African explorer. The first edition of fifteen hundred copies sold out in 1799, one month after publication. By year's end, three editions had been issued. A French translation appeared in 1799 and, ten years later, a sixth edition appeared. An American edition and a German translation came out in 1800. Since then, the work, which began the great search for the source of the Niger, has never been out of print.[19]

Livingstone, Stanley, Speke, and Burton opened up the dark interior, discovered the sources of the Nile, and answered other geographical questions. In volume after volume, they encouraged what British explorer Joseph Thomson viewed as the "phenomenal interest in all things African."[20]

One of the most popular books on African exploration was

Livingstone's *Missionary Travels and Researches in South Africa.*
Published in 1857, the first edition of twelve thousand copies
was oversubscribed before it appeared. Ten thousand copies
were sold in four years in the 6s. edition and thirty thousand
copies were produced in seven years in the guinea edition,
making Livingstone wealthy and famous.[21] In spite of his success, Livingstone complained that writing was "irksome and
laborious." On completing this three hundred thousand-word
book in six months, he lamented, "I would rather cross the
African continent again than undertake to write another book.
It is far easier to travel than to write about it."[22]

Livingstone's works were read around the world. The American edition of Livingstone's book, *Seventeen Years' Explorations
and Adventures in the Wilds of Africa,* influenced Martin R. De-
lany, a black American, to head an expedition to the Niger
valley in the hope of colonizing Africa with Afro-Americans.
Livingstone Memorial Hall was built at Fisk University in the
United States and, at Salisbury, North Carolina, Livingstone
College for Afro-Americans was established. In the centenary
of Livingstone's birth in 1913, the American black leader
Booker T. Washington declared, "Livingstone's life brought to
me as to many other coloured people in this country, not only
the first real knowledge of Africa and the African people but
the first definite interest in them."[23]

Explorers wrote not only travel accounts but novels and poems as well. Caught up in the glories of his younger days,
Frémont composed a poem in 1875 about his western explorations titled, "Written on Recrossing the Rocky Mountains in
Winter, After Many Years." In 1865 Burton, using the pseudonym Frank Butler, composed a poem, "Stone Talk," a satire
on Victorian hypocrisy. The cynicism Burton displayed in the
lengthy poem was based upon his bitterness toward the British
government, which he felt had treated him unfairly. In this
work, a paving stone in a London street comments on the ills
of British society and verbally attacks streetwalkers, philan-
thropists, shopkeepers, and liberals.[24]

Fifteen years later, Burton published his best poem, "The
Kasidah of Haji Abu El-Yezdi, a Lay of the Higher Law,"

under the pseudonym F. B. The poem went through sixteen editions in forty years. The name in the title was a variation of the Arabic name for Burton, Haji Abdullah. Burton expressed his anti-Christian views in this melancholy poem: "There is no God, no man-made God"; and

> There is no Heaven, there is no Hell
> these be the dreams of baby minds; Tools of the wily Fetisher
> To 'fright the fools his cunning blinds.[25]

Henry Stanley was one of the few explorers besides Livingstone who made money from his books on African exploration. *In Darkest Africa* was so successful that his publisher followed it with *How Stanley Wrote His Darkest Africa. In Darkest Africa* inspired a board game, "Snakes and Ladders," two musical compositions, and a popular stage review called "Africa."[26]

In 1873, a year after the publication of his successful book, *How I Found Livingstone,* Stanley wrote a fictionalized account of his loyal African servant Kalulu, *My Kalulu, Prince, King, and Slave,* one of the few books written about an African by a European. Based upon African folklore and Stanley's African adventures, the book was set in Central Africa and written for young readers. Although it went through a number of printings, the book did not sell, and Stanley never wrote fiction again.[27]

In his search for fame, Joseph Thomson composed what he believed would be "the great African novel." Thomson had been bothered by the errors and false ambiance in H. Rider Haggard's bestseller, *King Solomon's Mines.* Influenced by the works of Sir Walter Scott, Thomson attempted to give authentic color to his work. He collaborated with a school friend, Miss E. Harris Smith. In 1888, *Ulu: An African Romance* was published in two volumes. The tale centers on Mt. Kilimanjaro. Its hero is a brave hunter from Scotland, Tom Gilmour, who lives with the Chagga people and protects them from the Masai who attack their fields and steal their cattle. The love interest in the novel revolves around Gilmour, Ulu, a young Chagga maiden, and Kate Kennedy, the daughter of a missionary. The tale ends with the heroic death of Ulu in a fight with the Masai and the uniting of Kate and Gilmour.[28]

A number of young men who immersed themselves in explorers' accounts before becoming explorers themselves were considerably influenced by these works. Bruce's *Travels to Discover the Source of the Nile,* which started the nineteenth-century search for the sources of the Nile, made a lasting impression on William G. Browne, Mungo Park, John L. Burckhardt, and Friedrich Hornemann. René Caillié was stimulated by the accounts of Park as Cameron was excited by the works of Burton and Speke. Stanley talked about the effect Mayne Reid, a British author of popular adventure stories, had had on him.[29]

Thomson was influenced by fellow Scottish explorers Livingstone, Bruce, and Park, and Thomson's oldest brother and first biographer, James, remembered that, after reading about Stanley finding Livingstone, Joseph's mind began to wander "in a tender questioning way, over those large spaces on the map of that long neglected continent." Joseph Thomson decided that he was "doomed to be a wanderer."[30]

Explorers and their adventures influenced a number of writers, especially those of the romantic school of the late eighteenth and early nineteenth centuries. Captain Cook, the epitome of the dashing hero, was especially popular with the literati. His descriptions of vast oceans and distant lands had a considerable impact on the literature of the day.

The return of Cook's first expedition in 1771 inspired Oliver Goldsmith to write in the prologue to Joseph Cradock's *Zobeide: A Tragedy,*

> In these bold times, when Learning's sons explore
> The distant climate and the savage shore;
> When wise Astronomers to India steer,
> And quit for Venus, many a brighter here;
> While Botanists, all cold to smiles and dimpling,
> Forsake the fair, and patiently—go simpling.[31]

English poets William Wordsworth, Samuel Taylor Coleridge, and Robert Southey incorporated Cook's experiences into their works. These romantic poets were born in the 1770s, the decade of Cook's voyages. In his experiences they saw something basic to man's struggle for existence. A biographer of Coleridge wrote that seldom had Coleridge read anything that "fecundated his imagination so amazingly as that 257th page of Cook's second volume...."[32] The poems of Coleridge were influenced by the accounts of William Dampier, James Bruce, and William Bartram. The two latter explorers played a part in inspiring the exotic imagery of Coleridge's "Kubla Khan." Indeed, the model for the sacred river Alph came from Florida's Salt Springs Run.[33]

The works of Dampier, Park, Bartram, and Jonathan Carver can be detected in the poems of Wordsworth, who wrote to a friend asking him if he would collect travel books for him: "You would render me an essential service, as without much of such reading my present labours cannot be brought to any conclusion."[34] Certain lines from "She Was a Phantom of Delight" owe a great deal to Bartram's *Travels*. Bartram's influence can also be seen in Wordsworth's "Ruth," "The Excursion," "The Idiot Boy," and "The Complaint of a Forsaken Indian Woman." For this last poem, Wordsworth also made use of Canadian explorer Samuel Hearne's *Journey from Prince of Wale's Fort in Hudson's Bay to the Northern Ocean*." Dampier and Park were mentioned in notes to Wordsworth's "The Prelude," and Carver's *Travels* was used in *Poems in Two Volumes* and *Guide to the Lakes*.[35]

English poet and critic Algernon Charles Swinburne wrote two poems about Burton, "Elegy" and "On the Death of Richard Burton." He dedicated *Poems and Ballads, Second Series* to Burton and wrote "Dedication" for him.[36]

Victorian poet Roden Noel praised Livingstone in two of his most popular works, "Livingstone in Africa" and "The Death of Livingstone." An example of Noel's admiration can be seen in the latter poem:

A deep resolve, more grand than midnight skies
All wrathful elements hauled forth
Depart! He wades, he swims, he flounders; he is borne upon the
shoulders of dark men forlorn.[37]

American writers also made important use of explorers' works. Nineteenth-century American literature is largely a literature of mobility, and the central character of the great novels was often a traveler, a man or boy searching for a better life or in quest of himself. Huck Finn, Ishmael, Natty Bumppo are the most famous wanderers in American literature. In that century, a new literary hero appeared—the American Adam: separated from history, cut off from family, "an individual standing alone, self-reliant and self-propelling, ready to confront whatever awaited him with the aid of his own unique and inherent resources."[38] Not surprisingly, these words also describe the explorer.

Just as Cook was the favorite explorer of British authors, Frémont was the most popular among Americans. John Greenleaf Whittier glorified Frémont's western exploits in "The Pass of the Sierra" during the Pathfinder's 1856 presidential campaign. Whittier believed that Frémont, who so skillfully led his men in western exploration, could lead his nation just as skillfully.[39] Whittier's admiration for Frémont continued during the Civil War, as can be seen in the poem, "To John C. Fremont." In Frémont's attempt to abolish slavery in Missouri while he was military commander there and his subsequent removal by President Lincoln, Whittier and other radicals saw a symbol of what the war should be fought for and who should lead the abolitionist crusade. The Quaker poet wrote,

> Thy error, Fremont, simply was to act
> A brave man's part, without the statesman's tact,
> And, taking counsel but of common sense,
> To strike at cause as well as consequence.
> O, never yet since Roland wound his horn
> At Roncesvalles, has a blast been blown.[40]

Henry Wadsworth Longfellow used Frémont's report of his first expedition for scenic description of the prairie in "Evangeline." Basil Lajeunesse, a character in the work, was named for one of the French voyagers who traveled with Frémont on three of his five expeditions. A year before the publication of

"Evangeline," Longfellow read Frémont's account of the 1842 expedition and noted that Frémont had "touched my imagination; and I trust something may come of that."[41]

As a young child, Herman Melville dreamed of being a world traveler. When he turned to the word instead of the world, "The books from which he took off were not *Tristram Shandy* or Waverly but Mungo Park's *Travels in the Interior of Africa. . . .* " One of Melville's biographers asserted that Park "was almost certainly one of Melville's literary masters."[42] And well he should have been, for exploration became one of Melville's major themes. *Typee* and *Omoo* are exploration literature that owe a great deal to the exploits of Cook and Bougainville. In *Typee,* Melville's descriptions of the coco palm and the making of tapa were similar to those of Cook and Bougainville. In *Mardi,* the narrator Taji was believed by the natives to be an incarnation of their white God, a situation similar to Cook's experience when the Hawaiians mistook him for their returning deity, Lono.[43]

In 1846, with money from the sale of his first novel, *Typee,* Melville bought a copy of Wilkes's *Narrative of the United States Exploring Expedition* and used the work in writing *Omoo* and *Mardi.*[44] Much of the material about Queequeg and Fedallah in *Moby Dick* came from Wilkes. Queequeg's prototype was probably the New Zealand chief, Ko-towatowa, mentioned by Wilkes, and such incidents as the steward's sale of shrunken heads and a sea captain's faux pas at a native dinner were based on scenes from the *Narrative.*[45]

James Fenimore Cooper utilized the works of both Wilkes and Cook in *The Crater.*[46] The setting for this, America's first utopian novel, was the South Sea islands. Cooper's *The Sea Lions* was set in Antarctica. For this work, he lifted from Wilkes's *Narrative* information about the geography of Cape Horn and the dangers of sailing through ice fields, and he boldly borrowed from Wilkes the image of the iceberg as a translucent city.[47] Cooper used the works of Alexander Mackenzie, Pierre Charlevoix, Lewis and Clark, and Stephen Long in *The Last of the Mohicans* and *The Prairie.*[48] Cooper especially utilized the works of American explorers in the latter work, as is evident in the episodes concerning a mirage, boatbuilding, and cooking buffalo meat.[49]

More than any other American literary work, Edgar Allan Poe's *The Journal of Julius Rodman, Being An Account of the First Passage Across the Rocky Mountains of North America Ever Achieved by Civilized Man,* published in 1840, owes its inspiration to explorers. This picaresque parody recounted the journey of the first "civilized man" to cross the Rockies in 1792, antedating Mackenzie by one year and Lewis and Clark by twenty. Poe relied heavily on the journals of Lewis and Clark. He patterned his hero, Rodman, on Jefferson's description of Lewis, which appeared as a memoir in the journals. Poe lifted at least twelve pages directly from these journals, and paraphrased several other passages. Rodman sought escape in the unknown. "He was urged solely by a desire to seek, in the bosom of the wilderness, that peace which his peculiar disposition would not suffer him to enjoy among men. He fled to the desert as to a friend."[50]

For *The Journal of Julius Rodman,* Poe also drew from Irving's *Adventures of Captain Bonneville* and *Astoria;* the characteristics of the French voyageurs in the novel were taken from Irving's comments in *Astoria.* Poe used the overland journal of fur trader Wilson Price Hunt as a basis for his description of Rodman's ascent of the Missouri River.[51] Another source of Poe's *Rodman* was Mackenzie's *Voyages from Montreal,* from which Poe used a description of the preparation of pemmican.[52] Indeed, Poe used more glue than ink in this work, and it may be the most plagiarized novel ever written by a major American author.

To Henry David Thoreau, the West was a land of romance, an idealized place from whence would come America's renewal. Thoreau used exploration and discovery as metaphors for self-discovery in *Walden* when he wrote,

What does Africa,—what does the West stand for? Is not our own interior white on the chart? black though it may prove, like the coast, when discovered. Is it the source of the Nile, or the Niger, or the Mississippi, or a Northwest Passage around this continent, that we would find? Are these the problems which most concern mankind? Is Franklin the only man who is lost, that his wife should be so earnest to find him? Does Mr. Grinnell know where he himself is? Be rather the Mungo Park, the Lewis and Clark and Frobisher, of your own streams and oceans; explore your own higher latitudes. . . . Nay, be a Columbus to whole new continents and worlds within you, opening new channels, not of trade, but of thought. . . . What was the meaning of that South-Sea Exploring Expedition, with all its parade and expense, but an indirect recognition of the fact that there are continents and seas in the moral world to which every man is an isthmus or an inlet, yet unexplored by him, but that it is easier to sail many thousand miles through cold and storm and cannibals, in a government ship, with five hundred men and boys to assist one, than it is to explore the private sea, the Atlantic and Pacific Ocean of one's being alone.[53]

Thoreau concluded, "Explore thyself. Herein are demanded the eye and the nerve."[54]

Exploration literature has been placed in three categories: quests, odysseys, and ordeals. The accounts dealing with the quest focused on the search for a specific goal, such as the source of a river. This type of work emphasized the explorer's concentration on a single accomplishment, with everything and everyone else becoming secondary to this pursuit. In this literature, the mental and physical abilities of the explorer are stressed, placing him outside the realm of mortal man.

The odyssey was an expedition to gain a larger view of the unexplored world and its inhabitants. Here the general overview was more important than any specific objective, whether river, mountain, or pass. Such works placed their emphasis on the explorer's abilities to adapt to and learn from a new environment; here his personal awakening through travel is clearly revealed.

The ordeal focused on the explorer's will power and strength of character when he came close to death or died on an expedition. Here was sometimes seen the search for martyrdom. Bruce and Speke's exploration to discover the key to the Nile would fit the first category; the expeditions of Lewis and Clark, Frémont, Pike, and Long fit the second; and Livingstone, and Park on his second expedition, would fall into the third. Generally speaking, American expeditions would fit into the odyssey category, while African expeditions could be placed more easily into the other two.[55]

Writers of exploration literature in the nineteenth century were generally men lacking in literary power who dealt with new and unusual experiences; as one writer explained, explorers had "no more literary intention than a mating loon." They were better known as explorers than authors, for what they told than for their manner of telling it. Indeed, few readers expected much literary merit from their works.

Writers of travel literature, on the other hand, were often talented. Their personalities and descriptive abilities were as important as their themes. The traveler wrote "for a circulating library, and for the unthinking portion of mankind, who will not be bothered with details, and accuracy was sometimes a casualty."[56] Adventure and drama, basic to exploration literature, was often missing in travel books. Perhaps the real difference between the literature of the explorer and that of the travel writer was that the latter emphasized words over deeds, while the former emphasized deeds over words. The travel writer was basically a tourist who remained unchanged by his travels, and the reader was usually addressed in the second person as if he were along on the trip. Facts were planted in anecdotes of native life to make them more palatable, and the material, offered to a new literate middle class that enjoyed receiving its thrills vicariously, was simple if exotic.

The sixteenth and seventeenth centuries were the pioneer period in travel literature. During this time, numerous accounts of voyages came from the presses of England. Besides sailors William Dampier and George Anson, other distinguished British travel writers were John Windus and Lancelot Addison, who wrote about North Africa, Paul Rycaut and Henry Maundrell, who described the Near East, and Robert Beverley and John Lawson, who depicted North America.

Only novels were more popular than travel literature in Britain, where knowledge of travel books was considered vital to the well-rounded gentleman's education. Multi-volume travel collections as well as maps were found in many country homes. An English intellectual writing in 1710 noted that travel accounts were "the chief materials to furnish out a library.... These are in our present days what books of chivalry were in those of our forefathers...."[57]

The success of this literary genre in Britain in the eighteenth and nineteenth centuries was brought about in part by Britain's hope of recapturing the glorious days of Queen Elizabeth I, and it was believed that voyages and explorations by land would gain for Britain greater respect around the world. The need for opening new areas to trade was also strongly felt by the British government. It was believed that explorers would not only open up these areas but aid Britain's race for world dominance. The British also had a desire to expand their intellectual vistas. As explorers educated and uplifted the backward peoples of the globe, they performed valuable educational services. They cooperated with geographical and scientific societies and, through their publications and contributions to "useful knowledge," widened the intellectual horizons of their own countrymen.

The next great age of travel literature was launched by the exploits of Cook in the Pacific and the travels of Bruce in Ethiopia. Among the more popular travel books of this period were Edward Clarke's spirited letters and diaries of adventure in Asia and Africa, John Burckhardt's *Travels in Nubia* and *Travels in Arabia,* and John Barrow's *Travels in China* and *A Voyage to Cochin-China.*

A few decades later, another distinguished group of travel writers emerged. Among the most famous travel accounts in the nineteenth century was Edward Robinson's *Biblical Researches in Palestine,* which appeared in 1841 and won for the American college professor the prestigious Patron's Medal of the Royal Geographical Society. One of the most startling accounts was Charles M. Doughty's *Travels in Arabia Deserta,* published in 1888, in which the author described his travels in Arabia from 1876 to 1878. It was a brilliant work, containing sensitive and sure descriptions of seldom-seen towns and detailed information about the desert life of the Bedouin.

Among the most famous American travel writers of the

nineteenth century were John L. Stephens, Bayard Taylor, and George W. Kendall. In the 1830s Stephens traveled in Europe, the Middle East, and Central America. The latter region was a neglected area in travel literature until Stephens published *Incidents of Travel in Central America, Chiapas, and Yucatan* in the 1840s. Taylor was a correspondent for the New York *Tribune,* and his travels to California, Mexico, Europe, and Africa provided him with a wealth of material for his numerous popular travel books, one of which was *A Journey to Central Africa.* Kendall, a New Orleans newspaperman, wrote about his harrowing experiences in Texas and Mexico in the 1840s.

The public's hunger for travel information is evidenced in the number of lectures and lyceum programs devoted to travel. Bayard Taylor made thousands of dollars from his travel books and thousands more from his lectures. Perhaps Americans found in travel books and lectures a continuity that was lacking in a nation unconcerned with its past. In describing other areas of the world, travel writers helped Americans define more clearly their new land and their own identity.

Two of America's most famous nineteenth-century hoaxes involved the explorers Frémont and Park. When the showman P. T. Barnum was in Cincinnati in 1848, he read a handbill announcing the exhibit of a "woolly horse," a freak covered with fine hair that resembled wool. Recognizing the financial possibilities in the animal, he bought it.[58] He saw an even greater opportunity to exploit the "woolly horse" when he read of Frémont's disappearance in the Rocky Mountains, and he placed a story in the New York papers stating that Frémont and his men had captured a "woolly horse" near the Gila River.

Col. Fremont's Nondescript or Woolly Horse will be exhibited for a few days at the corner of Broadway and Reade street, previous to his departure for London. Nature seems to have exerted all her ingenuity in the production of this astounding animal. He is extremely complex—made up of the Elephant, Deer, Horse, Buffalo, Camel, and Sheep. It is the full size of a Horse, has the haunches of the Deer, the tail of the Elephant, a fine curled wool of camel's hair color, and easily bounds twelve or fifteen feet high. Naturalists and the oldest trappers assured Col. Fremont that it was never known previous to his discovery. It is undoubted by 'Nature's last,' and the richest specimen received from California. To be seen every day this week. Admittance 25 cents; children half price.[59]

Several huge transparencies depicting Frémont and his men chasing the horse over the plains were posted on the building where the horse was displayed. Barnum recollected in his autobiography,

The public appetite was craving something tangible from Colonel Fremont. The community was absolutely famishing. They were ravenous. They could have swallowed anything, and like a good genius, I threw them, not a "bone," but a regular tit-bit, a bon-bon—and they swallowed it at a single gulp![60]

English-born journalist Richard Adams Locke was responsible for creating two of the most famous hoaxes of the nineteenth century. While working for the New York *Sun* in 1835, he invented the famous "Moon Hoax" which described the discovery of men on the moon. His second hoax, the "Lost Manuscript of Mungo Park," told of the discovery of the Scottish explorer's diary, which added new and exciting but false stories to the history of Park's last expedition. But the earlier "Moon Hoax" had brought Locke's credibility into question and thus prevented him from committing a second deception successfully.[61]

The exploits of the explorers had a profound impact on literature. Stories of travel and exploration have always attracted a large audience. *The Odyssey* was the prototype of this genre. Odysseus—who returned home "spirit gladdened and riper in knowledge"—like the great explorers was courageous, determined, and resourceful. In his encounters with strange cultures, fabulous animals, and new worlds, he set the pattern that distinguished this type of literature.

In the nineteenth century, poets and novelists captured the driving dreams of the explorers. Writers like Byron and Coleridge understood the high drama and lasting significance of exploration; they noted as well the Christian allegory of the journey of life. To the readers of exploration literature there was a fascination with the search for the unknown, whether described by an explorer or a writer of fiction. An African proverb states, "Those who have tasted the waters of Africa must return to quench that thirst," and those entertained and excited by tales of new worlds had a thirst that was unquenchable.

"The Great Explorers—Lewis and Clark," by Frederic Remington (Free Library of Philadelphia).

Above, left: Merriwether Lewis (Independence National Historical Park Collection).

Above: William Clark (Independence National Historical Park Collection)

Left. Portrait of Zebulon Montgomery Pike by Charles W. Peale (Independence National Historical Park).

Above. Portrait of Stephen Long by Charles W. Peale (Independence National Historical Park Collection).

Above, right. Charles Wilkes (Purdue University Calumet)

Right. John Charles Frémont, the Pathfinder (Bancroft Library, University of California at Berkeley).

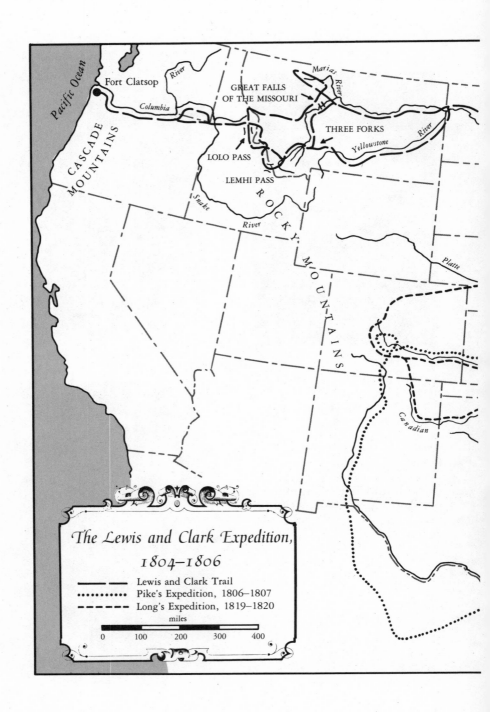

Pacific Ocean

River

Fort Clatsop

Columbia

GREAT FALLS
OF THE MISSOURI

Marias River

THREE FORKS

Yellowstone River

CASCADE MOUNTAINS

LOLO PASS

LEMHI PASS

ROCKY MOUNTAINS

Snake River

Platte

Canadian

The Lewis and Clark Expedition,
1804–1806

—————— Lewis and Clark Trail
•••••••••• Pike's Expedition, 1806–1807
– – – – – Long's Expedition, 1819–1820

miles

0   100   200   300   400

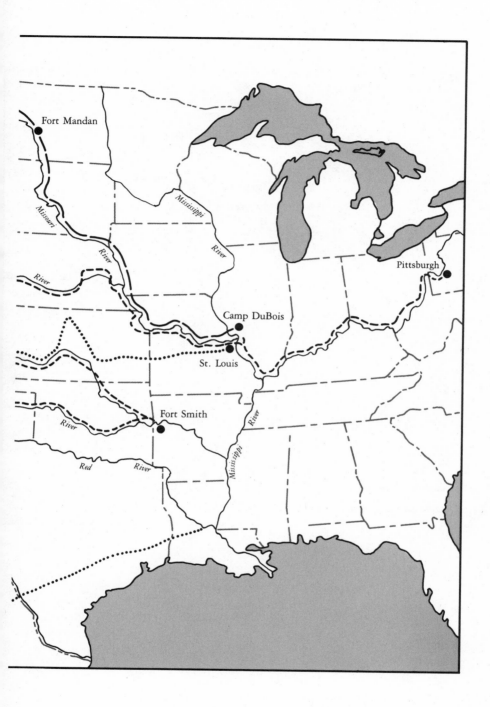

Fort Mandan

Missouri River

Mississippi River

Pittsburgh

Camp DuBois

St. Louis

River

Fort Smith

River

Red River

Mississippi River

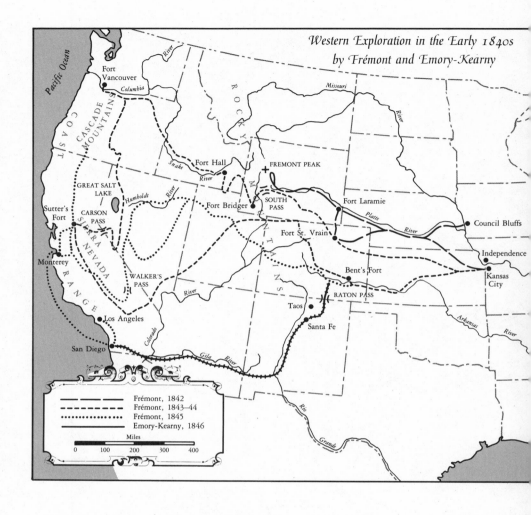

Western Exploration in the Early 1840s
by Frémont and Emory-Kearny

Pacific Ocean

Fort Vancouver

Columbia

COAST

CASCADE MOUNTAINS

ROCKY

Missouri

River

River

Snake

Fort Hall

FREMONT PEAK

River

Missouri

GREAT SALT LAKE

Humboldt

River

Fort Bridger

SOUTH PASS

Fort Laramie

Council Bluffs

Sutter's Fort

CARSON PASS

SIERRA

Platte

River

Fort St. Vrain

Independence

Monterey

NEVADA

WALKER'S PASS

Bent's Fort

Kansas City

RANGE

River

RATON PASS

Los Angeles

Colorado

Taos

Santa Fe

Arkansas

River

San Diego

Gila

River

Rio

Grande

Miles

	Frémont, 1842
	Frémont, 1843–44
	Frémont, 1845
	Emory-Kearny, 1846

0   100   200   300   400

MOUNTAINS

CENTRAL

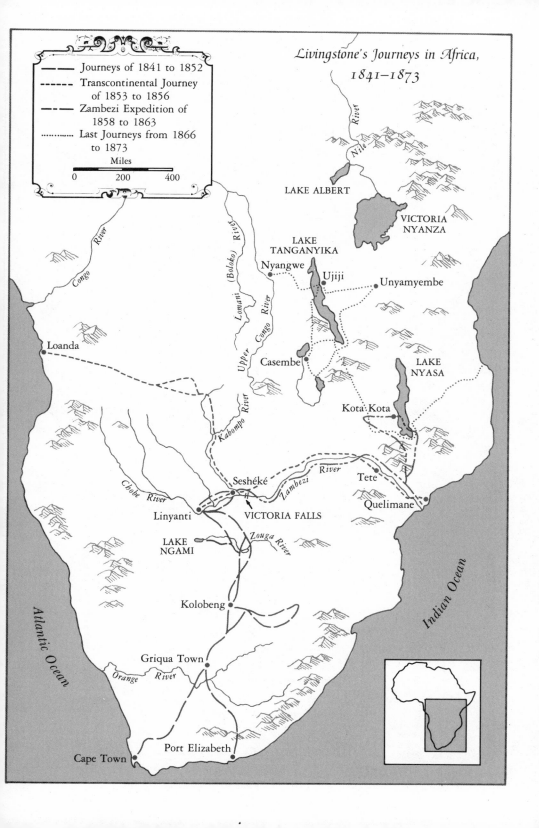

Livingstone's Journeys in Africa,
1841–1873

Congo River

Nile River

LAKE ALBERT

VICTORIA NYANZA

Lomani (Bolobo) River

Upper Congo River

LAKE TANGANYIKA

Nyangwe

Ujiji

Unyamyembe

Loanda

Casembe

LAKE NYASA

Kabompo River

Kota Kota

Seshéké

River

Zambezi

Tete

Quelimane

Chobe River

VICTORIA FALLS

Linyanti

LAKE NGAMI

Zouga River

Kolobeng

Griqua Town

Orange River

Atlantic Ocean

Indian Ocean

Cape Town

Port Elizabeth

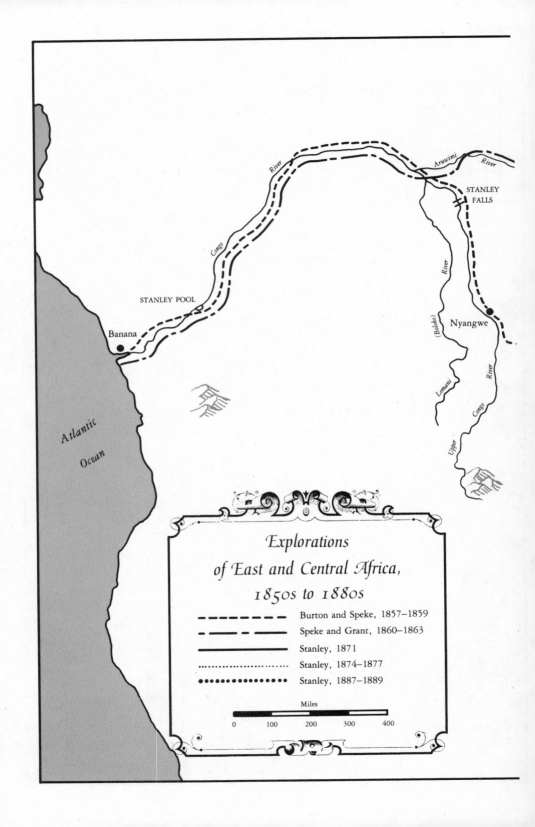

Explorations
of East and Central Africa,
1850s to 1880s

– – – – –	Burton and Speke, 1857–1859
— · — · —	Speke and Grant, 1860–1863
—————	Stanley, 1871
··············	Stanley, 1874–1877
••••••••••	Stanley, 1887–1889

Miles

0   100   200   300   400

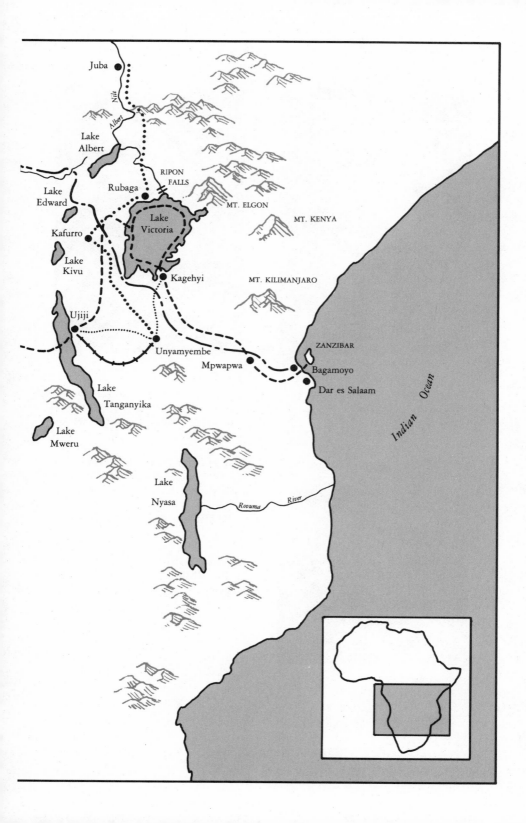

Above, left. Portrait of James Bruce of Kinnaird by Pompeo Batoni (National Galleries of Scotland).

Above. Engraving of a portrait of Sir Joseph Banks by Benjamin West (British Museum).

Left. Mungo Park (British Museum)

Opposite. Mungo Park's death at Bussa Rapids, 1806 (British Museum).

Above, left. Portrait of Capt. Hugh Clapperton by an unknown artist (National Galleries of Scotland

Above. Richard F. Burton (British Museum)

Left. John H. Speke (British Museum)

Left. David Livingstone, 1864
(National Galleries of
Scotland).

Right. Joseph Thomson (British
Museum).

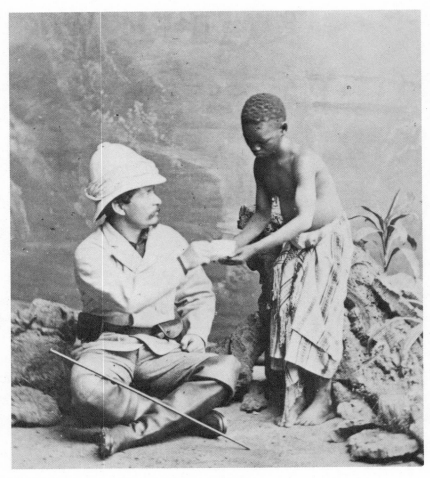

Henry Morgan Stanley with his African valet, Kalulu, 1872.
(National Galleries of Scotland).

CHAPTER SEVEN

The Explorers

THE AGE OF THE EXPLORER was also the age of the revolutionary. Both represented radical breaks with the past and opened up new and exciting vistas. It is more than coincidence that America's greatest revolutionary, Thomas Jefferson, was also her greatest patron of exploration. The success of both explorer and revolutionary lay in their ability to adapt to the demands of new situations and their devotion to a cause. In the late eighteenth century, both underwent changes in image. In the case of the explorer, this was a transformation in the way he was perceived, from deviant and vagabond to world celebrity. For the revolutionary, the image changed from that of rebel and radical to that of founding father.

The late eighteenth century was to James Bruce the golden age of exploration because explorers were interested in "humanity and science," and were "employed in the noblest of all occupations, that of exploring the distant parts of the Globe." Bruce noted significant differences between explorers in the early part of the eighteenth century and those of the later part. In the earlier period, explorers such as William Dampier had been "rated as little better than the buccaneer, or pirate, because they had . . . in manner been nearly similar." They displayed reckless cruelty and greed instead of generosity, and showed little concern for the native or the spark of a larger purpose. In the age of Cook, due largely to that noble captain's character and his emphasis on science, the public's attitude toward the explorer changed, and Cook was transformed into a romantic hero.[1]

The traits that Sigmund Freud used to define a great man—"decisiveness of thought, the power of will, the forcefulness of his deeds," and especially "self-reliance and independence" and "his divine conviction of doing the right thing, which may pass into ruthlessness"—were among the most important traits of the great explorer. Indeed, Freud described himself as "an adventurer . . . with the curiosity, the boldness and the tenacity that belong to that type of being."[2] Carl Jung said of Freud's love of knowledge that it "was to lay open a dark continent to his gaze."[3]

The hero's rite of passage—separation, initiation, and return—could describe the standard path of the explorer's great adventure. Joseph Campbell, a student of mythology, noted that this formula included the basic ingredients of the monomyth: "A hero ventures forth from the world of common day into a region of supernatural wonder: fabulous forces are there encountered and a decisive victory is won: the hero comes back from this mysterious adventure with the power to bestow boons on his fellow man." Some of the themes that Campbell developed for the heroic adventurer—"The Call to Adventure," "Crossing the First Threshold," and "Woman as the Temptress"—would be appropriate titles for an explorer's journal. The hero-explorer found that one of the most difficult parts of the exploratory experience was the return and reintegration into society, where he was often confronted with jealousy, skepticism, and misunderstanding. The difficult experiences that Bruce, Park, Lewis, Speke, and Stanley faced on their return paralleled the mythical hero's return.[4]

The explorer was a stranger not only to natives but, in a sense, to his own society, especially if he had been away for a long time or had undergone significant changes. The acceptance of the white explorer by the natives often depended upon the kind of society he visited. Most native societies were small, with a population consisting of anywhere from a few families to a few thousand people. The smaller societies seldom had strong, centralized political institutions, which sometimes made it difficult for the explorer to win tribal acceptance, even though he might be befriended by individuals. This type of political community was often found along the Pacific Coast, especially in California, and along Africa's east coast. In the interiors of both continents, however, the tribes were usually larger and more highly structured. If the stranger could win the friendship of the king or chief, his success was usually assured. Obviously, the explorer behaved differently in the warlike Buganda kingdom, with a population of over one million, than he did upon meeting a small, disease-wracked east coast tribe.[5]

An important difference between the two great periods of discovery and exploration (the late fifteenth and early sixteenth centuries and the late eighteenth and early nineteenth centuries) was that there was greater international cooperation during the second period, as seen in Franklin's aid to Cook's expedition and Bank's support of a French expedition. There was also less violence connected with the second age of exploration, even though weapons were more lethal and more available. Explorers of the later age were less violent toward one another and less brutal to the natives than in the days of Columbus and Magellan, or even of Dampier. Although Burton and Stanley treated the Africans harshly, they were generally more humane toward natives than Cortés and Pizarro had been. Bernal Díaz del Castillo, a soldier in Hernan Cortés's army that conquered the Aztecs in the sixteenth century, wrote that his purpose in exploring was to "serve God and his Majesty, to give light to those in darkness and also to get rich." Sir Walter Raleigh's purpose was "to seek new worlds, for golde, for prayse, for glory." In the second age of exploration, there was less rush for quick profits and for civilizing the benighted heathen in God's name and, as Bruce noted, less of the pirate and buccaneer and more of the scientist involved with exploration.

What made men want to explore? If their approach toward the natives in the nineteenth century was different from that of an earlier time, were their reasons for exploring different?

Did they do it to increase commerce? Trade was more a result of exploration than a reason. Even David Livingstone, who put so much faith in trade, linked it with God's work and Christian ethics.

Was it because of religious zeal? For Livingstone, the Christianization of the natives played a vital role and, although he was only one of many explorers who had God as his constant spiritual guide, his intensity set him apart. And even Livingstone hinted that his travels were much more than a religious excursion to save souls.

Was it for money? This also appears unlikely, although a few explorers made money from the publication of their journals. Explorers were often sent out by their governments or associations in underfunded expeditions; if they were military men, their pay remained the same and, if they were private citizens, the wages for their dangerous travels were minimal. There was no longer any rich Aztec Empire to conquer, nor Inca gold to fill a room.

One of the main reasons explorers explored was to discover, describe, and list everything that they observed, from aardvarks to the Zambezi. And while their work was usually toilsome and sometimes dangerous, few were happy doing anything else. In fact, the more difficult the undertaking, the more they enjoyed it. If anything, the dangers they encountered urged them on.

In that age, no experience partook so much of individual enterprise and initiative as did exploring. Few achievements could bring more stature, recognition, or fame to an individual than discovering an unknown river or mountain. As Paul Du Chaillu noted, there were occasions when "the objective instinct in the explorer as an observer was blunted by the quest for heroic stature which sometimes distorts perception."[6] Exploration was one of the last refuges of the hero, or at least it was one of the quickest ways of becoming one, Horatio Alger and Samuel Smiles notwithstanding.

What other compulsions moved these men to leave family and friends who seldom understood their urgent need to explore? Was it patriotism that made them face death? John

Speke said that he would rather suffer death a hundred times than let a foreigner take from England "the honour of the discovery." Was it caused by the romanticism of the age? Joseph Thomson told a friend that the age of romance was not yet over. Were they seeking freedom from constraints, recognition, or a recapturing of a lost innocence in an age of increasing industrialization and complexity? Were they akin to Herman Melville's Ishmael, who remarked,

Whenever I find myself growing grim about the mouth; whenever it is a damp, drizzly November in my soul; whenever I find myself involuntarily pausing before coffin warehouses, and bringing up the rear of every funeral I meet . . . then, I account it high time to get to sea as soon as I can.[7]

Were they "tormented with an everlasting itch for things remote," with a "love to sail forbidden seas and land on barbarous coasts"? Were they like Ulysses, who said that nothing

> could conquer in me the restless itch to rove
> And rummage through the world exploring it
> All human worth and wickedness to prove.[8]

A nephew of Sir Francis Drake believed that

ever since Almighty God commanded Adam to subdue the earth, there have not wanted in all ages some heroicall spirits which, in obedience to that high mandate, either from manifest reason alluring them, or by secret instinct forcing them thereunto, have expended their wealth, imployed their times, and adventured their persons, to finde out the true circuit thereof.[9]

Drake revealed his thoughts on exploring in this prayer: "O Lord God, when thou givest to thy servants to endeavor any great matter, grant us also to know it is not the beginning, but the continuing of the same untill it be thoroughly finished, which yieldeth the true glory."[10]

James Cook wished not just to travel farther than anyone had ever gone before "but as far as possible for man to go."[11] Yet Cook recognized a paradox in the explorer's quest:

The world will hardly admit of an excuse for a man leaving a Coast unexplored he has once discovered, if dangers are his excuse he is then charged with *Timorousness* and want of Perseverance and at once pronounced the unfitest man in the world to be employ'd as a discoverer; if on the other hand he boldly encounters all the dangers and obstacles he meets and is unfortunate enough not to succeed he is then charged with *Temerity* and want of conduct.[12]

In explaining the exploring instinct, J. R. L. Anderson in *The Ulysses Factor* noted that there is something in man, some type of unique adaptation, which encourages a few to adventures which, however senseless, "are of value to the survival of the race." He called this the "Ulysses factor" and felt it was unique to man. Other animals possess a sense of adventure, but taking risks to pursue some goal of little real value resides only in man.[13]

Rudyard Kipling caught some of the explorers' unconscious impulses with these words from his poem "The Explorer:"

> Something hidden
> Go and find it.
> Go and look,
> Behind the Ranges—
> Something lost behind the Ranges.
> Lost and Waiting for you. Go![14]

Perhaps it was the continuation of childhood fantasies or the discovery of hidden treasure which urged explorers on. Tales like "Ali Baba and the Forty Thieves," "Aladdin and the Magic Lamp," and "The Tinder Box" are based on some of the oldest dreams of the human race. These longings live in the memory of man. To uncover the mystery, to become famous, to find the treasure—these are the daydreams of both child and man.[15]

Discovery was Richard Burton's mania.

Of the gladdest moments in human life, methinks, is the departure upon a distant journey into unknown lands. Shaking off with one mighty effort the fetters of Habit, the leaden weight of Routine, the cloak of many Cares and the slavery of Home, man feels once more happy. The blood flows with the fast circulation of childhood. Excitement lends unwonted vigour to the muscles, and the sudden sense of freedom adds a cubit to the mental stature. Afresh dawns the morn of life; again the bright world is beautiful to the eye, and the glorious face of nature gladdens the soul. A journey, in fact, appeals to Imagination, to Memory, to Hope—the three sisters Graces of our moral being.[16]

Starting out thousands of miles from home with little hope of surviving, Burton asked himself " 'Why?' and the only echo was 'damned fool! . . . the Devil drives!' "[17] Exploring for Burton was in part a rejection of England and the English. Burton disclosed that England was the only nation where he never felt at home.[18] When a clergyman asked the cynical Burton if he had ever killed a man in Arabia, he replied, "Sir, I'm proud to say that I have committed every sin in the Decalogue."[19] Burton enjoyed shocking Victorian society, and he continued to upset English sensibilities from the frontiers of Africa with his graphic descriptions of the natives' sexual mores. But, for all his cynicism, Burton longed for the honor of discovering the source of the Nile.

In describing the joy of exploration, that practical idealist Livingstone said on the start of another trip to Africa that he felt "exhilarated. . . . The mere animal pleasure of traveling in a wild unexplored country is very great."[20]

Joseph Thomson enjoyed the adventure and the unlimited sense of freedom. Like Burton, he was bored with life in England after the excitement of exploring Africa. Even on his deathbed Thomson said that, if he were well enough to dress and walk a few yards, "I would go to Africa yet!"[21] Samuel Baker, explaining his need to explore, believed there was "a wandering spirit . . . in my marrow, which forbids me rest . . . Africa has always been in my head."[22] Baker had fallen prey to the malady known as "Afromania," a disease that acted on the sanest man like a powerful drug. Still he could wonder whether he had placed too much emphasis on discovery: "Had I wasted some of the best years of my life to obtain a shadow?"

Richard Lander wrote that there was something charming in the very word "Africa" that made his "heart flutter on hearing it mentioned."[23]

Henry Stanley explained simply that he saw "no sign that ever I shall love civilization better than I love roving." Mungo Park hoped to distinguish himself, to have "a greater name than any ever did."[24] He also saw more profit in Africa than in his medical practice in Scotland. John Speke revealed his obsession with exploration when he wrote to the president of the Royal Geographical Society, Sir Roderick Murchison, that he felt "like one goaded by all the eyes of Europe behind whilst hell is gaping at his feet, yet it requires but one strong resolve to leap the fire and win Paradise beyond."[25] James Grant believed that there was always something new from Africa.[26] John Charles Frémont defined exploration as "the true Greek joy in existence, in the gladness of living."[27] While surveying the magnificent western landscape, Frémont's guide, William Dixon, expressed the feeling of ecstasy and enthrallment which exploration stirred: "You wanted geography; look—there's geography for you!"[28]

Viewing something that no one has ever seen before is one of the greatest thrills that man can have, an instant of exalted vision. On first sighting the falls he named Victoria, Livingstone mused that, since it had never before been seen by Europeans, "This . . . (was) the most wonderful sight I had witnessed in Africa."[29] Samuel Baker, when he first saw the lake he christened Albert, felt

the glory of our prize burst suddenly upon me! There, like a sea of quick-silver, lay far beneath the grand expanse of water, a boundless sea . . . glittering in the noon-day sun. . . . It is impossible to describe the triumph of that moment;—here was the reward for all our labour. . . . England had won the sources of the Nile!

Lewis on viewing the Great Falls of the Missouri for the first time was ecstatic over the "sublimely grand spectacle." He believed that, if he were an artist, he would be able to give the world "some just idea of this truly magnificent and sublimely grand object which has from the commencement of time been concealed from the view of civilized man."[30]

Africanist Robert Rotberg wrote that no single motivation can explain the reason for exploring. What is needed is "a wide and penetrating range of psychoanalytically relevant data, detailed autobiographical statements, revealing biographies, the candid reminiscenses of associates or relatives" before serious conclusions can be reached.[31] A study of West African explorers revealed that they were obsessed with curiosity about the natives and the land, with a desire to discover and a nationalistic need to open Africa to European culture and contact.[32] These men were complex figures, and no single explanation of their motives will suffice. Some exhibited unbelievable persistence; a few seemed to be searching for death. With typical panache, Baker noted that only death could keep him from discovering the sources of the Nile. Burton believed that Speke, tired of living, had journeyed to Africa to die. Many thought that Livingstone was really searching for death in Africa.[33]

To others, the quest became almost a religious experience. A few returned to the wilds time and time again, as if to prove themselves worthy. After spending time in civilization, the explorer longed for the freedom found in exploring and knew he had to go out again. A few went just once, had their excitement and glory, and never returned. Seldom did they explore for the sake of the native, although Livingstone did explore as much for the African as for the European. A scholar of African explorers has stated that the mystery of Africa attracted the adventurer, but it also offered an escape from the rigors of western society. Explorers were extraordinary eccentrics. Flamboyant individuals, loners or dissenters, lacking sympathy for and often, like Burton, excluded by " 'proper' society, they sought relief and redress in the comforting loneliness provided by the wilds of Africa."[34]

Explorers offered many reasons for their urge to explore: to develop self-awareness, to test their mettle, or, as Alexander von Humboldt believed, to go out and witness something new. Since his youth, Humboldt had had a deep desire to journey to distant lands, a desire which he believed was a characteristic of his age, when life was an expanding horizon "and when we find an irresistible attraction in the impetuous agitations of the mind, and the image of positive danger."[35]

Explorers sometimes built up their confidence by comparing their expeditions to others'. On leaving Fort Mandan in April, 1805, Meriwether Lewis noted, "This little fleet, altho' not quite so respectable as those of Columbus or Captain Cook, were still viewed by us with as much pleasure as those deservedly famed adventurers ever beheld theirs." Forgetting the pains and sacrifices that Cook and Columbus had suffered, Lewis continued, "I·could but esteem this moment of my departure as among the most happy of my life."[36]

The explorer was devoted to his quest. Defying tradition and sometimes rebellious, he justified his eccentric behavior in the name of a higher ideal, be it science, nationalism, or religion. Religion was one of the main forces behind Livingstone's explorations. He described himself as a "missionary heart & soul," and he would not accept the accolades of the public for himself: "The Great Power being my helper, I shall always say that my success is all owing to His favour."[37] For Livingstone, there was no significant dichotomy between his work as a missionary and that as an explorer.

Most explorers were men of common piety. A towering figure in American exploration, Jedediah Smith, explained to his brother, "It is, that I may be able to help those who stand in need, that I face every danger. . . ."[38] Although an explorer might miss home and hearth and complain, "I am so tired of exploration without a word from home or anywhere else for two years," his devotion was to his quest.[39] Home was often on his mind. Samuel Baker dreamed of English beefsteak and pale ale. As he lay dying, Hugh Clapperton sang English and Scottish songs with his servant, Richard Lander, and Lander played his bugle. "How often have the pleasing strains of 'Sweet, sweet Home,' resounded through the melancholy streets of Soccatoo?"[40]

There was often a love-hate relationship toward the unknown. This was especially evident in the African explorers.

Joseph Thomson said that he would die "with the spirit of Africa on my lips." Baker knew that Africa was no heaven, but rather "hell itself." But he also believed that "The hard soil of Africa is a more fitting couch for the last gasp of an African explorer than the down-pillow of a civilized home." Speke noted, "I . . . felt as if I only wanted a wife and family, garden and yacht, rifle and rod, to make me happy here for life, so charming was the place."[41]

The question, What made an explorer great?, yields no easy answer. Was it the number of discoveries he made, the heroic deeds he inspired, or the miles he traveled? Livingstone traveled over twenty-nine thousand miles and opened one million square miles of new territory. Certainly his greatness lay not only in those figures but in the totality of his achievements, his skill in publicizing his expeditions, an ability to link his exploratory feats to a Christian destiny, and the power to inspire a generation of explorers.

One of the best descriptions of a great explorer was Thomas Jefferson's of Meriwether Lewis:

Of courage undaunted, possessing a firmness & perseverance of purpose which nothing but impossibilities could divert from it's direction, careful as a father of those committed to his charge, yet steady in the maintenance of order & discipline . . . with all these qualifications as if selected and implanted by nature in one body, for this express purpose. . . .[42]

In *The Ulysses Factor*, J.R.L. Anderson listed qualities which he felt comprised the exploring instinct. Among these were courage, selfishness, physical strength, a powerful imagination, and the ability to lead.[43] In writing about Lewis and Clark, Bernard De Voto included leadership, bravery, and skillfulness, and "the quality that must be insisted on is intelligence."[44] According to De Voto, besides Lewis and Clark only Canadian explorers Alexander Mackenzie and David Thompson possessed such intelligence, but to a lesser degree. If any one characteristic defined the great explorer, it was purposeful determination. Explorers were single-minded to the point of being "almost like a separate species of man, or men set apart by some strange mental condition."[45] It has been said that the explorer needed a stoic's ability to bear suffering, the self-control of an American Indian, the patience of a saint, and the constitution of a camel. A student of British explorers in Africa believed that two characteristics particularly common to them were intense powers of observation and a firm will not to be defeated. Certainly if Stanley, Livingstone, and Park had any basic characteristics in common, they were tenacity and a singleness of purpose.[46] Enticed by Livingstone's reports about the need to Christianize the Africans, European missionaries were drawn to this pagan land; dozens would die of fevers, and others would follow them and die too. Even after Livingstone's wife, Mary, died of fever in Africa, he remained there to continue his work.

The secrets of the Nile held as much fascination for African explorers as did the Northwest Passage for those in America. Livingstone, as quoted by Horace Waller in his 1880 book on his last journey, noted that these two searches brought out similar qualities in explorers but, because it was an ancient quest, the discovery of the Nile's sources "possesses, moreover, an element of interest which the North-west Passage never had."

Burton and Speke's deep commitment to discovering the headwaters of the Nile was clearly evident as they launched the first major exploration into the interior of East Africa in the 1850s. "I feel myself practically bedded with, and instinctively impelled on to the prosecution of geographical research, the same way as formerly the attainment of sport was the culminating point of my ambition," noted the enthusiastic Speke.[47] After discovering the source of the Nile, Speke was even more excited at the prospect of returning to Africa. "I felt as much tantalised as the unhappy Tantalus must have been when unsuccessful in his bobbings for cherries in the cherry-orchard, and as much grieved as any mother would be at losing her first-born, and resolved and planned forthwith to do everything in my power to visit the lake again."[48]

The unknown drew explorers like a magnet. A British travel writer noted that the object which moved these men to put themselves "in these various attitudes of discomfort and danger, has, in the majority of cases, been simply—'the fun of the thing'—a love of adventure."[49] Burton "turned lovingly towards Africa."[50]

Johann Krapf, Johannes Rebmann, and Livingstone were missionary explorers, a type not found in the nineteenth-century American exploration; others, like Cook, Bruce, and Frémont, were scientific. And there were those such as Long and Pike who went forth primarily for military reasons. Stanley's second journey was a political expedition. But these are simple ways to categorize a complex process and explain the external reasons for exploration, and they overlook the explorer's inner urge. The explorer's dedication, while remarkable, sometimes led to tragedy. The disastrous expeditions associated with Park, Livingstone, and Frémont were partly the result of their overweening ambition and insufficient concern for the welfare of their men.

Frémont tried to regain some of the prestige which he had lost due to his court-martial. The court-martial had come out of a dispute over who was in command in California during the Mexican War—General Stephen W. Kearny or Commodore Robert F. Stockton. When Kearny learned that he was in command, Frémont, who had supported Stockton, was arrested, court-martialed, and convicted. Frémont launched his fourth western expedition in 1848 to discover a new route across the San Juan Mountains at the 38th parallel. By mid-December, the party was in the mountains and the snow was deep, but still the impetuous Frémont pushed ahead. When the guide, "Old Bill" Williams, lost his way and the mules began to drop, the party decided to split up. A relief party finally arrived but, by that time, ten men were dead. Frémont seemed oblivious to the tragedy when, a year later, he noted, "The result was entirely satisfactory. It convinced me that neither the snow of winter nor the mountain ranges were obstacles in the way of the (rail) road."[51] Commenting on the singlemindedness of explorers, a writer believed that they "illustrate human purposefulness in such extreme and naked fashion as to take on a symbolic meaning."[52]

Mungo Park's second expedition, sponsored by the Colonial Office, was a disastrous example of blind optimism and needless risk. The Africans called this expedition *Doummoulafong,* or "a thing sent to be eaten." When Park left the West Coast of Africa in 1805, he had no African porters and had to depend upon thirty-five inexperienced soldiers whom he had hired at Goree. To the natives, Park's expedition looked like a conquering army. In a move that recalls Frémont's tragic timing, Park began his expedition at the start of the rainy season. Like Frémont, Park was no novice; he had traveled in Africa before, yet there were few greater urges than to start an expedition. This fact led him to the disastrous decision to begin the expedition in the spring.

The rains came, the donkeys faltered, and the soldiers died. In these desperate circumstances, this knight-errant of African exploration maintained his energy and courage. What remained of the party finally reached the Niger. "Lonely and friendless" in the wilds of Africa,[53] Park could, like Frémont, dismiss his difficulties in a letter to Lord Camden of the Colonial Office: "I am afraid your lordship will be apt to consider matters as in a very hopeless state, but I assure you that I am far from desponding. . . . I shall set sail to the east with the fixed resolution to discover the termination of the Niger or perish in the attempt."[54] Because he refused to pay the natives the *hongo,* or toll, and fired at anyone who approached in a threatening manner, Park's voyage down the Niger was a continual battle with the tribes. At Bussa Rapids, his craft became jammed between two rocks. The natives attacked from the banks and, his escape cut off, Park jumped into the swirling waters and drowned.[55]

In many ways, British and American explorers matched the characteristics of their societies. Optimism, a worship of power, and a smug feeling of racial superiority predominated in Victorian England and nineteenth-century America, and these traits were also found in the explorers. Furthermore, the Horatio Alger and Samuel Smiles self-help ethic was part of the way of life of most famous explorers. They were truly men of their time, even though their actions and fame set them apart.

Who were these explorers? What was their background? Did they share similar life stories? Of the thirty African and thirty American explorers studied, all were male, although women were involved with exploring in Africa; among them were David Livingstone's wife, Mary, Samuel Baker's mistress, and two explorers, Mary H. Kingsley and Alexandrine Tinne.

The oldest explorer in the sample was Jonathan Carver, who was born in 1710; Harry Johnston and Joseph Thomson, both born in 1858, were the youngest. The average age of the explorer on his first expedition was thirty.[56] While the American explorers came from different areas of the United States and a few were from Europe, 50 percent of them were born in Virginia, Massachusetts, or New York. Fifty percent of the British explorers were born in Scotland, mainly in the Lowlands. The most famous Scottish explorers were Park, Bruce, Livingstone, Cameron, Clapperton, Grant, and Thomson. A nationalistic urge touched Thomson, who felt that he had to explore because he was a countryman of the others. Six of the twelve founders of the African Association were Scotsmen. An old English proverb went that in every port there was a rat, a Newcastle grindstone, and a Scot.

Why this rugged and impoverished land gave so many men to African exploration is a question impossible to answer completely. In the late eighteenth century, Scotland was changing from a peasant to an industrial society. Upheavals in the cotton industry and agriculture sent repercussions throughout the land. Between 1780 and 1830 the nation witnessed a period of social transformation.[57] Although Scotland's economy boomed in the late eighteenth century and technology was emerging, the poverty of the land undoubtedly played a role in influencing some of its sons to explore. The religious devoutness and abolitionist sentiment in the Scotch mind also influenced the urge to explore.

The Scottish Enlightenment emphasized the scientific study

of society. Scottish philosophers were involved in formulating a science of society, and were thus interested in the orgins of civilization as well as in a comparison of different societies and in the rise and fall of civilizations. All of these were incentives to exploration. Lord Monboddo, a figure in the Scottish Enlightenment, studied African apes to better understand man because he believed that orangutans were undeveloped human beings.

The American economist John Kenneth Galbraith's characterization of the Scot as "godfearing but unfrightened"[58] is appropriate in defining the nineteenth-century explorer. Determination and individualism, two notable Scotch traits, were among the most important characteristics of successful explorers. The Scotsman's personal world needed a larger dimension in which to develop, and his desire to leave the drabness of his everyday surroundings for something better, even if it took him to darkest Africa, was a motivating factor.

Of the thirty Africian explorers studied, seven came from poor families, thirteen from middle-class families, seven from upper-class families, and three from families whose financial records were unobtainable. David Livingstone, Walter Oudney, Hugh Clapperton, and Henry Stanley were born into poverty. One of seven brothers and sisters, Livingstone began work in the cotton mills at Blantyre at the age of ten. He labored six days a week, twelve and a half hours a day, as a "piecer," putting together threads that were separated on the spinning jenny. Livingstone put this drudgery to good use; he propped a book on the jenny and read while he worked. Years later, in Africa, he attributed his ability to block out distracting sounds, "so as to read and write with perfect comfort amid the play of children or near the dancing and songs of savages," to the concentration he had developed in the cotton mills.[59]

Of the thirty American explorers studied, two came from poor families, eighteen from middle-class families, five from upper-class families and five from families whose financial records were unobtainable. Most of the explorers had some education. Frémont, Fredinand V. Hayden, Edwin James, Clarence King, James A. Grant, Harry H. Johnston, Joseph

Thomson, William B. Baikie, Gordon Laing, Livingstone, Burton, and Mungo Park attended college. Stephen Long received a classical education at Dartmouth, where he was elected to Phi Beta Kappa. George H. Derby, William H. Emory, and Joseph C. Ives went to West Point, and Long taught there for a short time. Jim Bridger, William Clark, Stanley, Kit Carson, and Clapperton had practically no formal education. A few African explorers were medical doctors—Park, Livingstone, Oudney, and Thomas Ritchie. Park told his friend Sir Walter Scott that "He would rather brave Africa and all its horrors than wear out his life in long and toilsome rides over cold, lonely heaths, assailed by the wintry tempest, for which the remuneration was hardly enough to keep body and soul together."[60]

The fathers of Burton, Speke, Lewis, Clark, and Pike had served in either the army or the navy. In fact, the fathers of half of the British explorers served in the military, and 50 percent of the American explorers themselves had served in the U. S. Army, the most prominent of these being Emory, Long, Pike, Frémont, Lewis, and Clark. Stanley fought on both sides during the American Civil War. Several British explorers had seen service in the military: Cameron, Clapperton, and Tuckey were in the Royal Navy, while Speke, Burton, Grant, and Houghton came from the army. Speke, Burton, and Grant served for years in India. A number of them—Ledyard, Hayden, Carson, Bridger, King, Frémont, Thomson, and Tuckey—suffered the deaths of their fathers at an early age. Stanley was thirteen when his father died, although he later maintained he was only a few weeks old. Livingstone, Stanley, Richard Lander, Ledyard, and Frémont had unhappy childhoods, and in part they explored to escape their pasts and gain recognition. Frémont and Stanley were both born out of wedlock. As a child, Frémont suffered from his illegitimacy, poverty, and uncertainty about the future. He was five when his father died, leaving the family without economic resources. He reminisced, "Going out into the excitement of strange scenes and occurrences I would be forced out of myself and for long intervals could forget what I left behind."[61]

Stanley was christened John Rowlands. At the age of six, he was sent to a workhouse where he remained for nine years. In later life, he seldom wrote about these early years and, when he did, it was in Swahili. Stanley disliked his drunken father, and his mother refused to have anything to do with him. One of the chapters in his *Autobiography* was entitled, "I Find a Father." Stanley had two father substitutes: Henry Stanley, a Louisiana businessman from whom Rowlands took his name, and Livingstone. Exploration helped Stanley forget the workhouse and his family problems. He took to it almost as a religious quest to remove those stigmas and prove his worth. The violence he suffered as a child did not lessen the brutality he showed the Africans; in fact, if anything, it may have increased his violent nature. He compared himself to a feudal lord controlling a great territory, and he boasted that he owned this vast land inhabited by noble animals: "Here I possessed, within reach of leaden ball, any one I chose of the beautiful animals, the pride of the African forests!"[62]

Tensions and problems at home increased the need for some to find ways out of their difficulties. Those deeply hurt by death or rejection, such as Stanley and Frémont, sought surcease in the solitude of the wilds of Africa or America. Through a rebirth and the prestige lavished upon them, they could attempt to sublimate their unhappy pasts.

The adventurous romanticism of the period was an encouragement to exploration. What could be more romantic than a journey to Timbuktu or realizing Columbus's dream of discovering a Northwest Passage? An exuberance for life and an unleashing of emotional energy carried expeditions through agonizing ordeals. "New truths were welcomed in free minds, and free minds make brave men," wrote an English author of that age.[63] "Nearly all [explorers] were hopelessly romantic," observed Robert Rotberg.[64]

Most explorers dealt with one or two specific, unanswered geographical questions such as the source of the Nile, the existence of the Northwest Passage, the directional flow of the Niger—questions which, because of their importance and dramatic consequences, became part of the nineteenth century's romantic sensibilities. The spirit of romanticism was tied closely to exploration, to man in nature. It was during this period in American and European history that nature cast its haunting spell, even though the mighty tread of western civilization was heard throughout the newly-discovered lands. The age of Frémont and Burton was also that of Scott and Byron. Vistas were sublime and virtue pure. In the wake of the explorers came poets, novelists, and artists who identified closely with this age of romantic nature.

One of the basic tenets of romanticism was a change in the prevailing mode of thought from uniformitarianism to diversitarianism. The concept of diversity could be seen nowhere more clearly than in the different societies, landscapes, and cultures which the explorers viewed. Few persons were more cosmopolitan than the explorer; none had seen more. Romanticism stressed exotic scenes and multifaceted views, creating a religion of multitudes. The American philosopher Arthur O. Lovejoy described this romantic and optimistic mood, which he defined as "the principle of plenitude": "One thing alone is needful: Everything."[65] Knowledge was based on variety. Diversity was the basis for excellence. everything was thought to be related, and all was part of a grand, cosmic consciousness. To Louis Agassiz, the great Swiss zoologist, the whole world was arranged according to God's plan, and "a physical fact is as sacred as a moral principle."[66] "Geography is the science of facts," wrote Bougainville. And a young Thoreau cautioned, "Let us not underrate the value of a fact; it will one day flower in a truth."[67]

Of all the culprits in the swift outbreak of modernization—the railroad, the factory, the steamboat—the explorer was considered the initiator.[68] As he opened up the unknown, it was defiled and destroyed by the march of civilization which he had unleashed. Like Daniel Boone, the explorer was both builder and destroyer. In America, William Cullen Bryant, James Fenimore Cooper, Thomas Cole, and Asher Durand denounced the consequences of exploration.

Nature's grandeur was a national experience in America, whereas in Britain it was seen as an individual and aesthetic experience. For America, nature was the basis of its growth; indeed, the United States was a nation committed to and molded by nature. "America," wrote the American historian Perry Miller, "can progress indefinitely into an expanding future without acquiring sinful delusions of grandeur simply because it is nestled in Nature, is instructed and guided by mountains, is chastened by cataracts."[69]

The bold, optimistic men who led exploring expeditions hungered for discovery and were taken captive by faraway places. Their motto could have been, "Any place but here." Exploring was their life, and sometimes their death. They went forth for one final time in search of the world's last great secrets.

During the closing moments of the age of exploration, the explorers displayed many traits both positive and negative. But no one could gainsay their amazing energy, their unbelievable will to survive, and a bravery comparable to that of Ulysses. These new heroes were romantic and practical men— romantic in their interest in the remote and primitive, yet practical enough to recognize the supreme importance of the printed page and the well-drawn map.

Because of their calling, their fervor, and their independent spirit, they may be considered the last pilgrims. They endured trials seldom dreamed of by Christian martyrs; death was their constant companion. Seldom did they turn back; rarely did they admit defeat. They were gamblers who accepted nature's invitation.

CHAPTER EIGHT

The Exploration Experience

BEFORE TURNING HIS ATTENTION to the study of heredity, the English scientist Francis Galton published *The Art of Travel,* in which he wrote that the success of an expedition usually depended "on a chain of minor successes, each link of which must be perfect; for where one fails, there must be an end of further advance." Recalling the fable of the tortoise and the hare Galton warned exploring parties not to travel too fast, that it was preferable for both men and animals to become gradually acclimated. Using Park's disastrous second expedition as an example, Galton offered, as a general rule, that small parties fared better than large; they excite less terror, "do not eat up the country, and are less delayed by illness."[1]

Galton also believed that a knowledgeable interpreter was vital to a successful expedition, "for so great is the poverty of thought and language among common people that you will seldom find a man, taken at hazard, able to render your words with any correctness."[2]

Effective communication with the natives was a major problem in both the American West and Africa, and its breakdown led to heated words and misunderstandings.[3] Sign or gesture language among the Plains Indians eased the problem in the West. Meriwether Lewis described the method he used to communicate with the Shoshoni:

the means I had of communicating with these people was by way of Drewyer who understood perfectly the common language of jesticulation or signs which seems to be universally understood by all the Nations we have yet seen. It is true that this language is imperfect and liable to error but is much less so than would be expected. The strong parts of the ideas are seldom mistaken.[4]

Richard Burton learned Indian sign language on a trip to the American West in 1860 and later taught it to Africans. Burton rarely had to worry about language, since he spoke twenty-nine languages and over a dozen dialects.[5]

Like Burton, Henry Stanley traveled in the West, as a correspondent for a St. Louis newspaper. There he met Colonel George A. Custer, whom he admired for his courage and impetuosity. It was in the West in the 1860s that Stanley first became aware of the cultural conflicts between different civilizations, and he viewed the American Indians with the same mixed feelings he later had for the Africans. In 1867, Stanley was assigned by his editor to cover General William Tecumseh Sherman, a member of a United States peace commission who was sent west to deal with the Plains Indians. A few years later, Stanley met Sherman in Paris and quoted to the general the speech Sherman had given the Indians. Stanley told Sherman that he had used that same speech in negotiating with Africans on his trek to find Livingstone.[6]

African and American explorers were dependent upon native guides. The Indian Sebastian was essential to the Garcés and Anza expeditions. Indian guides were important to the Escalante and Domínguez exploration of the Great Basin in 1776. Sacajawea, a Shoshoni Indian, became well known as guide and translator to Lewis and Clark. William Clark recognized the importance of guides while traveling through the Rocky Mountains, for without them "I doubt whether we who had once passed them could find our way to Traveler's Rest in their present situation, for the marked trees on which we had placed considerable reliance are much fewer and more difficult to find than we had apprehended."[7]

Mountain man Jedediah Smith was guided by Indians on many of his explorations; and native guides were included as regular members of the Hudson's Bay Company explorations. Delaware Indians served as guides and hunters on Frémont's journeys. Peter Skene Ogden recognized the importance of Indian guides; he knew that the guides had the explorers at their mercy, and that few persons understood how much anxiety an Indian guide could cause.[8]

Often the explorer's dilemma lay not so much in discovering a pass or a river as in finding a native willing to lead him there. One candid observer remarked that he "discovered, as we white men say when we are pointed out some geographical feature by an Indian who has been familiar with it since childhood."[9]

Indians not only guided the explorers, they supplied food, horses, and boats. They were usually friendly, but Indian attacks were always a possibility, as two bloody attacks on Jedediah Smith's men attest: ten of his men were killed by Mohaves in 1827, and the next year Indians on the Umpqua River massacred fourteen.[10] Lewis and Clark succeeded in preventing a Sioux attack by the use of firmness. They were fair in their dealings with the Indians and, in fact, the attachment that the Nez Perce had for whites began with the Lewis and Clark expedition and lasted for seventy years.[11]

One of the major problems of explorers was controlling their own men. During the first weeks of the Lewis and Clark expedition, the captains used severe disciplinary measures on their men for any infraction of the rules. In the early weeks of the expedition strict discipline proved effective, for the relationship between Lewis and Clark and their men was excellent throughout the expedition.

In Africa native support was more crucial to the explorer than in America, because there the tsetse fly killed off the pack animals, necessitating a reliance upon native labor. Attempts to use Indian and African elephants proved unsuccessful.

African guides on the East Coast, called *kirangozi*, were essential to a successful expedition. Two men of the Yao tribe played key roles in European exploration. The devoted Chuma, a former slave who was with Livingstone, Thomson, and others, was an effective leader of East African caravans and could speak a number of African languages, as well as English. To Thomson, Chuma was "a treasure that cannot be valued too highly." Sidi Bombay was another former slave who guided several explorers, including Speke, Burton, Stanley, and Cameron. For his loyal service, the Royal Geographical Society awarded him a medal and a pension. Stanley said of him that he had weaknesses but also virtues: "He was brave and manly. He was faithful, and was incorruptible. . . ."[12]

An African caravan was a spectacle resembling a Fourth of July parade and an army on the march. The lack of beasts of burden forced the natives to carry heavy loads, and Galton observed that it was a good idea to have women along on an expedition, for "women were made for labor."[13] The guide was often dressed in a scarlet robe and fancy headdress and, on the East Coast, carried the red flag of the sultan of Zanzibar; next came the drummer beating the cadence for the march; then the porters or *pagazi;* and finally the leader, who kept an eye out for loafers and deserters.[14] Burton found that the best porters on the East Coast were the Nyamwezi who, for one hundred fifty years, were in the forefront of the ivory trade with the interior.[15] These men were able to carry seventy-pound loads while subsisting on little food. They impressed the explorers with their strength, intelligence, and endurance. Alongside the porters marched the soldiers or *askari* armed with swords, shields, and flintlocks. Cooks, servants, and interpreters were also part of the larger caravans.

Burton wrote that African expeditions were "campaigns on a small scale, wherein the traveller, unaided by discipline, has to overcome all the troubles, hardships, and perils of savage warfare. He must devote himself to feeding, drilling and showing his men the use of arms and to the conduct of a caravan. . . ." In exploring, as in warfare, taking advantage of an opportunity was extremely important.[16]

In response to European exploration, the sultan of Zanzibar began to assert more territorial claims to the mainland and, since Zanzibar was the gateway to East Africa, European explorers contracted with the sultan for supplies. British consuls like John Petherick also played important roles in the support of East African explorers; and Sir George Grey, governor of the Cape Colony and high commissioner for South Africa, who had explored Australia with Royal Geographical Society support, was able to offer considerable help to John Speke and James Grant as they began their expedition from Cape Town. Hammer Warrington, British consul in Tripoli, aided explorers who started their treks from North Africa.[17]

Beads from Venice, iron, brass, copper wire, silks, and cloth were used in payment of the African *hongo*, as was the popular crude cotton made in the United States and called *merikani* by the natives. These gifts were wrapped in bales that weighed about sixty pounds apiece.[18] The explorers lavished tribal chiefs with gifts because the success or failure of an expedition often depended upon their disposition. Park, Lander, and Caillié revealed that the umbrella was highly prized by Africans, who were fascinated with the way it opened and closed. The king of Katoba was presented with a dirk, glass beads, two bottles of rum, white muslin, twenty bars of amber, coral, eighteen bars of tobacco, and red cloth.[19] On one of Stanley's expeditions, his natives carried eight and a half tons of materials, mainly cloth and beads. In America, explorers brought along medals, knives, tomahawks, beads, mirrors, and cloth for the Indians.[20]

The first day of an African journey was a time of excitement and pandemonium.[21] With the firing of guns, shouts of joy, beating of drums, and the shrill of kudu horns, the caravan moved forward.[22] "Woe to the man in Africa who cannot stand perpetual uproar," one explorer exclaimed. "Few things surprised me more than the rarity of silence and the intensity of it when you did get it." Another remarked,

Perhaps of all evils that can afflict a sick person, noises of any kind are the greatest. In Africa, whether one is ill or well, it is exactly the same, nothing like peace or quiet is anywhere to be found. Independent of the continual fluttering of pigeons, the bleating of sheep and goats, and the barking of numerous half-starved dogs, we are still more seriously annoyed by the incessant clatter of women's tongues, which I really believe nothing less than sickness or death on their part can effectively silence.[23]

As the caravan moved out, the explorers' thoughts turned to home and to the great adventure before them. Thomson recalled Stanley who, besieged by thousands of savages, was forced to kill dozens to save his life. Would he have to do the same? He imagined Livingstone near death in the Bangweolo swamps: "Might such not be our own fate?"[24]

In Africa each day's travel would begin around 4:00 A.M. In an hour's time breakfast was eaten and the porters gathered to shoulder their daily loads. Deserters were a problem, "leaving the caravan-leader like a water-logged ship."[25] Trouble often arose when a porter felt that he was being given an unduly heavy load. Thomson reported that, on one occasion when some porters balked at carrying their loads, Chuma "danced about with indignation, seizing this man by the ear and that by the throat, and dragging him to his appointed load, while he volleyed out his threats, or lashed them with his satire." Thomson intended to have a good relationship with his party, so he decided to fine his porters for infractions rather than beat them. But they went on strike and demanded a return to the harsher system; they preferred the whippings to reduced wages. Thomson later used the whip at the start of another expedition, believing that it would lessen the need for future whippings. Harry Johnston had a problem with his men on the first day of a march from the East Coast to Mt. Kilimanjaro. This was the critical time, when the explorer either gained control of his men or lost his authority. As the Zanzibari looked on, he ordered one man to pick up his load and march. When he refused, Johnston's Indian servant grabbed him by his heels, "whilst I soundly trounced him with his own walking stick. . . ." As the porter begged that the beating stop, Johnston was counting the laying-on of the wand. The remaining men lifted their loads and began to march westward. There was sometimes "open mutiny" among the porters and when that happened, Thomson observed, "You discover that the erstwhile negro has degenerated into a *nigger*."[26] Galton reminded travelers that it was not useful to strike a black man on his skull with a stick, "as it is a fact that his skull endures a blow better than any other part of his person."[27]

Controlling the members of an exploring party was a greater problem in Africa than in America. Baker was once confronted with the mutiny of his men. The ringleader informed Baker that they would no longer travel with him. "Lay down your gun!" Baker thundered, "and load the camels!" When the surly porter refused, Baker lashed out with his right hand and knocked him down. The animals were soon loaded and the caravan was on its way. In another incident, Baker was surrounded by menacing porters. Just then his mistress appeared. The men were surprised by her sudden emergence, which gave Baker time to order the drummer to beat fall-in, and the men did. Based on experiences such as these, Baker noted that sometimes everything depended "upon one particular moment; you may lose or win according to your action at that critical instant." A Russian proverb avers that heroism is endurance for one moment more.[28]

Barring any delays, the expedition party would be underway by 5:00 A.M. and, depending upon the type of caravan (an Arab caravan traveled more slowly than the Nyamwezi), the average pace was two miles an hour. A typical day's march in Africa covered five to ten miles. Speke and Burton averaged just over three miles a day, and the restless Stanley advanced seven.[29]

The size of the party varied. American expeditions were generally smaller than African. Lewis and Clark's caravan consisted of thirty-two people, and Pike had twenty-three with him when he left Belle Fontaine in July, 1806. Long had twenty-two men when he set out for the Platte River in 1820; Frémont took two dozen men on his first expedition and about forty each on his second and fourth. Park was nearly alone on his first expedition and, because of this, fared much better than on his second, larger expedition. Livingstone also traveled better with smaller expeditions. Speke and Grant in 1859 had 213 people when they started; Burton and Speke led 132 from Bagamoyo in the summer of 1857. Stanley's New York *Herald* expedition to find Livingstone started out in 1871 with 187 men; in 1874 he had 356 when he left Zanzibar on his exploration of the Congo. In 1879, on his second Congo expedition, he had sixty-eight Zanzibaris in his party, three-fourths of whom had been with him on his earlier Congo expedition. Thomson had 113 with him in 1882.

The success of an expeditionary party depended to a large degree upon effective management. Problems with members of the caravan and the different tribes were daily concerns of the explorers. Although the guide had important responsibilities, the explorer was in charge. He had to know how far to push ahead, how to allot loads among the porters, when to punish and when to forgive. Sometimes these daily decisions were made while he was delirious with fever. Fights, pilfering, and desertions were everyday occurrences. Burton compared his problems with a caravan to "driving a herd of wild cattle." He was willing to use any means to move the caravan: "by dint of promises and threats, of gentleness and violence, of soft words and hard words, occasionally backed by a smart application of the 'bakur'—the local 'cat.' "[30]

Nearly all African explorers used slaves as porters on their expeditions. Nevertheless, explorers showed an antipathy to slavery, "a subject which strikes home to the heart of every Englishman,"[31] and which Livingstone called the "great open sore of the world."[32] Mungo Park was an exception to the hostility toward slavery. Given the circumstances and conditions of slavery in Africa, he wondered if the effects of ending slavery "would . . . be so extensive or beneficial as many wise and worthy persons fondly expect."[33]

The African caravan would usually make a stop at about 8:00 A.M. when the sun reached past the tree tops, and by midday the march would end because of the intense heat. Leaders of caravans, like wagonmasters in the American West, preferred to end their day fording a stream rather than face it in the morning after a night of rain.[34]

Tents were thrown up, food was prepared, and the African explorers took time to write up the day's adventures. The main meal of the day would be served at 4:00 P.M. Bedtime was heralded around 8:00 P.M. with the repeated cry of *Lala!*, "Sleep!"; often the porters would sing and dance until much later. Distant drums were sometimes heard, loud, then soft, the wild, weird sounds of Africa, as common as the toll of church bells in Europe. Burton presented a romantic picture of a jungle bivouac.

The dull red fires flickering and forming a circle of ruddy light in the depths of the black forest, flaming against the tall trunks and defining the foilage of the nearer trees, illuminate lurid groups of savage men, in every variety of shape and posture. Above, the dark purple sky, studded with golden points, domes the earth with bounds narrowed by the gloom of night.[35]

Then, as the flames died, stillness returned. The contrast between hullabaloo and silence was especially great in Africa.

The camel was the beast of burden in North Africa, the ox in South Africa, but in Central Africa there was no animal that could be used effectively. In spite of the known danger of the tsetse fly, pack animals were sometimes brought along, and they would quickly die. A few were killed by wild animals, and some would run away. The donkey was the animal most commonly used. For his exploring, Livingstone used oxen and camels, but they all died from disease and overloading.[36]

When African natives became aroused over the lack of payment of the *hongo* or some other matter, explorers dealt with them in different ways. Stanley's two golden rules for African travel were, "Do not fire the first shot," and do not fire "until you see the first spear, and then take good aim." Stanley was not reluctant to use his firepower if he felt threatened; he explored by means of private warfare. On his second expedition, from 1876 to 1877, he had thirty-two battles with Africans. Two were especially bloody. At Bumbiri Island, forty Africans were killed. In his largest skirmish, at the junction of the Congo and the Aruwimi, Stanley's party was attacked by fifty war canoes, but rifle bullets destroyed the attackers' advantage in numbers. Surrounded by the blood and cries of the dying, Stanley's party seemed possessed: "Our blood is up now. It is a murderous world, and we feel for the first time that we hate the filthy, vulturous ghouls. . . ."

"Fire," Stanley boasted, "had a remarkable sedative influence on their nerves." Pursuing Africans to their homes, "I skirmish in their streets, drive them pell-mell into the woods beyond, and level their ivory temples; with frantic haste I fire the huts."[37] Burton remarked to John Kirk, British consul at Zanzibar, "Of course you have seen Stanley, who still shoots negroes as if they were monkeys."[38]

Firmness was the best policy to use with the natives so that there might be no question about who was in charge. Even Livingstone, who believed, "He who goes gently goes safely; he who goes safely goes far," could use the cane when his patience wore thin. But he considered it degrading and preferred not to perform the punishment himself. With Livingstone as his hero, the humane and gentle Joseph Thomson traveled fifteen thousand miles in Africa with no defections and no shots fired. Only on his sixth trip did the first loss of life occur. On his return, Thomson told fellow Scotsmen that his greatest boast was not that he had marched over land never seen by whites but that he was "able to do so as a Christian and a Scotchman, carrying everywhere goodwill and friendship, finding that a gentle word was more potent than gunpowder. . . ."[39]

The conflict between whites and natives existed partly because of a native belief that whites were cannibals and the slave trade was only an excuse to gather up Africans in order to eat them.[40] Another difficulty involved the overbearing attitude shown by many explorers toward the natives. But most problems occurred within the caravan. Insolence, mutiny, and dumping crucial provisions along the trail were some of the problems with the natives that explorers faced. On Speke's second expedition, he started with 176 men and, by the time he returned, 150 had deserted. The death of Livingstone can in all likelihood be traced to a deserting Yao porter who carried off the doctor's medical supplies. When Livingstone learned of this, he wrote, "I felt as if I had now received the sentence of death. . . ."[41] When Burton and Speke reached Ujiji on Lake Tanganyika in 1858, their porters deserted, leaving Burton partially paralyzed and Speke temporarily blind.[42]

On occasion, African explorers were forced to accompany Arab caravans, some of which dealt in slaves. Cameron considered the Arabs contemptible creatures because they traded in slaves, and Mungo Park, who was haunted by his captivity in the Moorish camp at Benoum, viewed them as "the rudest savages on earth."[43] The Arab slave trader Tippu-Tib and his men, however, aided Stanley on his expedition to the Congo. And Burton, a well-known supporter of Arab culture, felt that Islam had improved the black African both morally and physically. He believed that the Moslem faith won more African converts by accepting rather than attempting to end African vices, and he felt at home with the Arabs. Stanley, Baker, and Thomson also praised them.[44]

The Moslem success in proselytizing the Africans was of some concern to other explorers. Many abhorred the Moslem religion for allowing polygamy, which Europeans considered a sexual insult to women. Livingstone hoped to destroy the influence of the Arabs, who he felt neglected missionary and educational programs and emphasized commerce. He displayed an even greater dislike for the Portuguese, whom he blamed for the failure of his Zambezi expedition. He considered them indolent and apathetic, an example of the tropics' influence.[45] Heinrich Barth, a German explorer in the service of the British, noted that in Arab society "The camel is man's daily companion, and the culture of the date-tree his chief occupation."[46]

Considering the diverse native tribes they encountered and the dangers they faced, it is remarkable that so few explorers were killed by the natives. Of the thirty British explorers studied, only Mungo Park, Richard Lander, and Gordon Laing met this fate.[47]

This is not to say that the natives did not attack the explorers; they did on a number of occasions, as the accounts of Stanley, Speke, and Burton attest. Speke suffered eleven spear wounds at Berbera. Native bearers and attackers generally suffered the greatest casualties, while the low number of casualties among the explorers was due to their firearms, the divisiveness among the tribes, and luck.

Because many explorations were military expeditions, they were armed accordingly. The Lewis and Clark party was well supplied with muskets and rifles. In fact, a new American rifle, Model 1803, was first put to the test on their expedition. Of all the weapons they had, Lewis's air gun was special. It was an unending mystery to the Indians because it fired so often but used no powder; they considered it "Big Medicine."[48] Gun accidents were not uncommon. Meriwether Lewis was accidentally shot in the butt by one of his men; George Hunter shot himself in the hand while loading his pistol.

Joseph Thomson used a galvanic battery to give the Africans shocks, and he extricated himself from a dangerous situation with the Masai by displaying his false teeth. An African leader was taken with James Grant's photographs, especially one of a buffalo's head, and his lucifer matches. Clever use of a music box and a magnet increased Paul Du Chaillu's popularity among the Africans. When Samuel Baker became governor of Equatoria, he took with him fireworks, a magic lantern, music boxes, and a magnetic battery, which he used to convince tribal chiefs of the white man's power. On an earlier expedition, Baker impressed the natives with a full-dress Highland kilt, sporran, and Glengarry bonnet. Hugh Clapperton delighted the natives when he fired some Congreve rockets.[49]

The muzzle-loading Brown Bess was the standard weapon of the British army; but because its range was limited and it took at least sixty seconds to reload, it was not effective in African exploration. Experiments in rifling and the introduction of the percussion cap marked a revolution in long guns. By the 1850s, the Brown Bess was replaced by the Enfield rifle, which fired the new cylindroconoidal bullets. Its range was five times that of the Brown Bess. In the next few years it would be succeeded by breechloaders, and the Martini-Henry would become the standard weapon for the British army. A few explorers, such as Livingstone and René Caillié, did not carry arms when they traveled in Africa, but most traveled as if they were on military maneuvers. Baker had sixteen hundred men with him in the Sudan and enough arms and ammunition to fight for years. Baker was a gun collector, and on his expedition to the Nile, he had a double-barreled No. 24, two No. 10 polygroove rifles, and an elephant gun which he called "Baby" and which the natives called "Child of a cannon." Its recoil was so powerful that every time he fired it he "spun round like a weathercock in a hurricane."[50] As mentioned before, Stanley was not reluctant to use his heavy firepower on the Africans. But explorers generally brought only enough weapons to bag game.

Sometimes tragic incidents grew out of the cultural contrasts, especially when the western world imposed its technology on the natives. James Grant recalled the story of a native ruler who received a rifle as a present. If he was unable to find any game when he went hunting, he tested his marksmanship on his subjects.[51]

Henry Stanley, who had traveled in the American West before he explored Africa, believed that

The lessons derived from the near extinction of the Indian are very applicable to Africa, and it was my principal reason for advocating the prohibition of trade in breech-loading rifles with Africans. To produce the same effects on the African aborigines as have resulted in the almost total destruction of the North Americans, all we need do is to freely permit the carriage of modern rifles and their ammunition into Africa, and in a few years we shall find the same rapid process of depopulation going on there. Savages have the minds of children and the passions of brutes, and to place breech-loaders in their hands is as cruel an act as to put razors in the hands of infants.[52]

The steamboat was one of the technological innovations that aided African exploration. The first steamboat appeared on the Senegal River in 1818. The Lairds of Birkenhead were pioneers in building British steamboats, and, soon after Richard Lander's exploration along the Niger, Macgregor Laird organized the African Inland Commercial Company to take advantage of Lander's discoveries. In 1832 Laird and Lander, aboard two steamers, sailed up the Niger as far as the Benue, thereby pushing British influence and commerce deeper into Africa.

Of the forty-nine whites on that expedition, forty died of

malaria. The African variety of malaria, caused by the *Plasmodium falciparum,* was the deadliest. By the mid-nineteenth century, the role of the anopheles mosquito was understood, and with the discovery of quinine prophylaxis more of Africa was opened to European penetration.[53] Disease, not the natives, was the primary killer of British explorers. Of the thirty explorers studied, fifteen died from disease in Africa and three died from diseases contracted in Africa. Every African explorer was stricken by disease.[54] In 1847, Alexander Bryson wrote *A Report on the Climate and Principal Diseases of the African Station* in which he revealed that the mortality rate on the West Coast had been cut in half by giving the men regular doses of quinine and avoiding the disease-ridden island of Fernando Po. Dr. William B. Baikie proved the effectiveness of quinine as a prophylactic on his 1854 expedition to the Niger.

Thereafter, explorers such as Stanley, Speke, Cameron, and Burton always carried supplies of quinine with them. And even though they still suffered from malaria, they survived to explore another day. Livingstone had his own concoction made from calomel, quinine, rhubarb, and jalap. In James Grant's medicine chest were "Brown's blistering tissue, plaster, quinine, lunar caustic, citric acid, julap, calomel, rhubarb, blue pill, colocynth, laudanum, Dover's powders, emetic essence of ginger." Burton believed in the curative powers of "Dr. Warburg's Drops." Then there was always brandy for medicinal purposes. Baker began making a whisky from sweet potatoes. He called his enterprise "King Kamrasi's Central African Unyoro Potato-Whisky Company, Unlimited," and maintained, "I found an extraordinary change in my health from the time that I commenced drinking the potato-whisky. I became strong, and from the time to the present day my fever left me. . . ."[55]

Dr. Benjamin Rush added little to Meriwether Lewis's list of medicines, which included four ounces of calomel, a quarter ounce of tartar emetic, fifteen pounds of the powdered bark, a half pound of jalap, two pounds of saltpeter, and ten pounds of Glauber's salts. The famous Philadelphia physician's major contribution was six hundred pills of his own creation and a potent physic consisting of ten grains of calomel and ten of julap, named by the men "Rush's thunderbolts."[56]

In Africa the explorer was not "setting out upon a mere promenade." During his search for Livingstone, Stanley suffered numerous attacks of fever.[57] Burton's condition on his return from East Africa left a memorable imprint on his fiancee: "I shall never forget Richard as he was then; he had had twenty-one attacks of fever, and had been partially paralyzed and partially blind; he was a mere skeleton, with brown yellow skin hanging in bags, his eyes protruding, and his lips drawn away from his teeth."[58]

Many native porters died on these expeditions, but explorers were concerned mainly with the health of the white members of the expedition. Verney Cameron lost two of three white colleagues; five whites on Stanley's first two expeditions died. Of the forty-four Europeans in Park's second expedition to the Niger, thirty-five died of malaria. On Captain James Tuckey's expedition to the Congo in 1816, he had with him forty-four Europeans, of whom twenty-one died from fever.

The average age of American explorers at death was sixty-one, but for African explorers it was forty-seven. Two famous explorers died under strange circumstances. Meriwether Lewis was either murdered or committed suicide on the Natchez Trace in 1809. John Speke probably died from a bullet wound suffered in a hunting accident in 1864, although some believe it was suicide. In noting the irony of Bruce's death, whose end came as a result of a fall down a flight of stairs, Burton remarked, "After a life of hazard and of dangerous enterprise, [Bruce] perished by the slipping of his foot."[59]

Of the thirty American explorers studied, only Captain John W. Gunnison and Jedediah Smith were killed by natives. Like the Africans, Indians launched a number of attacks against explorers, but the danger to the explorers from the natives was generally far less than was the danger to the natives from the explorers.[60] Lewis had a skirmish with Piegans in 1806 in which two Indians were killed. If one does not count the three men killed by Shivwits Indians on John Wesley Powell's first exploration of the Colorado River, only one person who took part in the Great Surveys of the 1860s and 1870s died violently.

The Lewis and Clark expedition was stricken almost daily by illness. For over a month, the party was "troubled with boils, and occasionally with the dysentry . . . and disorders of the stomach." Lewis, who suffered from dysentry, also had terrible pains and a high fever.[61] Dysentery incapacitated several members of the Long party.[62]

Diseases brought to the uncivilized land by the white man wrought havoc among the Indians. This biological intrusion killed tens of thousands of previously-isolated natives. Smallpox was carried up the Missouri in the 1830s, and it struck practically every tribe from the river to the Pacific Ocean. This American Black Death reduced the Mandan tribe from sixteen hundred to thirty in one devastating winter. The number of Blackfeet, the tribe American trappers feared most in the upper Missouri valley, was reduced by three-fourths.

Explorers suffered from near-starvation in America and Africa. Stanley lost seventy-six pounds during his search for Livingstone, and Livingstone had to pull in his belt to stave off hunger pangs:[63] "In changing my dress this morning," he wrote, "I was frightened at my own emaciation."[64] The natives charged outrageous prices for elephant meat, but Livingstone had to pay them or starve to death.[65] The African explorer had an exotic variety of meat from which to choose, including eland and giraffe, but a starving man would eat rotten zebra meat or the dirty, saliva-covered remains of an animal left by a lion. The Europeans on Stanley's Emin Pasha expedition ate monkey, donkey, rat, snake, and insects in order to survive.

Wild animals ordinarily posed no threat to the explorer, but the grizzly bear, true to its name (*Ursus horribilis*), is a frightening creature. It weighs half a ton and is extremely fast despite its size. Coming upon huge tracks, the men of the Lewis and Clark party were anxious to view the animal. Presently Lewis and a companion spotted two grizzlies and emptied their rifles into the beasts. One animal wandered off, but the other went after Lewis. The bear pursued Lewis for one hundred yards across the plain before it was brought down; Lewis remarked, "These bear being so hard to die reather intimedates us all; I must confess that I do not like the gentlemen and had reather fight two Indians than one bear." Lewis had a second encounter with a grizzly. He was on a buffalo hunt and, after killing a buffalo, turned to see a huge bear moving toward him. Since he was alone and his gun was empty, Lewis started running for a tree three hundred yards away. The bear charged, and Lewis, realizing that he would never reach the tree in time, plunged into the Missouri River. Fortunately, when Lewis pointed his espontoon at him, the animal gave up the chase and retreated.[66]

Pike found that grizzlies would not attack unless provoked, but would "defend themselves courageously." In the Powder River country in 1823 Jedediah Smith was attacked by a large grizzly. The bear grabbed Smith by his head and threw him to the ground. Smith's skull was opened and his right ear left hanging. He recovered but bore the scars for life.[67]

The Lewis and Clark party had an unsettling experience with another animal. Lewis recounted,

Last night we were all allarmed by a large buffaloe Bull, which swam over the opposite shore and coming along side of the white perogue, climbed over it to land, he then allarmed ran up the bank in full speed directly towards the fires, and was within 18 inches of the heads of some of the men who lay sleeping before the centinel could allarm him or make him change his course, still more allarmed, he took his direction immediately towards our lodge, passing between 4 fires and within a few inches of the heads of one range of the men as they yet lay sleeping.

The buffalo finally lumbered off and, luckily, no one was hurt.[68]

An African animal that created a great deal of excitement was the gorilla. Since the Carthagenian voyage of Hanno to Africa, a legend had surrounded the animal, which was first sighted in Gabon. Hanno thought gorillas were humans covered with long hair. Three female gorillas were killed and their skins taken to Carthage and put on display at the temple of Astarte.

In the 1850s, Paul Du Chaillu was sent to West Africa by the Academy of Natural Sciences of Philadelphia. For four years he explored along the Gabon River, the first white man to do so since the seventeenth century. During the expedition, he discovered the source of the Ogowe River and killed a gorilla. When he published his travel account in 1861, many readers questioned his stories about the gorilla. Heinrich Barth doubted that Du Chaillu had traveled into the interior, although Burton supported many of Du Chaillu's observations. But his claim of having been the first white man to hunt gorillas and study them in their natural state was proved correct, even if he did exaggerate the ferocity of the animal. He was also doubted when he told of his encounter with the Obengo tribe of pygmies.[69] Asked what was the most difficult problem he faced as an explorer, Du Chaillu replied, "To keep my reputation."

Livingstone and Thomson were nearly killed by wild animals. Livingstone observed lions in Bechuanaland and had, in fact, seen a woman eaten by one, but "The sense of danger vanishes when you are in a country of lions."[70] One day natives came to Livingstone complaining that a lion was killing their sheep and they asked for his help. Rushing off with only one gun and no armed natives for protection, Livingstone fired both barrels at the lion. The wounded animal charged Livingstone, grabbed him, and shook him as a terrier would a rat. He was near death when one of his men diverted the animal. Livingstone's comment on the attack: "The shake annihilated fear, and allowed no horror in looking round at the beast. The peculiar state is probably produced in all animals killed by the carnivores; and if so, is a merciful provision by our benevolent Creator for lessening the pain of death."[71]

In late December, 1883, near Mount Elgon, Joseph Thomson was looking for something to shoot for dinner. Spotting two water buffalo, he fired from fifty yards away, hitting one near the heart. The animal ran off. Thomson pursued and sent a bullet into its shoulder, but it refused to fall until Thomson hit it in the head with his last shot. Foolishly, Thomson moved forward, believing the animal to be "completely *hors de combat.*" He was six yards away when the dying buffalo got to its feet and charged. The animal threw Thomson on its horns and he landed dazed and hurt, with one thought streaking through his mind: "If he comes for me again I am a dead man." As the buffalo was about to charge, a headman's bullet brought it down.[72] Charging bull elephants nearly killed Livingstone, Thomson, and Baker. On the Nile a hippopotamus attacked Baker's canoe and lifted it out of the water. Fortunately for the crew the vessel was righted, for crocodiles were swimming on either side.[73]

Mosquitoes were a serious problem for the members of the Lewis and Clark expedition. Sacajawea's baby, Baptiste, suffered from numerous bites, and Sergeant Ordway's face and eyes swelled up from the insects' poison. Long's party suffered from mosquitoes in Missouri.[74] Livingstone was attacked by red ants when he stepped on one of their nests: "The bites of these furies were like sparks of fire, and there was no retreat. I jumped about for a second or two, then in desperation tore off all my clothing, and rubbed and picked them seriatim as quickly as possible." An attack by African bees disrupted one exploring party and killed a horse.[75]

Even worse was John Speke's experience. During a severe storm, he lit a candle in his tent and the interior filled with black beetles. After Speke fell asleep, a beetle entered his ear. When Speke attempted to remove it, he pushed it further in and it began to gnaw at the inside of his ear. Desperate with pain, he poured melted butter into his ear. He managed to quiet the beetle with a penknife but severely injured his ear. Speke suffered excruciating pain and became nearly deaf. The remains of the beetle fell out, six months later.[76]

To be a successful explorer, one needed a new awareness of the environment; to survive, one had to relearn sights and sounds. It was crucial to be constantly on guard. Was that sound distant thunder, native drums signaling an attack, or a roaring waterfall waiting to be discovered? Silence took on a language of its own. Vistas expanded, visions became confused. Were those trees or buffalo or natives?

In their unrelenting searches, explorers were often too intense, too caught up in their goals and, through an exaggerated belief in themselves, too optimistic. Inexperience increased the novice's optimism, and the seasoned explorer trusted his previous experiences to forestall the hazards of the trek.

The essence of exploration was discovery. The first sighting, the sound of a waterfall, was sublime. In their passion for discovery, explorers often abused their men and took needless risks. Their ambition sometimes led to the goal sought; at other times it resulted in death.

CHAPTER NINE

The Impact
of Exploration

THE EXPLORERS HAD A SIGNIFICANT and lasting effect on their societies. The information they brought back stimulated a new look at man and his environment. Based upon explorers' reports, new maps and geographical reports were drawn. James Rennell studied the journals of the African explorers and wrote knowledgeable essays on geography for the African Association. In the United States, the Topographical Bureau initiated a program of investigation and mapping that would become a model for its time. From the reports of explorers it sent out, the bureau published a relief map in 1850, "The United States and Their Territories Between the Mississippi and the Pacific Ocean," the first accurate map of the West's physiographic features.

Few expeditions had the impact of Lewis and Clark's. Two dozen Indian tribes, one hundred twenty animals, and over one hundred seventy-five new plants were discovered by its members. The grizzly bear, pronghorn antelope, prairie dog, and mule deer were among the mammals first described by Lewis and Clark. Lewis, who carried with him two books written by Linnaeus, named the mule deer and the whistling swan. Although the grizzly bear had been described earlier by Canadian explorers, Lewis and Clark were the first to write about the animal's range, habits, and physical characteristics.

Lewis and Clark were honored with the creation of the genera Lewisia and Clarkia. Newly-discovered birds were named

Clark's nutcracker and the Lewis woodpecker; two species of herbs were named clarkia and lewisia. The Latin name for the ragged robin was *Clarkia pulchella*. Three new species were Lewis's wild flax (*Linum lewisii*), Lewis's monkey flower (*Mimulus lewisii*), and Lewis's syringa (*Philadelphus lewisii*).[1] Other animals newly discovered by Lewis and Clark were the white sturgeon and the steelhead trout, the horned toad and the prairie rattler, and the western meadowlark and the sage grouse.

John Charles Frémont also had flora and fauna named for him, including Fremont cottonwood, Fremont pine, and Fremont's squirrel. A pass in Colorado and a peak in Wyoming bear his name, along with a number of towns and counties. A low-quality ore, "marcylite," was named for army explorer Randolph B. Marcy.

Explorers named hundreds of geographical locations. Lewis and Clark named the Marias, Milk, Gallatin, Madison, and Jefferson rivers. They named Council Bluffs, were among the first to use the word "prairie," and described the extensive area of rolling, treeless country as the Great Plains. Frémont named the Great Basin, the Golden Gate, and the Humboldt River. Zebulon Pike named a mountain Grand Peak; later it would be called Pike's Peak. Stephen Long was the first to use the expression, "the Great American Desert."

In Africa, explorers gave names to the land, even though Richard Burton wrote that nothing was "so absurd as to impose English names on . . . the remote interior parts of Africa." A member of the Royal Geographical Society complained about seeing "the name of our great and gracious sovereign insulted and degraded, in giving names to places in this most barbarous and degraded country."[2] John Speke named the source of the White Nile Lake Victoria and, because of the support he received from the Royal Geographical Society, named the falls at its north end Ripon for the society's president. Samuel Baker discovered and named Lake Albert for the prince consort and Murchison Falls for the former president of the Royal Geographical Society. Henry Stanley was the first to popularize the sobriquets "Dark Continent" and "Darkest Continent." He left his name on Stanley Pool, Stanley Falls, and Stanleyville, and he named the falls on the Congo River after David Livingstone. A settlement on Lake Nyasa was called Livingstonia.

Three species of gazelle were named for James Grant, Joseph Thomson, and Speke. A giraffe was named for Grant and a bushy-tailed rat for Speke. Two birds were called the *Okapi johnstoni* and the *Gallirex johnstoni* for Harry Johnston.

In that age of nationalism, exploration—or the possibility of exploration—by one country often forced another to send out its own expedition. Indeed, after Paul Du Chaillu reported that he had solved the Ogowe River question, the French government dispatched a party of explorers to the area. Mungo Park was sent by Joseph Banks on his second expedition because of a book published by a Frenchman who supported his nation's expansion into West Africa. Jefferson was concerned about British penetration in the West when he sent out Lewis and Clark. Lewis noted that if the United States built a post on the Yellowstone River it could stop the expansion of the British North West Company, for

if this powerful and ambitious company are suffered uninterruptedly to prosecute their trade with the nations inhabiting the upper portion of the Missouri, and thus acquire an influence with those people, it is not difficult to conceive the obstructions which they might hereafter through the medium of that influence, oppose to the will of our government or the navigation of the Missouri.[3]

Explorers played a vital role in shaping expansion in America and Africa. In the mid-nineteenth century, American explorers were important to the rise of Manifest Destiny. A few decades later, the influence of British explorers was evident in the Scramble for Africa. When most of the basic exploration had been accomplished, explorers became involved with expansionism, diplomacy, and settlement.

During Jefferson's presidency, the United States government played an active role in organizing expeditions. Government sponsorship of expeditions continued into later administrations as well. In his first message to Congress in

1825, President John Quincy Adams stated that America must assume "her station among the civilized nations of the earth." He continued,

The voyages of discovery prosecuted in the course of that time at the expense of those nations have not only redounded to their glory, but to the improvement of human knowledge. . . . One hundred expeditions of circumnavigation like those of Cook and La Pérouse would not burden the exchequer of the nation fitting them out so much as the ways and means of defraying a single campaign in war. But if we take into account the lives of those benefactors of mankind of which their services in the cause of their species were the purchase, how shall the cost of those heroic enterprises be estimated, and what compensation can be made to them or to their countries for them? Is it not by bearing them in affectionate remembrance? Is it not still more by imitating their example—by enabling countrymen of our own to pursue the same career and to hazard their lives in the same cause?[4]

The War of 1812 made the United States government aware of the need for topographical engineers, and in 1817 the Topographical Corps was established; the Topographical Bureau was organized the following year. From then on the government had a corps of professionally trained soldier-engineers to explore the American West scientifically. The Army Corps of Topographical Engineers was reorganized in 1838 and, although it was made up of only three dozen officers, no other agency of the United States government was as important in exploring and opening the West. The corps was the scientific advance agent for Manifest Destiny.[5]

Many of America's leading scientists, including Asa Gray, James Dana, and Titian Peale, were involved with exploratory expeditions. The emergence of a community of professional scientists paralleled and was intertwined with American exploration. A scientific inventory was being taken of the West. A half century after Long's 1820 expedition, Asa Gray remarked that the contributions of its scientists were the beginnings of the history of botany in the West.[6]

Explorers, army officers, and scientists came to the West in increasing numbers in the 1840s. These professionals launched expeditions to discover and classify western flora and fauna. They were especially useful because the emphasis was shifting away from simply locating new geographical wonders and toward the intensive study of natural resources and ethnological studies of native peoples.

Through explorations and surveys and the resulting press coverage, another frontier was opened up—tourism. John Wesley Powell, Ferdinand Hayden, and George Wheeler were associated with touring parties and the promotion of the scenic beauties of the West. Tourists were especially attracted to Clarence King's *Mountaineering in the Sierra Nevada*, published in 1872.[7] Explorers' accounts served to encourage the establishment of national parks. The Washburn-Doane and Hayden expeditions of the early 1870s and the ensuing publicity helped build sentiment for the creation of Yellowstone National Park in 1872.[8]

The explorer was becoming increasingly involved with national policies affecting the West. Because he possessed the geographical expertise needed in treaty-making, more and more he was pulled into diplomatic negotiations. And even though he was not always directly involved in these negotiations, the data he brought back from his expeditions were used in making the decisions that rounded out the American continent in the 1840s and 1850s.

William H. Goetzmann, who has written extensively on this subject, remarked that "The explorer, perhaps as much as anyone else, helped to shape the exact contours of America's Western domain."[9] The American explorers who played the greatest roles in expanding American involvement in the West were Charles Wilkes, John C. Frémont, and William H. Emory. One of the major promoters of the Wilkes expedition was Jeremiah N. Reynolds, special agent for the secretary of the navy, who wanted to test John Cleves Symmes's theory that the earth consisted of five concentric spheres with a hollow core and polar openings into which ships could safely sail. Reynolds was also interested in the prestige that the United States would gain in launching such an expedition.[10] The United States Exploring Expedition, which set sail in 1838, was the first government-sponsored overseas expedition. Under the command of Captain Wilkes, it spent nearly six months off the coast of Oregon in 1841.

With the expedition's return to New York in June, 1842, Wilkes was convinced of the importance of the Pacific Northwest to the United States. Because he had spent a great deal of time there, making more surveys than ordered, Wilkes became an authority on the area. When he lost his vessel, the *Peacock*, while she was crossing the sandbar at the entrance to the Columbia, Wilkes encouraged the occupation of the region above 49° where better harbors, notably Puget Sound, could be found.[11] Wilkes wrote:

Mere description can give little idea of the terrors of the bar of the Columbia: all who have seen it have spoken of the wildness of the scene, and the incessant roar of the waters, representing it as one of the most fearful sights that can possibly meet the eye of the sailor.[12]

Farther northward Wilkes found that

nothing can exceed the beauty of these waters, and their safety: not a shoal exists within the Straits of Juan de Fuca, Admiralty Inlet, Puget Sound, or Hood's Canal, that can in any way interrupt their navigation by a seventy-four gun ship. I venture nothing in saying, there is no country in the world that possesses waters equal to these.[13]

Wilkes viewed San Francisco Bay with equal zeal. He boasted that it was "one of the finest, if not the very best harbour in the world," large enough to contain all of the navies of Europe.[14] His grandiloquent boasts about agricultural successes in California were used by the propagandists of Manifest Destiny.[15]

Wilkes believed that in a few years upper California would probably separate from Mexico and unite with Oregon to form one state with two of the world's greatest harbors, San Francisco Bay and the Straits of Juan de Fuca. He further believed that trade between these points and Pacific Ocean ports would become extremely profitable and that the West

Coast, "evidently destined to fill a large space in the world's future history," would be taken by the Americans, for there were no rivals save those "indolent inhabitants of warm climates. . . ."[16] A scholar of American expansion has credited Wilkes, along with other travelers to the Pacific Northwest, with convincing Washington to establish 49° as the line dividing Canada and the United States in the Treaty of 1846 with Great Britain.[17]

John C. Frémont was even more influential than Wilkes in American expansionism. According to Goetzmann, Frémont's three expeditions between 1842 and 1845 were "the outstanding examples, in American history, of the calculated use of exploring expeditions as diplomatic weapons."[18] The purpose of these expeditions was to advertise the West, bring back information about the land, and encourage settlement. Frémont personified the romantic mood of the country in the mid-nineteenth century. Dashing, adventurous, and young, he was the American Byron. His illegitimate birth even added a touch of scandal that appealed to the American public.

Frémont had been commissioned a second lieutenant in the Topographical Corps in 1838, in the same year he joined Joseph N. Nicollet to survey the area from the upper Mississippi River westward along the Minnesota River. Born in France, Nicollet came to the United States in 1832. He was a skilled astronomer and mathematician and introduced Frémont to several new scientific techniques. Nicollet considered Frémont extremely qualified and predicted that, if he lived long enough, he could "carve out for himself a distinguished position among the *savans* of the age."[19]

Adding further to Frémont's romantic image was his elopement with Senator Thomas Hart Benton's beautiful daughter Jessie. Benton became a strong supporter of Frémont's explorations and helped him head his first expedition to the Rocky Mountains. That expedition departed from St. Louis in 1842 and traveled along the Oregon Trail as far as Wyoming. In the Wind River Range, Frémont, with an eye for the dramatic, climbed what he believed to be the highest peak and left a flag as symbol of eventual American occupation.

Aided by his wife, Frémont published a report of the expedition that would become valuable to the western expansionists. One of the most notable features of the report was Frémont's description of the western plains not as a "Great American Desert," as they had been called by earlier explorers, but as a fertile land. Western poet Joaquin Miller caught the nationalistic sentiment when he wrote, "I fancied I could see Frémont's men, hauling the cannon up the savage battlements of the Rocky Mountains, flags in the air, Frémont at the head, waving his sword. . . ." Miller concluded, "Now I began to be influenced with a love of action, adventure, glory, and great deeds. . . ."[20]

In a book about his experiences, Frémont excited the public with his dramatic account of western adventure, and as a work of propaganda and romance it was grand. A member of the United States Senate made a motion that one thousand extra copies of the report be printed for public distribution.

In 1843, Frémont was given command of a second western expedition to link his earlier expedition with the Pacific Coast surveys of Wilkes, "so as to give a connected survey of the interior of our continent. . . ."[21] Frémont was to travel west by way of the Oregon Trail, designating the important areas along the route for future pioneers.

The party left St. Louis in May, 1843. Among its thirty-nine members were Tom Fitzpatrick and Kit Carson. Carson's connection with Frémont's explorations heightened interest in the travels and, among exploring partners, only a few—Lewis and Clark, Stanley and Livingstone, and Grant and Speke—shared the friendship and fame that Frémont and Carson enjoyed. On reaching the Great Salt Lake, Frémont explained, "I am doubtful if the followers of Balboa felt more enthusiasm when, from the heights of the Andes, they saw for the first time the great Western ocean."[22]

After exploring the lake for a few days, the party continued on to Fort Hall and then to Oregon. With most of their work completed, they moved south into the Great Basin, where Frémont hoped to find the San Buenaventura River. Crossing the Sierras in the winter, they reached Sutter's ranch on the American River. From there the party traveled back to Missouri.

With the publication of his second report in 1845, Frémont, like Wilkes, revealed the agricultural potential of California. He believed that the Sacramento Valley, covered with groves of evergreen and white oak, was unrivaled in its beauty. As for the San Joaquin Valley, Frémont described it as "beautiful with open groves of oak, and a grassy sward beneath. . . ."[23] In his report on Oregon, Frémont recalled the passage to India theme.

Commercially the value of the Oregon Country must be great, washed as it is by the north Pacific ocean—fronting Asia—producing many of the elements of commerce—mild and healthy in its climate—and becoming, as it naturally will, a thoroughfare for the East India and China trade.[24]

Frémont's journal of the 1843–1844 exploration was broad in coverage, and the map drawn by Charles Preuss was one of the great achievements in western cartography. Carl I. Wheat, a scholar of western maps, was convinced that this map "changed the entire picture of the West, and made a lasting contribution to cartography." Frémont not only advertised the West but encouraged emigration there. The Mormons, who had suffered the murder of their leader, Joseph Smith, and the collapse of their Nauvoo, Illinois, settlement, were prompted by Frémont's narrative to move to the valley of the Great Salt Lake in order to establish the state of Deseret.[25] Frémont's writings also sparked enthusiasm for the South Pass route to the West. Describing the easy ascent through the pass, he compared the passage to the "ascent of the Capitol hill from the avenue, at Washington."[26]

Frémont's achievements, in addition to supplying much new information, increased interest in Manifest Destiny. On this third expedition, in 1845, Frémont played a part in the conquest of California when he joined forces with Americans there in the Bear Flag Rebellion which overthrew Mexican control.

One of the most important military reconnaissances of the West was undertaken by Lieutenant William H. Emory. Emory had been born into a wealthy Maryland family and graduated from West Point in 1831. He was appointed lieutenant in the Corps of Topographical Engineers in 1838, the year of Frémont's appointment to the corps. During the Mexican War, Emory made an important expedition to California from Santa Fe while he was with General Stephen W. Kearny's Army of the West. The Southwest, although explored since the days of Coronado, had never been effectively mapped, and when Emory's findings were published America had its first scientific report of the area. Emory's task, wrote a historian, "was to ascertain whether or not the Southwest was worth taking by force and, if so, whether or not it was worth keeping!"[27]

Ten thousand copies of the Emory report were published, and it became a major work on the Southwest and a handbook for hundreds of overlanders in the next few years.[28] His report was also valuable in the diplomatic maneuvering between Mexico and the United States. Emory advised the Polk administration that the southern boundary should encompass the area south of the Gila River for an eventual railroad route. In 1851, Emory was appointed chief astronomer and surveyor of the United States–Mexico Boundary Survey. The commission was retired after the 1852 presidential election, but the next year Emory was given the task of drawing that boundary as commissioner of the Gadsden survey, further demonstrating the importance of the explorer to American expansionism in the 1840s and 1850s.[29]

African explorers also activated an interest in that continent by adding to the information available about its interior. Like the American explorers, those in Africa opened the way for British expansionism. Explorers Samuel Baker, Harry Johnston, and Henry Stanley became administrators in Africa. John Speke's works were well known to British imperialists like Frederick D. Lugard and William Mackinnon. In his journals, Speke mentioned the vast resources of the areas he visited and the interest of the natives in developing trade with

Europe. After spending time with Mutesa I, kabaka of Buganda, Speke found the chief knowledgeable and friendly. The explorer noted that, since Mutesa had Abyssinian blood in his veins, he was practically "civilized." Thus was born the "Hamitic myth," which held that the Hamites of the north were the people who civilized black Africa. Harry Johnston also believed in a division of Africans between the superior Hamitic and the inferior Negro. Speke's answer to the problems he witnessed in East Africa was to encourage British control over the natives like that already established in India. The resultant imperial push into East Africa showed the effects of Speke's words on the British.[30]

The politically astute Verney Cameron laid claim to the Zambezi and Congo basins for the British Crown, believing the area to be rich in natural resources. He showed how easy it was to change roles from African explorer to advocate for British imperialism in Africa. In his outspoken propagandizing, Cameron established the British Commercial Geographical Society in 1884, the objectives of which were centered on opening markets and sources of raw materials and discovering new trade routes.[31] In 1885, Cameron published *Across Africa*, in which he stated, "It is our bounden duty as Britons to do our utmost in every possible way toward the opening up of the country." A practical humanitarian, Cameron believed that the Africans needed British aid and encouragement. He wished to make "the darkest corners of Africa . . . as light as the day."[32] Revealing a flair for historical imagery, Cameron described his own exploratory endeavors: "Following the example of the adventurers of the Elizabethan era, of Cook, and many other worthies, I planted the Union Jack in the very midst of the heart of Africa, and then proclaimed the rule and dominion of Her Most Gracious Majesty Queen Victoria."[33]

Joseph Thomson explored Africa in the 1870s and 1880s, the period between the last days of African exploration and the start of European imperialism. He played a leading role in colonization by making treaties with native rulers in northern Nigeria for the National African Company, a trading firm in West Africa. Describing his new part in this incipient imperialism, the pragmatic Scot commented that he became a diplomat "at the expense of a few pounds and a demoralised stomach."[34] While in the service of the imperialist Cecil Rhodes and the British South Africa Company, Thomson negotiated more than a dozen treaties with Africans.[35]

Another precursor of British imperialism was James Grant, who was connected with a number of activities to open up Africa to commerce and civilization. He was a delegate to the 1876 International African Conference convened by King Leopold II of Belgium, and he also worked with businessmen interested in Africa like shipping magnate William Mackinnon. Grant became involved with the African Exploration Fund (set up by the Royal Geographical Society to support further exploration) and with a plan to build a transcontinental telegraph line. This last proposal anticipated Cecil Rhodes's Cape to Cairo connection by over a decade. Grant took pride in the fact that his son worked for Rhodes. In the words of his eulogist, England was "preparing to reap the harvest" for which Grant and other explorers had "sowed the seed."[36]

In 1869, Samuel Baker was sent by Ismail Pasha, viceroy of Egypt, to lead an expedition of sixteen hundred men and fifty-eight ships to the upper Nile. Baker's major objective was to crush the slave trade and extend Egyptian control farther south into the Sudan. Harsh in his methods, Baker left for England after three years of conflict, but his adventures had an impact on Britain: his reports attracted those with political and economic interests in the Sudan. When he left, his successor as governor of Equatoria (Southern Sudan) was General Charles G. Gordon. By the late 1890s, the British controlled the Sudan.[37]

Following his explorations, Henry Stanley was also interested in opening up Africa to European control. Stanley believed that Africa's problems could be more easily solved if Europeans became involved. His second expedition in Africa, which lasted from 1874 to 1877, answered many of the geographical questions asked by Livingstone during his final years.

This second expedition, called "the first of the new political expeditions," was a precursor of the Scramble for Africa in the 1880s.[38] Stanley, who recognized the political consequences of his expeditions, urged Britain to move into the Congo basin. When Britain failed to move, Leopold II and his International African Association entered the picture and hired Stanley in 1879 to halt the French advance. Through his road building, diplomacy, and establishment of stations, the energetic Stanley was partially responsible for the birth of the Congo Free State in 1885.

In a statement that recalls American expansionism in the era of Manifest Destiny, Stanley wrote that God "surely intended that Africa should be reserved until the fulness of time for something higher than a nursery for birds and a storeplace for reptiles."[39]

Like his good friend Stanley, Livingstone linked commerce to civilizing the Africans, and, more than any other explorer, he put Africa "on the map." With Livingstone's death in 1873, a renewed interest in Christianizing Africa appeared. In November, 1875, Stanley praised Livingstone's heroism in a letter to the London *Daily Telegraph*, which further encouraged missionaries to spread the gospel in Central Africa. The next year, an Anglican bishop wrote that so many missionaries were flooding into Africa that "the natives all suppose that their country is being mapped out for a grand military attack."[40]

Livingstone's attempt to establish a highway for traders and missionaries in the heart of Africa ended in the disastrous Zambezi expedition. Livingstone noted the gold and copper mines in Katanga, but he was more interested in the potential of cotton production. These economic and Christian enterprises, he felt, would revolutionize Africa. Livingstone's last seven years of exploration were the most significant of any European's in the nineteenth century. His forceful personality, immense suffering, and martyrdom proved to be of greater value to African trade than his geographical discoveries. Livingstone's graphic descriptions of the slave trade and the generally deplorable situation of the African prompted many Englishmen to become involved in African colonization and in establishing law and order there. Livingstone was one of the greatest abolitionists of the mid-nineteenth century.

The British signed treaties with the Africans in part because of the information from Livingstone's reports of the slave trade. Redeeming the native became a justification for British incursion.

Explorers were both precursors and progenitors of imperialism. In the 1860s, Livingstone talked about annexing the area around Lake Nyasa to Britain, and three decades later Nyasaland was established. A supporter of British imperialism boasted that the Royal Geographical Society, in sending out Grant, Burton, and Speke, had helped establish a protectorate over Uganda.[41]

A new interest in race developed in both England and the United States in the early nineteenth century, and a variety of theoretical avenues of study was adopted. Many of the scientific ideas about race, distinctions between species and varieties, and debates between monogenists and polygenists were sparked by exploratory endeavors.

Besides the African Association, a number of other groups were organized as a result of the scientific information brought back by the explorers. The Ethnological Society of London and the British and Foreign Aborigines' Protective Society debated such questions as whether blacks were a separate race. Burton attacked the Protective Association for being too sympathetic to the African and, to refute many of their views, he helped found the Anthropological Society of London in 1863. This group emphasized the field of physical anthropology and pointed out inherent racial differences. By supporting the polygenetic theory, it hoped to show the clear separation of the black and white races. Burton pushed for retrenchment in the funding for missionary activity in Africa, believing it would do the African no good.[42]

Americans and the British approached the native with an ethnocentric, mid-Victorian attitude. They conceived of a ladder of civilization based on the laws of evolution, with the Anglo-Saxons at the top and Africans and Indians at the bottom. Filled with a sense of superiority and moral self-righteousness and suffused with noble intentions, they believed that they could lift these backward aborigines to greater heights.

Warfare, paganism, and cultural backwardness were anomalies that had to end, and the establishment of law and order was a basic justification of imperialism.

Explorers were influential as purveyors of facts and stimulators of imagination, and because of their searches empires were created. The drama of their experiences and their dreams of adventure, as much as any policy or program, stimulated the advance of imperialism.

Yet some sensed that these changes were not necessarily for the better. Joseph Thomson noted that the "iron heel of commerce" had destroyed the romance of African travel; one no longer looked at trees for their beauty but for their economic worth.[43]

Although there are clear differences between exploring Africa and exploring North America—for example the African explorer faced large, powerful native populations, while American explorers often went for days without seeing a native—there are also many similarities. Britain and America were caught up in an era of expansion at about the same time. Both nations rationalized their actions as their manifest destiny to civilize and elevate what were thought to be some of the most degraded peoples of the world. Much of this sentiment was based on feelings of racial superiority and national fervor. But the end result was the same: land was taken from the natives, their culture was eroded, and their dignity was trampled. In his subordination of the natives the white man, who had expected gratitude and obedience, engendered only hatred.

CHAPTER TEN

Conclusion

THERE ARE PROBABLY as many differences as similarities between African and American exploration, but the story of daring, driven individuals and their effect upon native cultures remains basic to the history of exploration. Nineteenth-century exploration is a mosaic of individual enterprise, personal bravery, scientific interest, and national ambition. Even though the technology of exploration changed, the goal of replacing myth with reality was constant.

The images of Africa and America at the beginning of the nineteenth century were largely characterized by geographical ignorance, but within the next six decades most of the misconceptions would be removed. America reached the peak of her exploration in the 1840s with the journeys of Frémont and Wilkes. Their achievements completed the early exploration of the Mountain Men and also sparked a new interest in national expansion. The great age of African exploration occurred between the 1850s and the 1870s when the two greatest African explorers, Livingstone and Stanley, made their famous discoveries.

Not before or since has so much of the earth been discovered in such a brief period. Having found the solutions to the geographical puzzles, the explorers turned the land over to diplomats and military men to solve the geopolitical problems.

In the 1880s and 1890s another breed of explorer was moving into a new and even more dangerous area, as newspapermen, photographers, and social critics penetrated the mysterious and hidden byways of the urban slums. City streets were sometimes more dangerous than jungle paths, and the natives of the city became more interesting than the natives encountered by explorers. The novels of Charles Dickens told of the terrors of London life. In America, Horatio Alger's character Ragged Dick noted the dangers of city life: "A fellow has to look sharp in this city, or he'll lose his eye teeth before he knows it." "We have a new literature of exploration," wrote American religious leader Walter Rauschenbusch. "Darkest Africa and the polar regions are becoming familiar; but we now have intrepid men and women who plunge for a time into the life of the lower classes and return to write books about the unknown race that lives in the next block."[1]

Salvation Army founder William Booth published *In Darkest England and the Way Out* in 1890, a few months after Stanley's *In Darkest Africa* appeared. Depicting the plight of England's "submerged tenth," the work began with a contrast between "darkest Africa" and "darkest England." "The lot of the negroes in the Equatorial Forest is not, perhaps, a very happy one, but is it so much more than that of many a pretty orphan girl in our Christian capital?" As Stanley had rescued Emin Pasha, so Booth proposed Stanley-like expeditions to "rescue . . . the miserable wanderers from their captivity, and bring them out into the larger liberty and the fuller life."[2]

But while these urban explorers wanted to launch reforms, destroy darkness, and replace mystery with information and reason, they never caught the imagination of the public as did the Frémonts, Stanleys, and Livingstones. No group of men played a more important role in the nineteenth century than the explorers. Their effects on geography, literature, ethnology, and foreign affairs were lasting. Would that they had known their impact. But it is doubtful that it would have made a difference in their actions.

These knights-errant were seduced by the unknown and fascinated by the glamor of adventure. They followed their dreams and were envied for the glories of exploration. They lived in a world beyond, a world that could never be again, where lively colors and intense emotion burned under the savage sun and the land was clean and new. The monotony and clutter of civilization was left behind for the monotony of the trek—wake, eat, march, stop, cook, eat, march, sleep. The sounds of civilization were displaced by the sounds of silence, at least until nightfall when the wild, weird drumbeats matched the beat of one's heart.

And if there was a touch of madness to their deeds, these brave fools who entered the immense world of the unknown were admired for their lunacy. As men, they followed their natural bent, committed to pursuing childhood dreams. If they tempted death and died of fever it was their decision; they elected to take that final pilgrimage into fierce solitude.

Was it strange that they were labeled liars? They had seen sights that others could not even imagine. Generally more intelligent, more daring, more single-minded than those they left behind, they were men apart, men often as inscrutable as the land they searched for. They advanced knowledge and offered their lives for the future, yet moved back in time to a primitive world. They discovered new outer worlds, yet made journeys within themselves. But as they trudged down new trails, breaking for all time the savage silence, they brought with them the threat of civilization. From the pure and innocent dreams of discovery to the horrors of invasion and massacre, it all happened with such speed. Explorers were the forerunners of change, carrying with them the blessings of civilization, of commerce, of conquest. Was it to be a better future for the natives, or the beginning of a long nightmare?

From the compulsions of explorers came the expansion of nations. From self-discovery came the discovery of new lands. A personal triumph for the explorer became a national goal for his country. But how many lives would be lost in the name of civilization? How many natives massacred, how much disease spread, how many cultures destroyed as a consequence of the explorers' dreams?

What had begun so simply became suddenly so complex. What had begun with a man going into the wilderness ended with colonization, wars, and imperialism. Of the tragedies caused by the new imperialism, Joseph Conrad wrote in *Heart of Darkness*, "The conquest of the earth, which mostly means the taking it away from those who have a different complexion or slightly flatter noses than ourselves, is not a pretty thing when you look into it too much."[3]

Notes

Preface

1. William H. Goetzmann, *Exploration and Empire: The Explorer and the Scientist in the Winning of the American West* (New York, 1967), p. xi; John Kirtland Wright, "Where History and Geography Meet: Recent American Studies in the History of Exploration" in *Proceedings* of the Eighth American Scientific Congress IX (1943): 20; for a different view of discovery, see Samuel Eliot Morison, *Portuguese Voyages to America in the Fifteenth Century* (Cambridge, Mass. 1940), pp. 5–6. See Paul Dickson, *Think Tanks* (New York, 1972), p. 7, for a discussion of the differences between basic and applied research that parallel distinctions between discovery and exploration. Increased scientific training came with the Age of Exploration; for examples of the lack of specialization and preparation during the Age of Discovery, see Samuel Eliot Morison, *The European Discovery of America: The Southern Voyages*, A.D. *1492–1616* (New York, 1974), pp. 346–47, and J. H. Parry, *The Age of Reconnaissance* (New York, 1964), pp. 84–85.

2. Daniel J. Boorstin, *The Exploring Spirit: America and the World, Then and Now* (New York, 1976), pp. 6–7; see also Wilcomb E. Washburn, "The Meaning of 'Discovery' in the Fifteenth and Sixteenth Centuries," *American Historical Review* 68 (October, 1962): 1–21.

Chapter One

1. Oswald Spengler, *The Decline of the West* (2 vols, New York, 1970) II, p. 501.

2. Ibid., I, p. 333; Bailey W. Diffie, *Prelude to Empire: Portugal Overseas Before Henry the Navigator* (Lincoln, Neb., 1967), ch. 9.

3. J. H. Parry, *The Establishment of the European Hegemony 1415–1715: Trade and Exploration in the Age of the Renaissance* (3rd ed. rev.,

New York, 1966), pp. 26–27; Gomes Eannes de Azurara, *The Chronicle of the Discovery and Conquest of Guinea*, trans. C. R. Beazley and Edgar Prestage (2 vols., London, 1896) I, 12–15.

4. Carlo M. Cipolla, *Guns, Sails, and Empires: Technological Innovation and the Early Phases of European Expansion 1400–1700* (n.p., 1965), pp. 81–82; Boies Penrose, *Travel and Discovery in the Renaissance 1420–1620* (New York, 1962), pp. 334–39; J. H. Parry, *The Age of Reconnaissance*, (New York, 1964), ch. 3, 4.

5. Luis Weckmann, "The Middle Ages in the Conquest of America," *Speculum* 26 (January, 1951): 131–32. Anatomical geography is also applied to rivers; e.g., arm, head, mouth.

6. Samuel Eliot Morison, *Admiral of the Ocean Sea: A Life of Christopher Columbus* (2 vols., New York, 1962) II, p. 546. For more on this, see Clarence J. Glacken, *Traces on the Rhodian Shore* (Berkeley, 1976), p. 358; and Samuel Eliot Morison, *The European Discovery of America: The Southern Voyages* A.D. *1492–1616* (New York, 1974), p. 286.

7. Homer, *The Odyssey*, trans. E. V. Rieu (Baltimore, 1961), p. 79.

8. V. S. Naipaul, *The Loss of El Dorado: A History* (Middlesex, 1977) Part One; also see John Hemming, *The Search for El Dorado* (New York, 1979). Paradoxically, Raleigh, influenced by Sir John Mandeville's *Travels*, believed in the existence of a race of headless mortals.

9. Morison, *The European Discovery of America*, p. 5. Marco Polo and Odoric of Pordenone looked for Prester John on their travels to Asia.

10. E. Denison Ross, "Prester John and the Empire of Ethiopia," in *Travel and Travellers of the Middle Ages*, ed. Arthur Percival Newton (London, 1926), p. 175. See Bede's view of the earth before the Fall in Glacken, *Traces*, p. 206, n. 101.

11. Genesis 2:10–14.

12. Ross, "Prester John," p. 175.

13. For more on Prester John, see A. H. M. Jones and Elizabeth Monroe, *A History of Ethiopia* (London, 1968), pp. 59–63; Penrose, *Travel and Discovery*, pp. 17–18; also see Vsevolod Slessarev, *Prester John: The Letter and the Legend* (Minneapolis, 1959); Robert Silverberg, *The Realm of Prester John* (Garden City, 1972); Ronald Sanders, *Lost Tribes and Promised Lands; The Origins of American Racism* (Boston, 1978).

14. H. C. Heaton, ed., *The Discovery of the Amazon* (New York, 1934), pp. 214, 220–21, 434. See Irving A. Leonard "Conquerors and Amazons in Mexico," *Hispanic American Historical Review* 24 (November, 1944): 561–79. For a North American version of the Amazons, see William P. Cumming, ed., *The Discoveries of John Lederer* (Charlottesville, Va., 1958), p. 30.

15. Fawn M. Brodie, *The Devil Drives: A Life of Sir Richard Burton* (New York, 1969), p. 251; Richard Burton, *A Mission to Gelele: King of Dahome* (New York, 1966), ch. 13; Duarte Barbosa, *The Book of Duarte Barbosa* (2 vols., London, 1918) I, pp. 12–13.

16. William Shakespeare, *The Second Part of Henry the Fourth,* ed. Allan G. Chester (Baltimore, 1974) p. 136.

17. Robin Hallett, *The Penetration of Africa: European Exploration in North and West Africa to 1815* (New York, 1965), p. 55. René Caillié, *Travels Through Central Africa* (2 vols., London, 1930) II, p. 49. Hugh Clapperton, who had heard grand descriptions of Kano by the Arabs, was equally disappointed on arriving in that important trading center.

18. Alfred Lord Tennyson, *Poems,* ed. Mildred M. Bozman (2 vols., New York, 1962) I, p. 1. These lines were attributed to George Chapman but were written by Tennyson for his poem "Timbuctoo."

Chapter Two

1. Henri Baudet, *Paradise on Earth: Some Thoughts on European Images of Non-European Man* (New Haven, 1965), p. 6. See Bernard De Voto, *The Course of Empire* (Boston, 1962) for Emery Heywood's quote, "Even more than other history the Age of Discovery is man come upon strangeness and traveling it mostly in dream." In Australian history, the period before the Europeans arrived is called the Dream Time. In May, 1806, Meriwether Lewis, on seeing the Rocky Mountains for the first time, wrote, "I thought it might be a dream"; see Robert Edson Lee, *From West to East: Studies in the Literature of the American West* (Urbana, Ill., 1966), p. 24.

2. John Dryden, "The Conquest of Granada," in *Selected Dramas,* ed. George R. Noyes (Chicago, 1910), p. 22. This positive view of the Native American can also be seen in Papal Bulls such as *Sublimis Deus,* in the works of Bartolomé de Las Casas, and in Spain's New Laws of 1542–43.

3. Alexander Pope, 'An Essay on Man,' in *Selected Poetry,* ed. Martin Price (London, 1970), p. 126; Robert F. Berkhofer, Jr., *The White Man's Indian: Images of the American Indian from Columbus to the Present* (New York, 1978), pp. 72–80; Bernard W. Sheehan, *Savagism and Civility: Indians and Englishmen in Colonial Virginia* (Cambridge, England, 1980), ch. 1; Salvador De Madariaga, *The Fall of the Spanish American Empire* (rev. ed.; New York, 1963), pp. 206–09.

4. Aphra Behn, *Oroonoko: or, The Royal Slave: A True History* (New York, 1973), p. 3; also see Benjamin Bissell, *The American Indian in English Literature of the Eighteenth Century* (New Haven, 1925).

5. Michel de Montaigne, "Of Cannibals," in *Selected Essays,* ed.

Blanchard Bates (New York, 1949), p. 79. The quote is from Seneca's *Epistles*.

6. Ibid., p. 87. See Pope's "Essay," p. 146, and William Shakespeare's primitive savage Caliban in *The Tempest* for the Bard's view of primitism.

7. Thomas Jefferson, *Notes on the State of Virginia*, ed. William Peden (New York, 1972), p. 140; also see William P. Cumming, ed., *The Discoveries of John Lederer*, (Charlottesville, Va., 1958), p. 14, on Indian oratory.

8. Jefferson, *Notes*, p. 62; also see John Chester Miller, *The Wolf by the Ears: Thomas Jefferson and Slavery* (New York, 1977), pp. 64–73, and Bernard W. Sheehan, *Seeds of Extinction: Jeffersonian Philanthropy and the American Indian* (New York, 1974), ch. 4 and 5, especially pp. 109–110n. for two different interpretations of Logan's speech. Jefferson's view of the Indian was part of his defense of America brought on by the calumnies of the Comte de Buffon; for more on this, see Antonello Gerbi, *The Dispute of the New World: The History of a Polemic, 1750–1900* (Pittsburgh, 1973).

9. Roy Harvey Pearce, *Savagism and Civilization: A Study of the Indian and the American Mind* (Baltimore, 1971), p. 5; also, Sheehan, *Savagism and Civility*, ch. 2.

10. David B. Quinn, *The Elizabethans and the Irish* (Ithaca, 1966), especially ch. 9, "Ireland and America Intertwined"; Gary B. Nash, *Red, White, and Black: The Peoples of Early America* (Englewood Cliffs, N.J., 1974), pp. 39–41. For the negative view of the Native American by the English traveler, see R. W. Frantz, *The English Traveller and the Movement of Ideas, 1660–1732* (Lincoln, 1967), pp. 101–04; for the positive view, see pp. 106–17. For a recent article on ambivalence toward the Indian, see Alden T. Vaughan, " 'Expulsion of the Salvages:' English Policy and the Virginia Massacre of 1622," *William and Mary Quarterly*, 3rd Series, 35 (January, 1978): 57–84.

11. André Thevet, *New Found Worlds* (London, 1568), p. 5; on the Wild Men of Europe, see Richard Bernheimer, *Wild Men in the Middle Ages: A Study in Art, Sentiment, and Demonology* (New York, 1970); Richard G. Cole, "Sixteenth-Century Travel Books as a Source of European Attitudes Toward Non-White and Non-Western Culture," *Proceedings* of the American Philosophical Society 116 (February, 1972): 62. See Gerbi, *Dispute*, for more on the inferiority of the Native American, especially ch. 3.

12. Herodotus, *The Histories*, trans. Aubrey de Selincourt (Middlesex, England, 1974), p. 334.

13. Katherine George, "The Civilized West Looks at Primitive Africa: 1400–1800, A Study in Ethnocentrism," *Isis* 49 (March, 1958): 63. Philip D. Curtin, *The Image of Africa: British Ideas and Action*

1780–1850 (2 vols., Madison 1973) I, p. 23, writes that "the reporting often stressed precisely those aspects of African life that were most repellent to the West and tended to submerge the indications of a common humanity." J. M. Degerando, "Documents Anthropologiques," *Revue D'Anthropologie*, 2nd series, XII (1883): 159, wrote, "Ils nous ont transmis des descriptions bizarres qui amusent l'oiseuse curiosité du vulgaire, mais qui ne fournissent aucune instruction utile a l'esprit du philosophe."

14. H. Alan C. Cairns, *The Clash of Cultures: Early Race Relations in Central Africa* (New York, 1965), p. 53.

15. Richard Eden, comp., *The First Three English Books on America* (Birmingham, 1885), p. 23; Cole, "Sixteenth-Century Travel," pp. 59–67.

16. Genesis, 9:22, 25; Winthrop D. Jordan, *White Over Black: American Attitudes Toward the Negro, 1550–1812* (Baltimore, 1969), pp. 17–19; Thomas F. Gossett, *Race: The History of an Idea in America* (New York, 1971), p. 5; Joseph E. Harris, *Africans and Their History* (New York, 1972), pp. 11–19.

17. Montaigne, "Of Cannibals," p. 77; see Pearce, *Savagism*, p. 106, on John Adams's skeptical view of the depiction of Indian life.

18. George, "Civilized West," p. 69.

19. Ibid., p. 70. E. A. Ayandele, *African Exploration and Human Understanding* (Edinburgh, 1971), p. 10; *New-York Daily Tribune* (October 9, 1855) 4:3; although this is dated 1855, it applies as well to an earlier period:

Modern exploration is intelligent, and its results are therefore positive and permanent. The traveler no longer wanders bewildered in a cloud of fables, prepared to see marvels and but too ready to create them; he tests every step of his way by the sure light of science, and his pioneer trail became a plain and easy path to those who follow. The pencil, the compass, the barometer, and the sextant accompany him; geology, botany, and ethnology are his aides, and by these helps and appliances, his single brain achieves results now which it would once have required an armed force to win.

20. J. M. Reid, *Traveller Extraordinary: The Life of James Bruce of Kinnard* (New York, 1968), ch. 9; Dixon Denhan, *Narrative of Travels and Discoveries* (3rd ed., London, 1826), p. 85. It has been suggested that Bruce was actually a prisoner of the Ethiopian royal family.

21. Ayandele, *African Exploration*, p. 13. Mungo Park, *Travels in Africa* (London, 1969), p. 201; for support of Park's position, see Hugh Clapperton, *Journal of a Second Expedition* (London, 1966),

p. 13, on lack of theft. For a different view, see Richard F. Burton, *Zanzibar; City, Island, and Coast* (2 vols., London, 1872) II, p. 78; see J. J. Tobias, *Urban Crime in Victorian England* (New York, 1972), and Douglas Hay, et al, *Albion's Fatal Tree: Crime and Society in Eighteenth-Century England* (New York, 1975), on European crime. One of the most common criticisms of the American Indian by explorers was their propensity to steal.

22. Park, *Travels*, p. 151. Since he also made critical comments about Africans, Park's writings were used by both abolitionists and anti-abolitionists in Britian.

23. Horace Waller, ed., *The Last Journals of David Livingstone in Central Africa* (New York, 1875), pp. 517–41. The fear the natives had of being accused of murdering Livingstone helps account for this action.

24. Elliott Coues, ed., *New Light on the Early History of the Greater Northwest* (3 vols., New York, 1897) I, pp. 367, 58; see also Richard Glover, ed., *David Thompson's Narrative 1784–1812* (Toronto, 1962), p. 177, on the Mandan; Lewis O. Saum, *The Fur Trader and the Indian* (Seattle, 1965), especially ch. 1, is most helpful on this topic.

25. Bernard De Voto, ed., *The Journals of Lewis and Clark* (Boston, 1963), p. 51. See also Samuel Hearne's comments on Indian women in *A Journey from Prince of Wales Fort* (Toronto, 1958), p. 83.

26. De Voto, *Journals*, p. 52.

27. John Bakeless, *Lewis and Clark: Partners in Discovery* (New York, 1947), p. 269. There was a rumor that Lewis had been captivated by a Nez Perce woman.

28. Reuben Gold Thwaites, ed., *Original Journals of the Lewis and Clark Expedition* (8 vols., New York, 1904–05) I, pp. 248, 250; Bakeless, *Lewis and Clark,* pp. 183, 256.

29. De Voto, *Journals*, pp. 48, 52; Elliott Coues, ed., *History of the Lewis and Clark Expedition* (3 vols., New York, n.d.) I. pp. 159, 164; Donald Jackson, ed., *Letters of the Lewis and Clark Expedition with Related Documents, 1783–1854* (Urbana, 1962), pp. 503, 539; Eldon G. Chuinard, *Only One Man Died: The Medical Aspects of the Lewis and Clark Expedition* (2nd ed.; Glendale, 1980), pp. 258–60.

30. Coues, *New Light* II, p. 749; Ross Cox, *The Columbia River,* ed. Edgar I. Stewart and Jane R. Stewart (Norman, 1957), p. 71.

31. W. Kaye Lamb, ed., *The Journals and Letters of Sir Alexander Mackenzie* (Cambridge, England, 1970), p. 240; also pp. 183–84 on a graphic description of male dress.

32. Gabriel Franchère, *Adventure at Astoria, 1810–1814* (Norman, 1967), pp. 110–11. This journal was used by Thomas Hart Benton to support his demands for the American acquisition of Oregon. Washington Irving also used it for his *Astoria.*

33. Thomas Simpson, *Narrative of the Discoveries on the North Coast*

of America (London, 1843), p. 347; J. B. Tyrrell, ed., *David Thompson's Narrative of His Explorations in Western America, 1784–1813* (Toronto, 1916), p. 22.

34. J. B. Tyrrell, ed., *Journals of Samuel Hearne and Philip Turnor* (Toronto, 1934), p. 458; David Williams, "John Evans' Strange Journey," *American Historical Review* 54 (April, 1949): Part II, 521; Alexander Ross, *Adventures of the First Settlers on the Oregon or Columbia River* (London, 1849), p. 329.

35. Donald Jackson and Mary Lee Spence, eds., *The Expeditions of John Charles Frémont* (3 vols., Urbana, 1970) I, p. 487.

36. Ibid., p. 687.

37. Grant Foreman, ed., *Adventure on Red River* (Norman, 1968), p. 122; see the dependable guide story, pp. 122–23; also see J. N. B. Hewitt, ed., Edwin Thompson Denig's "Indian Tribes of the Upper Missouri," Bureau of American Ethnology Forty-Sixth Annual Report (1928–29) (Washington, 1930), pp. 527–28.

38. E. E. Rich, ed., *Moose Fort Journals, 1783–85* (London, 1954), p. 28; "First Journals of Simon Fraser from April 12th to July 18th, 1806," Dominion of Canada, *Report* of the Public Archives for the Year 1929, p. 145.

39. Lamb, *Mackenzie*, p. 255; also see the account of the problems Mackenzie's guide had, p. 300.

40. Coues, *New Light* II, pp. 449–50.

41. Frederick Merk, ed., *Fur Trade and Empire: George Simpson's Journal* (Cambridge, Mass., 1968), p. 74.

42. "Journals of Simon Fraser," p. 145.

43. Lamb, *Mackenzie*, p. 153.

44. Coues, *Lewis and Clark Expedition* II, pp. 527, 556, 503. For Indian bestiality, see Sheehan, *Savagism and Civility*, ch. 3.

45. Ross, *Adventures of the First Settlers*, p. 94.

46. Maurice S. Sullivan, ed., *The Travels of Jedediah Smith: A Documentary Outline. . . .* (Santa Ana, Calif., 1934), p. 5.

47. Peter Skene Ogden, *Traits of American Indian Life and Character* (San Francisco, 1933), p. 91.

48. A. P. Nasatir, ed., *Before Lewis and Clark: Documents Illustrating the History of the Missouri 1785–1804* (2 vols., St. Louis, 1952) II, p. 412.

49. Walter Sheppe, ed., *First Man West: Alexander Mackenzie's Journal of His Voyage to the Pacific Coast of Canada in 1793* (Berkeley, 1962), p. 166; LeRoy R. Hafen and W. J. Ghent, *Broken Hand: The Life Story of Thomas Fitzpatrick, Chief of the Mountain Men* (Denver, 1931), p. 225.

50. Cairns, *Clash of Cultures*, p. 147.

51. Arthur O. Lovejoy, *The Great Chain of Being: A Study of the History of an Idea* (Cambridge, Mass., 1976), pp. 197, 234–35, 363n.

17; Loren Eiseley, *Darwin's Century: Evolution and the Men Who Discovered It* (Garden City, 1961), pp. 260–261. For travelers' accounts of the Hottentots, see Frantz, *English Traveller*, p. 104.

52. John H. Speke, *Journal of the Discovery of the Source of the Nile* (London, 1969), pp. 54, 59, 64. Speke believed this backwardness was largely due to the slave trade; Richard Burton, *The Lake Regions of Central Africa* (New York, 1860), pp. 489, 226. See Burton, *Zanzibar* II, pp. 96, 1, 101, for his harsh criticism of the Wanyika tribe.

53. David Patterson, "The Vanishing Mpongwe: European Contact and Demographic Change in the Gabon River," *Journal of African History* 16 (1975):221, 229–30.

54. Samuel White Baker, *The Albert N'Yanza: Great Basin of the Nile and the Explorations of the Nile Sources* (2 vols., New York, 1962) I, pp. 51, 57, 174, 208–13. Cairns, *Clash of Cultures, p. 79, 161;* for more on the negrophobia of Baker see pp. 203–05. Christine Bolt, *Victorian Attitudes to Race* (London, 1971), pp. 121–24; Frederick Bradnum, *The Long Walks: Journeys to the Sources of the White Nile* (London, 1970) p. 250.

55. David Livingstone, *Narrative of an Expedition to the Zambesi* (London, 1865), p. 416. For the use that a proslavery Southerner made of Livingstone's critical views of the Africans in *Missionary Travels and Researches in South Africa,* see Daniel R. Hundley, *Social Relations in our Southern States* (Baton Rouge, 1979), pp. 303–10, 328–29, 350.

56. Joseph Thomson, *Through Masailand*, ed. Roland Young (Evanston, 1962), p. 42; Robert I. Rotberg, ed., *Africa and Its Explorers; Motives, Methods, and Impact* (Cambridge, Mass., 1973), pp. 311, 317; Bolt, *Victorian Attitudes,* p. 133. David Livingstone's favorite tribe was the Makololo; Stanley was partial to the Zanzibari.

57. David Livingstone, *Missionary Travels and Researches in South Africa* (New York, 1857), p. 34.

58. Rotberg, *Africa,* p. 44; Cairns, *Clash of Cultures,* pp. 149–50, 192; Burton, *Zanzibar* II, p. 144.

59. Waller, *The Last Journals,* pp. 209, 108; Burton, *Lake Regions,* p. 265; Joseph Thomson, *Through Masai Land; A Journey of Exploration* (London, 1887), p. 250, on the "Apollo type" of native. Thomson considered the Fulani women beautiful.

60. Waller, *The Last Journals,* p. 209. In western literature, the only well-known black beauty was a horse.

61. Burton, *Lake Regions,* p. 44. Clapperton, *Journal,* p. 13. But admiration for African women did appear. Thomas Baines, *The Northern Goldfield Diaries,* ed. by J. P. R. Wallis (3 vols., London, 1946) I, p. 76, described the Matatole women as "models of beauty." Some explorers criticized the physiognomy of the African—especially the flat feet, curly hair, and odor; see Richard Francis Burton,

Wanderings in West Africa (2 vols., London, 1863) I, p. 178, and Burton, *Lake Regions,* p. 104. Livingstone pointed to Africans' light skin, "finely-shaped heads, straight or acquiline noses and thin lips, magnificent forms, with small feet and hands, graceful limbs; and barn-door mouths, prognathous jaws and lark-heels are never seen," in Bolt, *Victorian Attitudes,* p. 134.

62. Bradnum, *Long Walks,* p. 199; Cairns, *Clash of Cultures,* pp. 168–69; see rumors about whites, p. 169.

63. Park, *Travels,* pp. 41–42, 92, 100–01. On the experience of Dixon Denham, see *Missions to the Niger,* ed. E. W. Bovill (4 vols., Cambridge, England, 1964–1966) II, p. 266; Bolt, *Victorian Attitudes,* p. 134, states that Richard Burton and Harry Johnston mentioned that there was a preference for light skin among the Africans themselves. For the American Indian and white skin, see Franchère, *Adventures,* p. 108, and Stephen Long, *Account of an Expedition* in Reuben Gold Thwaites, ed., *Early Western Travels 1748–1846* (32 vols., Glendale, 1904–07) XVI, p. 207.

64. Park, *Travels,* p. 209; Waller, *The Last Journals,* p. 168; Burton, *Lake Regions,* p. 43. Also see John H. Speke, *What Led to the Discovery of the Source of the Nile* (Edinburgh, 1864), pp. 349–50. The same lack of geographical information was noted about the Arabs, Waller, *The Last Journals,* p. 186. For a different view, see Thomson, *Through Masailand,* p. 92.

65. Bolt, *Victorian Attitudes,* pp. 136–37; Baker, *Albert N'Yanza,* p. xliii.

66. Fawn M. Brodie, *The Devil Drives* (New York, 1969), p. 251.

67. Burton, *Zanzibar* I, p. 379.

68. Ibid., p. 135; Speke, *What Led to the Discovery,* p. 15.

69. Richard Hall, *Lovers on the Nile* (New York, 1980), p. 90. Byron Farwell, *The Man Who Presumed: A Biography of Henry M. Stanley* (New York, 1957), p. 68. For more on sex in the Victorian age, see Steven Marcus, *The Other Victorians* (New York, 1967), and Walter E. Houghton, *The Victorian Frame of Mind* (New Haven, 1976), pp. 353–72.

70. Tim Jeal, *Livingstone* (New York, 1974), p. 349; see Henry Morton Stanley, *Stanley's Dispatches to the New York Herald* ed. Norman Bennett (Boston, 1970), p. 101, on the story that Livingstone married an African princess. Burton made fun of Livingstone for "he never made a Kafir convert."

71. J. A. Hunter and Daniel P. Mannix, *Tales of the African Frontier* (New York, 1954), pp. 58–59, 51. When natives asked Thomson to help stop Masai attacks on their village, not wishing them to believe he was impotent, he cooked some fruit salts which the tribe drank. He fired his guns and photographed the stockades and the village, proving that he had done his job. See Cairns, *Clash of Cultures,* p. 183.

72. Margery Perham and J. Simmons, *African Discovery: An Anthology of Exploration* (London, 1957), pp. 97–105.

73. Bolt, *Victorian Attitudes*, p. 142.

74. Ibid., pp. 8, 143–144.

75. Cairns, *Clash of Cultures,* p. 69.

76. Ibid.

77. Joseph Thomson, *To the Central African Lakes and Back* (2 vols., London, 1968) I, p. 253; Henry M. Stanley, *How I Found Livingstone* (London, n.d.), p. 236.

78. Henry M. Stanley, *How I Found Livingstone* (New York, 1902), p. 412. For the social distance that should be maintained between a Southern slave owner and his slaves, see John W. Blassingame, *The Slave Community: Plantation Life in the Antebellum South* (rev. and enlarged ed., New York, 1979), p.239.

Chapter Three

1. John Kirtland Wright, *Human Nature in Geography* (Cambridge, Mass., 1966), p. 28.

2. John L. Allen, "Lands of Myth, Waters of Wonder: The Place of Imagination in the History of Geographical Exploration" in *Geographies of the Mind: Essays in Historical Geosophy*, ed. David Lowenthal and Martyn J. Bowden (New York, 1976), pp. 43, 45; Allen, "An Analysis of the Exploratory Process: The Lewis and Clark Expedition of 1804–1806," *Geographical Review* 62 (January, 1972): 13–39.

3. Allen, "Exploratory Process."

4. James Thomson, "Summer" from *The Seasons*, as quoted by Thomas Winterbottom, *An Account of the Native Africans in the Neighbourhood of Sierra Leone*, 2nd ed. (2 vols., London, 1969) I, 17; also see poetic quote on p. 3.

5. Hugh Murray, *Historical Account of Discoveries and Travels in Africa*, (2nd ed., 2 vols., Edinburgh , 1818) I, p. 29. Murray felt "the whole region was in a manner given up to fable."

6. Robin Hallett, "The European Approach to the Interior of Africa in the Eighteenth Century," *Journal of African History* IV (1963):193.

7. Quote is from Oliver Goldsmith's "The Deserted Village" in *The Poetical Works of Oliver Goldsmith* (London, 1927), p. 35. These lines applied to the dismal woods of Georgia; also see Goldsmith's "The Traveller" and "The Captivity"; William Blake's "The Tiger," and James Thomson's "The Seasons." For more on the American antiimage, see Howard Mumford Jones, *O Strange New World: American Culture; The Formative Years* (New York, 1967), pp. 39–70, and Richard Slotkin, *Regeneration Through Violence: The Mythology of the American Frontier* (Middletown, Conn., 1973).

8. *Proceedings* of the Association for Promoting the Discovery of the Interior Parts of Africa (2 vols., London, 1967) I, pp. 211–12. Similar problems confronted the explorers of Latin America—impenetrable jungles, the Chaco desert, the lack of navigable rivers, and tropical diseases; see Alistair Hennessy, *The Frontier in Latin American History* (Albuquerque, 1978), p. 18.

9. *Encyclopaedia Britannica,* (3rd ed., 18 vols., Edinburgh, 1797) I, p. 225; the same words were used in the 2nd edition in 1778.

10. Anna M. Falconbridge, *Narrative of Two Voyages to the River Sierra Leone During the Years 1791–1793* (London, 1967), p. 148; also see Winterbottom, *An Account of the Native Africans,* especially the new introduction by John D. Hargreaves and E. Maurice Backett; and Philip D. Curtin, *The Image of Africa: British Ideas and Actions, 1780–1850* (2 vols., Madison 1973) I, pp. 71–87, for an excellent discussion of African diseases.

11. Richard F. Burton, *Wandering in West Africa* (2 vols., London, 1863) I, p. viii.

12. Frederick Bradnum, *The Long Walks, Journeys to the Sources of the White Nile* (London, 1970), pp. 188–89.

13. Curtin, *Image of Africa* I, p. 72.

14. Philip D. Curtin, *The Atlantic Slave Trade: A Census* (Madison, 1970), p. 286; K. G. Davies, "The Living and the Dead: White Mortality in West Africa, 1684–1732," in Stanley L. Engerman and Eugene D. Genovese, eds., *Race and Slavery in the Western Hemisphere: Quantitative Studies* (Princeton, 1975), pp. 83–98; Curtin, *Image of Africa* I, pp. 72–87; Peter Burroughs, "The Human Cost of Imperial Defence in the Early Victorian Age," *Victorian Studies* 24 (Autumn, 1980):14–15.

15. Curtin, *Image of Africa* I, pp. 77, 223.

16. R. A. Adeleye, *Power and Diplomacy in Northern Nigeria 1804–1906* (New York, 1971), p. 120.

17. Thomas Astley, *A New General Collection of Voyages and Travels* (4 vols., London, 1745–47) II, pp. 145–49.

18. Richard Jobson, *The Golden Trade* (Teignmouth, England, 1904), p. 125; "The Journey of Cornelius Hodges in Senegambia, 1689–90," *English Historical Review* 39 (January, 1924): 89–95.

19. Harry H. Johnston, *The Nile Quest* (London, 1903), p. vii.

20. Herodotus, *The Histories* (Middlesex, 1974), p. 139; B. W. Langlands, "Concepts of the Nile," *Uganda Journal* 26 (March, 1962): 1–22. The Mountains of the Moon are now identified as the Ruwenzori Mountains.

21. Lucan, *The Civil War* (Cambridge, Mass., 1962), p. 5.

22. E. Denison Ross, "Prester John and the Empire of Ethiopia," in Arthur Percival Newton, ed., *Travel and Travellers of the Middle Ages* (London, 1926), p. 193.

23. John H. Speke, *What Led to the Discovery of the Source of the Nile*

(Edinburgh, 1864), p. 307; Richard Burton, *Zanzibar: City, Island, and Coast* (2 vols., London, 1872) II, pp. 389, 382.

24. Sanche de Gramont, *The Strong Brown God: The Story of the Niger River* (Boston, 1976), p. 12. Gramont described the Niger as curling "like a question-mark through West Africa."

25. Ibid., p. 43.

26. Peter Forbath, *The River Congo* (New York, 1977), p. 74. Today the Congo is once again called the Zaire by the Africans in an effort to erase the ugly historical connotations attached to the word "Congo." Interestingly, the first commercial company on the upper Congo was the Sanford Exploring Expedition, headed by an American.

27. J. N. L. Baker, *A History of Geographical Discovery and Exploration* (New York, 1967), p. 306; Murray, *Historical Account* I, p. vii. Jonathan Swift, "On Poetry: A Rapsody," in *Poetical Works*, ed. Herbert Davis (London, 1967), p. 574.

28. Leslie Stephen and Sidney Lee, eds., *The Dictionary of National Biography* (Oxford, 1921–22) 16, pp. 900–01. Clements R. Markham, *Major James Rennell and the Rise of Modern English Geography* (London, 1895); J. N. L. Baker, "Major James Rennell and His Place in the History of Geography," in Baker's *The History of Geography* (New York, 1963), pp. 130–57.

29. Wayne Franklin, *Discoverers, Explorers, Settlers: The Diligent Writers of Early America* (Chicago, 1979), p. 22. See Ray A. Billington, *Land of Savagery/Land of Promise: The European Image of the American Frontier in the Nineteenth Century* (New York, 1981), especially ch. 1 and 2.

30. David B. Quinn (ed.), *The Roanoke Voyages 1584–1590* (2 vols. London, 1955) I, p. 108.

31. John Lankford, ed., *Captain John Smith's America* (New York, 1967), pp. 17, 129. For comments on the obvious sexual allusion to the land, see Annette Kolodny, *The Lay of the Land: Metaphor as Experience and History in American Life and Letters* (Chapel Hill, 1975), ch. II. For the connection between the bounty of nature and the indolence of man, see Speke, *What Led to the Discovery*, p. 344.

32. Franklin, *Discoverers*, p. 33.

33. Clarence W. Alvord and Lee Bidgood, *The First Exploration of the Trans-Allegheny Regions by the Virginians* (Cleveland, 1912), p. 141; John Logan Allen, *Passage Through the Garden* (Urbana, 1975), pp. 199, 200. Also see Bernard De Voto, ed., *The Journals of Lewis and Clark* (Boston, 1963), p. 28.

34. David A. Dary, *The Buffalo Book* (New York, 1975), p. 21. Also see Raymond Darwin Burroughs, ed., *The Natural History of the Lewis and Clark Expedition* (East Lansing, 1961), ch. 7.

35. John Filson, *The Discovery, Settlement, and Present State of Kentucke* (New York, 1962), pp. 57–58, 54.

36. Ibid., p. 50; for more on antiimage, see Howard Mumford Jones, *O Strange New World*, ch. II.

37. George Catlin, *Letters and Notes on the Manners, Customs, and Conditions of the North American Indians* (2 vols., New York, 1973) II, p. 3; also see John Bakeless, *The Eyes of Discovery: The Pageant of North America as Seen by the First Explorers* (New York, 1961).

38. F. Scott Fitzgerald, *The Great Gatsby* (New York, 1953), p. 182. See R. W. B. Lewis, *The American Adam: Innocence, Tragedy, and Tradition in the Nineteenth Century* Chicago, 1959), and David W. Noble, *The Eternal Adam and the New World Garden: The Central Myth in the American Novel since 1830* (New York, 1963); Leo Marx, "The American Revolution and the American Landscape," in *America's Continuing Revolution* (Garden City, 1976).

39. Thomas Paine, *Common Sense and the Crisis* (Garden City n.d.), pp. 27, 34–35; Charles Francis Adams, *Familiar Letters of John Adams and His Wife Abigail* (Boston, 1875), p. 65. See Alexander Hamilton's six essays called "The Continentialist" in Harold C. Syrett, ed., *The Papers of Alexander Hamilton* (New York, 1961–) II, pp. 649–52, 654–57, 660–65, 669–75; III, pp. 75–82, 99–106.

40. Wright, *Human Nature in Geography*, p. 291. See E. G. R. Taylor, "Idée Fixe: The Mind of Christopher Columbus," *Hispanic American Historical Review* XI (August, 1931): 289–301.

41. John Bartlett Brebner, *The Explorers of North America, 1492–1806* (Garden City, 1955), ch. 22.

42. Gloria Griffen Cline, *Exploring the Great Basin* (Norman, 1972), pp. 46–50; C. Gregory Crampton and Gloria G. Griffen [Cline] "The San Buenaventura, Mythical River of the West," *Pacific Historical Review* 25 (May, 1956): 163–71; C. Gregory Crampton, "The Discovery of the Green River," *Utah Historical Quarterly* 20 (October, 1952): 299–312.

43. Brebner, *The Explorers*, ch. 19. Also see John Francis Bannon, *The Spanish Borderlands Frontier 1513–1821* (New York, 1970), pp. 110–11.

44. Henri Folmer, "Étienne Véniard de Bourgmond in the Missouri Country," *Missouri Historical Review* 39 (April, 1942): 279–98; David M. Hayne (ed.) *Dictionary of Canadian Biography* (Toronto, 1969) II, 645–47; Bannon, *Borderlands*, pp. 131–32.

45. Henri Folmer, "The Mallet Expedition of 1739 Through Nebraska . . ." *Colorado Magazine* 16 (September, 1939): 161–173; *Dictionary of Canadian Biography* II, pp. 423–24; Bannon, *Borderlands*, pp. 141–42.

46. G. Hubert Smith, *The Explorations of the La Vérendryes in the Northern Plains 1738–43* (Lincoln, 1980), pp. 3–6.

47. Bernard De Veto, *The Course of Empire* (Boston, 1962), p. 197; *Dictionary of Canadian Biography* III, pp. 247–54.

48. Nellis M. Crouse, *La Vérendrye: Fur Trader and Explorer* (Ithaca, 1956); Christine Bolt, *Victorian Attitudes to Race* (London, 1971), p. 133. To Richard Burton, the Fon poeple of Gabon resembled Europeans because of their fine features and light complexions.

49. David Williams, "John Evans' Strange Journey," *American Historical Review* 54 (January–April, 1949): I, 290; II, 525–26.

50. John L. Allen, "Pyramidal Height-of-Land: A Persistent Myth in the Exploration of Western Anglo-America," *International Geography* I (1972): 395–96; see also his *Passage Through the Garden*, passim, and "Division of the Waters: Changing Concepts of the Continental Divide, 1804–44," *Journal of Historical Geography* IV (1978): 357, 370.

51. John Cawte Beaglehole, *The Life of Captain James Cook* (Stanford, 1974), pp. 686–87.

52. Alexander Mackenzie, *Voyages From Montreal* (London, 1802), pp. xi–xii; Lawrence J. Burpee, *The Search for the Western Sea: The Story of the Exploration of North-Western America* (2 vols., Toronto, 1935) II, ch. 3; Walter Sheppe, ed., *First Man West: Alexander Mackenzie's Journal of His Voyage to the Pacific Coast in 1793* (Berkeley, 1962).

53. Baker, *Geographical Discovery and Exploration*, pp. 172, 174; George Vancouver, *A Voyage of Discovery to North Pacific Ocean* (3 vols., London, 1798); Bern Anderson, *The Life and Voyages of Captain George Vancouver: Surveyor of the Sea* (Seattle, 1960), ch. 11.

54. Donald Jackson, ed., *Letters of the Lewis and Clark Expedition with Related Documents, 1783–1854* (Urbana, 1962), p. 137; Allen, *Passage Through the Garden*, pp. 60–61.

55. Lewis P. Simpson, ed., *The Federalist Literary Mind: Selections from the Monthly Anthology and Boston Review, 1803–1811* (Baton Rouge, 1962), pp. 58–59; and John Quincy Adams's parody of the Barlow poem, pp. 58–62.

56. Ibid., p. 60; Linda K. Kerber, *Federalists in Dissent: Imagery and Ideology in Jeffersonian America* (Ithaca, 1980), p. 93.

57. Aubrey Diller, "James Mackay's Journey in Nebraska in 1796," *Nebraska History* 36 (June, 1955): 127; G. Malcolm Lewis, "Three Centuries of Desert Concepts in the Cis-Rocky Mountain West," *Journal of the West* 4 (July, 1965): 460; Annie Abel, "Trudeau's Description of the Upper Missouri," *Mississippi Valley Historical Review* 8 (June–September, 1921): 158.

58. Zebulon Montgomery Pike, *The Journals*, ed., Donald Jackson, (2 vols., Norman, 1966) II. p. 27. Examples of American explorers

and travelers using African images can be found in the following works: Elliott Coues, ed., *The Expeditions of Zebulon Montgomery Pike* (3 vols., New York, 1895) II, p. 525; Timothy Flint, *The History and Geography of the Mississippi Valley* (2 vols., Cincinnati, 1833) I, p. 459; Jean-Bernard Bossu, *Travels Through That Part of North America Formerly Called Louisiana* (2 vols., London, 1771) I, p. 230; Frederick Adolphus Wislizenus, *Memoir of a Tour to Northern Mexico* (Glorieta, N.M., 1969), p. 69; Reuben Gold Thwaites, ed., *Original Journals of the Lewis and Clark Expedition* (8 vols., New York, 1959) I, p. 147; and in Thwaites, *Early Western Travels, 1748–1846* (32 vols., Cleveland, 1904–07) XIII, pp. 228, 276; XVIII, p. 219; XXVI, p. 234; Henry Marie Brackenridge, *Views of Louisiana* (Pittsburgh, 1814), p. 35.

59. Pike, *Journals* II, 28; see Merlin P. Lawson, 'A Behavioristic Interpretation of Pike's Geographical Knowledge of the Interior of Louisiana," *Great Plains–Rocky Mountain Geographical Journal* I (1972): 58–64.

60. Cardinal Goodwin, "A Larger View of the Yellowstone Expedition, 1819–1820," *Mississippi Valley Historical Review* IV (December, 1917): 303.

61. Edwin James, *Account of an Expedition from Pittsburgh to the Rocky Mountains* (2 vols., Ann Arbor, 1966) II, p. 389.

62. Ibid., p. 361.

63. Martyn J. Bowden, "The Great American Desert and the American Frontier, 1800–1882: Popular Images of the Plains," in Tamara K. Hareven, ed., *Anonymous Americans: Explorations in Nineteenth-Century Social History* (Englewood Cliffs, N. J., 1971), pp. 48–79; Ralph C. Morris, "The Notion of a Great American Desert East of the Rockies," *Mississippi Valley Historical Review* 13 (September, 1926): 190–200.

64. Reuben Gold Thwaites, ed., *The Jesuit Relations and Allied Documents* (73 vols., New York, 1959) LVIII, p. 105.

65. Bossu, *Travels Through That Part of North America* I, p. 230.

66. Elliott Coues, ed., *The History of the Lewis and Clark Expedition* (3 vols., New York, n.d.) I. p. 67. The influence of Jefferson, who believed in the garden image, can be detected here.

67. David M. Emmons, *Garden in the Grasslands; Boomer Literature of the Central Great Plains* (Lincoln, 1971), p. 9.

68. Thomas L. Karnes, *William Gilpin, Western Nationalist* (Austin, 1970), ch. 8.

69. Allen, *Passage Through the Garden*, p. 114.

70. Irene M. Spry, *The Palliser Expedition* (Toronto, 1973), p. 283; for an excellent survey of this Canadian controversy, see John Warkentin, ed., *The Western Interior of Canada: A Record of Geographical Discovery 1612–1917* (Toronto, 1964), Part 6.

71. Arthur S. Morton, *A History of the Canadian West to 1870–71*, (2nd ed., Toronto, 1973), p. 835.

72. F. G. Roe, "Early Opinions on the 'Fertile Belt' of Western Canada," *Canadian Historical Review* 27 (June, 1946): 131–49, is critical of Macoun.

73. Ibid., p. 136.

Chapter Four

1. Peter Gay, *The Enlightenment: An Interpretation, The Rise of Modern Paganism* (New York, 1968) p. 129.

2. Ibid., p. 4; Ernst Cassirer, *The Philosophy of the Enlightenment* (Princeton, 1951), pp. 4–5.

3. A. Wolf, *A History of Science, Technology, and Philosophy in the 18th Century* (2 vols., New York, 1961) I, p. 27.

4. Peter Gay, *The Enlightenment: An Interpretation, The Science of Freedom* (New York, 1969) p. 6.

5. These lines are from Horace's *Epistles* I, 2, 40–41: "Dimidium facti qui coepit habet: sapere aude: Incipe!;" "To have begun is to be half done: dare to know; Start!"

6. A. S. Turberville, ed., *Johnson's England: An Account of the Life and Manners of His Age* (2 vols., Oxford, 1965) I, p. 3.

7. Robin Hallett, *The Penetration of Africa* (New York, 1965), p. 156.

8. James Bruce, *Travels to Discover the Source of the Nile. . . .* (6 vols., Dublin, 1790–91) I, p. 20.

9. Gay, *Science of Freedom*, pp. 51–55.

10. Norman S. Fiering, "The Transatlantic Republic of Letters: A Note on the Circulation of Learned Periodicals to Early Eighteenth-Century America," *William and Mary Quarterly* 33 (October, 1976): 644, 655.

11. Russel Blaine Nye, *The Cultural Life of the New Nation: 1776–1830* (New York, 1960), pp. 251–52. A Philadelphia paper had the august title of *Pennsylvania Gazette and Universal Instructor in All the Arts and Sciences*.

12. John C. Greene, "Science and the Public in the Age of Jefferson," *Isis* 49 (March, 1958): 19.

13. Max Savelle, *Seeds of Liberty: The Genesis of the American Mind* (Seattle, 1965), pp. 138–39, 411, 567; see Nye, *Cultural Life*, pp. 240–41, for a later period.

14. Gay, *Science of Freedom*, p. 321.

15. Hector Charles Cameron, *Sir Joseph Banks, K.B., P.R.S., The Autocrat of the Philosophers* (London, 1952), p. 150; Charles Coleman Sellers, *Mr. Peale's Museum: Charles Willson Peale and the First Popular*

Museum of Natural History and Art (New York, 1980), pp. 187, 206. William Clark put his mementoes of the expedition in a museum that he established in St. Louis.

16. Peter Gay, *The Party of Humanity: Essays in the French Enlightenment* (New York, 1971), pp. 154–56.

17. Walter Veit, ed., *Captain James Cook: Image and Impact* (Melbourne, 1972), pp. 91, 103.

18. Mark Van Doren, ed., *Travels of William Bartram* (New York, 1955), p. 385. Also see Robert Rogers, *Ponteach; or the Savages of America* (London, 1766) for more on the heroic Indian.

19. Henry Steele Commager, *The Empire of Reason: How Europe Imagined and America Realized the Enlightenment* (Garden City, 1977), pp. 57–59; for the popularity of Turkey, see p. 59.

20. Hallett, *Penetration*, pp. 160, 167.

21. Percy G. Adams, *Travelers and Travel Liars, 1660–1800* (New York, 1980), pp. 211–17. Bruce was ridiculed on the British stage when a popular burlesque of his African adventures appeared as "The Adventures of Baron Munchausen."

22. Richard Collier, *The General Next to God: The Story of William Booth and the Salvation Army* (London, 1965), p. 187.

23. J. H. Parry, *Trade and Dominion: The European Oversea Empires in the 18th Century* (London, 1974), pp. 321–22.

24. J. Paul Hunter, *The Reluctant Pilgrim: Defoe's Emblematic Method and Quest for Form in "Robinson Crusoe"* (Baltimore, 1966), pp. 15–16. Joseph Epes Brown, comp., *The Critical Opinions of Samuel Johnson* (New York, 1961), p. 249.

25. Brown, *Critical Opinions*, pp. 248–49; Johnson maintained that "books of travel will be good in proportion to what a man has previously in his mind; his knowing what to observe; his power of contrasting one mode of life with another," p. 250.

26. Commager, *Empire of Reason*, p. 263, n. 18 on the number of books on exploration that Defoe wrote; also see Harvey Swados's Afterword in Daniel Defoe, *Robinson Crusoe* (New York, 1961); Henri Baudet, *Paradise on Earth* (New York, 1965), pp. 41–42. In *Emile*, Rousseau offered *Robinson Crusoe* as that young person's first book. The French explorer René Caillié was greatly influenced by *Robinson Crusoe*; Paul Zweig, *The Adventurer* (New York, 1974), ch. 8, on "Robinson Crusoe, The Unadventurous Hero."

27. Mungo Park, *Travels in Africa* (London, 1969), p. 281. John Speke had nightmares involving lions and tigers; David Livingstone's memories of the slave traffic made him "start up at dead of night horrified by their vividness." Alexander Mackenzie suffered from nightmares in which he was with Death.

28. Timothy C. Blackburn, "The Coherence of Defoe's *Captain*

Singleton," Huntington Library Quarterly 41 (February, 1978): 119–36; R. W. Chapman, ed., *The Letters of Samuel Johnson* (3 vols., Oxford, 1952) I, p. 308; see J. N. L. Baker, "The Geography of Daniel Defoe," in his *The History of Geography* (New York, 1963), pp. 158–72. The search for a father was part of Singleton's quest as it would be for Henry M. Stanley and John Charles Frémont. Hugh Clapperton considered Richard Lander as if he were his son. A chapter in Stanley's *Autobiography* is titled, "I Find a Father."

29. Richard F. Burton, *Zanzibar; City, Island, and Coast* (2 vols., London, 1872) II, pp. 223–24.

30. Ibid., p. 141.

31. John Parker, ed., *The Journals of Jonathan Carver and Related Documents, 1766–1770* (St. Paul, 1976), pp. 38–44; John R. Cuneo, *Robert Rogers of the Rangers* (New York, 1959), pp. 177–80; Savelle, *Seeds of Liberty*, pp. 132–37.

32. Esmond Wright, *Fabric of Freedom, 1763–1800* (rev. ed.; New York, 1978), p. 160.

33. Lord Byron, *Don Juan* (Boston, 1958), p. 259.

34. Marshall Fishwick, *American Heroes: Myth and Reality* (Washington, 1954), p. 63.

35. Ibid., p. 64.

36. Donald Jackson, *Thomas Jefferson and the Stony Mountains* (Urbana, 1981), p. 82; Jared Sparks, *The Life of John Ledyard* (Cambridge, 1828), p. 172.

37. Edwin James, *Account of An Expedition from Pittsburgh to the Rocky Mountains* (2 vols., Ann Arbor, 1966) I, p. 2.

38. Before his expedition, Meriwether Lewis spent time in Philadelphia studying under Barton and Wistar.

39. Brooke Hindle, *The Pursuit of Science in Revolutionary America, 1735–1789* (New York, 1974), p. 302. Lettsom had written the first biography of Jonathan Carver and had helped turn out the third edition of Carver's travels.

40. *The New-Haven Gazette, and the Connecticut Magazine* 2 (Aug. 30, 1787): 222. The motto of this magazine was taken from Daniel 12:4, "Many shall run to and fro, and knowledge shall be increased." An influential American magazine stated "how boorish . . . is it to be ignorant of the general history of the elephant!" Greene, "Science and the Public," p. 19.

41. Benjamin Rush, "An Enquiry into the Utility of a Knowledge of the Latin and Greek Languages, As a Branch of Liberal Education . . . , " *The American Museum, Or, Universal Magazine* 5 (June, 1789): 531.

42. Leonard W. Labaree, ed., *The Papers of Benjamin Franklin* (New Haven, 1960–) II, p. 382. It is not surprising, therefore, that

the third man that Jefferson asked to explore the West was André Michaux.

43. Marquis de Chastellux, *Travels in North America in the Years 1780, 1781, and 1782* (2 vols., New York, 1827) II, p. 546.

44. Hindle, *Pursuit of Science*, p. 303. The American government did not become involved with the funding of exploration until Jefferson became president.

45. Ibid., pp. 303–04, 325; Merle Curti, *The Growth of American Thought* (2nd ed., New York, 1951), p. 130.

46. Hindle, *Pursuit of Science*, ch. 8; Harry Woolf, *The Transits of Venus: A Study of Eighteenth-Century Science* (Princeton, 1959); Raymond Phineas Stearns, *Science in the British Colonies of America* (Urbana, 1970), pp. 653–58.

47. Other discoveries in the sky would show that explorations were not necessarily limited to *terra firma*. William Herschel, German-born astronomer, had settled in England in 1757. Twenty-five years later he was made the king's astronomer by George III and began his "review of the heavens" from which he discovered the seventh planet from the sun beyond Saturn, Uranus. Twenty years later, Giuseppe Piazzi discovered the asteroid Ceres. In the early nineteenth century, Americans became interested in astronomy and published the results of their observations. See Giorgio Abetti, *The History of Astronomy* (New York, 1952), ch. 14.

48. Parry, *Trade and Dominion*, p. 331.

49. John Cawte Beaglehole, *The Life of Captain James Cook* (Stanford, 1974), p. 698.

50. Ibid., pp. 87–90.

51. *Proceedings* of the Association for Promoting the Discovery of the Interior Parts of Africa (2 vols., London, 1967) I, pp. 3–4.

52. Parry, *Trade and Dominion*, chs. 11 and 12.

53. Thomas Bankes, *A New, Royal, Authentic and Complete System of Universal Geography* (London, 1790), p. iii.

54. Savelle, *Seeds of Liberty*, pp. 131, 137.

55. Ibid., p. 134. R. V. Tooley, *Maps and Map-Makers* (New York, 1978), p. 114, stated that, by the nineteenth century, American cartographers had taken the place of European mapmakers as far as American cartography was concerned.

56. Hallett, *Penetration*, p. 139.

57. Adams, *Travelers and Travel Liars*, p. 212.

58. Burton, *Zanzibar* II, pp. 139–40.

59. Hallett, *Penetration*, pp. 193–216; A. Adu Boahen, "The African Association, 1788–1805," *Transactions* of the Historical Society of Ghana 5 (1961): 43–64. Ten of its twelve founders were members of the Royal Society. The membership of the association never num-

bered over 110. The association was also involved with Australian exploration. Societies similar to the African Association were founded in Spain and France in 1802.

60. Boahen, "The African Association," p. 57

61. Ibid., p. 62.

62. Ralph A. Austen and Woodruff D. Smith, "Images of Africa and British Slave-Trade Abolition: The Transition to an Imperialist Ideology, 1787–1807," *African Historical Studies* II (1969): 83.

63. Hindle, *Pursuit of Science*, ch. 7. In America the settler was often the explorer.

64. Albert H. Smyth, ed., *The Writings of Benjamin Franklin* (10 vols., New York, 1905–07) III, p. 228.

65. Daniel J. Boorstin, *The Lost World of Thomas Jefferson* (Boston, 1960), p. 11.

66. Whitfield J. Bell, Jr., "As Others Saw Us: Notes on the Reputation of the American Philosophical Society," *Proceedings* of the American Philosophical Society 116 (June, 1972): 272.

67. Smyth, *Franklin* VII, p. 242. Banks had shown a similar concern when the French scientific expedition under Chevalier D' Entrecasteaux was captured by the British. Banks helped return the scientific collections to the French. In the 1790s, Carlos IV of Spain gave the German scientist Alexander von Humboldt carte blanche to explore Spanish America. During the Schleswig-Holstein dispute in the 1860s, Sir Roderick Murchison of the Royal Geographical Society persuaded the Danes to lift the blockade on the Elbe River so that explorer Carl Von der Decken's boat could proceed to East Africa. For more on international cooperation in the eighteenth century, see Whitfield J. Bell, Jr., "A Box of Old Bones: A Note on the Identification of the Mastodon, 1766–1806," *Proceedings* of the American Philosophical Society 93 (May, 1949): 169–77; I. Bernard Cohen, "Science in America: The Nineteenth Century," in Arthur M. Schlesinger, Jr., and Morton White, eds., *Paths of American Thought* (Boston, 1970), p. 170; and especially Glen M. Rodgers, "Benjamin Franklin and the Universality of Science," *Pennsylvania Magazine of History and Biography* 85 (January, 1961): 50–69.

Chapter Five

1. Dumas Malone, *Jefferson the Virginian* (Boston,, 1948), pp. 23–24; Merrill D. Peterson, *Thomas Jefferson and the New Nation: A Biography* (New York, 1970), p. 6; Donald Jackson, *Thomas Jefferson and the Stony Mountains: Exploring the West from Monticello* (Urbana, 1981), ch. 1.

2. Jackson, *Jefferson*, p. 36; Malone, *Virginian*, p. 378.

3. Dumas Malòne, *Jefferson the President: Second Term, 1805–1809* (Boston, 1974), p. 212.

4. Donald Jackson, ed., *Letters of the Lewis and Clark Expedition with Related Documents, 1783–1854* (Urbana, 1962), pp. 654–55.

5. Ibid., 655–56; John Bakeless, *Lewis and Clark: Partners in Discovery* (New York, 1947), p. 81. The question of size was one of the most important for explorers: too small a party could be dangerous to its members; too large a party could be divisive.

6. Jackson, *Jefferson*, p. 46; Thomas Jefferson, *The Life and Selected Writings*, ed. Adrienne Koch and William Peden (New York, 1944), p. 70; Bernard De Voto, *The Course of Empire* (Boston, 1962), p. 279.

7. For more on Ledyard, see Helen Auger, *Passage to Glory: John Ledyard's America* (New York, 1946); James K. Munford, *John Ledyard: An American Marco Polo* (Portland, 1939); and Jared Sparks, *The Life of John Ledyard: The American Traveller* (Cambridge, 1828).

8. Ibid.

9. Sparks, *Ledyard*, p. 276; see Sparks's comparison of Ledyard with Mungo Park, p. 19. Stephen D. Watrous ed., *John Ledyard's Journey through Russia and Siberia 1787–1788* (Madison, 1966), p. 253. Besides Ledyard's classic understatement regarding his exploration, Lord Palmerston greeted James Grant on his return from the Nile with, "You have had a long walk, Captain Grant."

10. Allen Johnson (ed.) *Dictionary of American Biography* (20 vols., New York, 1928–1936) I, pp. 354–55.

11. Bakeless, *Lewis and Clark*, p. 86; Jackson, *Jefferson*, p. 76.

12. Mary P. Adams, "Jefferson's Reaction to the Treaty of San Ildefonso," *Journal of Southern History* 21 (May, 1955): 187; Jackson, *Lewis and Clark*, p. 13; Grace Lewis, "Financial Records, 'Expedition to the Pacific Ocean'," *Bulletin* of the Missouri Historical Society 10 (July, 1954): 465–89. The total cost of the expedition was about $40,000.

13. Jackson, *Lewis and Clark*, p. 12.

14. Ibid., p. 61.

15. Bernard De Voto, ed., *The Journals of Lewis and Clark* (Boston, 1963), pp. xxv–xxvi.

16. Ibid., p. xliii.

17. Jackson, *Lewis and Clark*, p. 50. Lewis's mother was a well-known amateur doctor. On the use of questionnaires in other explorations, see Philip D. Curtin, *The Image of Africa: British Ideas and Action, 1780–1850* (2 vols., Madison, 1973) I, pp. 14–15, 199, 211–12; II, pp. 331–34.

18 Bakeless, *Lewis and Clark*, p. 273.

19. Isaac Joslin Cox, "The Exploration of the Louisiana Frontier,

1803–1806," in Annual *Report* of the American Historical Association for the Year 1904, pp. 149–74. For more on Dunbar, see Arthur H. De Rosier, Jr., "William Dunbar: A Product of the Eighteenth Century Scottish Renaissance," *Journal of Mississippi History* 28 (August, 1966): 185–227; and De Rosier, "William Dunbar, Explorer," *Journal of Mississippi History* 25 (July, 1963): 165–85.

20. De Rosier, "William Dunbar, Explorer," p. 174; Milford F. Allen, "Thomas Jefferson and the Louisiana-Arkansas Frontier," *Arkansas Historical Quarterly* 20 (Spring, 1961): 53–54.

21. Ibid.

22. Donald Jackson, ed., *The Journals of Zebulon Montgomery Pike* (2 vols., Norman, 1966) II.

23. Ibid.

24 Roger L. Nichols and Patrick L. Halley, *Stephen Long and American Frontier Exploration* (Newark, 1980), p. 116. Another South Carolinian, Joel R. Poinsett, secretary of war under Van Buren, also encouraged exploration.

25. Henry Nash Smith, *Virgin Land: The American West as Symbol and Myth* (Cambridge, 1971), pp. 22–33.

26. Ibid., p. 25.

27. William Nisbet Chambers, *Old Bullion Benton: Senator from the New West* (Boston, 1956), p. 398. See Stephen Bonsal, *Edward Fitzgerald Beale: A Pioneer in the Path of Empire* (New York, 1912), p. 171.

28. Robin Hallett, ed., *Records of the African Association, 1788–1831* (London, 1964), p. 275; David Mackay, "A Presiding Genius of Exploration: Banks, Cook, and Empire, 1767–1805," in Robin Fisher and Hugh Johnston, eds. *Captain James Cook and His Times* (Seattle, 1979), p. 29.

29. Hector Charles Cameron, *Sir Joseph Banks, K. B., P. R. S.: The Autocrat of the Philosophers* (London, 1952), especially ch. 2.

30. Henry Steele Commager, *The Empire of Reason* (Garden City, 1977), pp. 5–6.

31. Cameron, *Banks,* p. 248.

32. Mackay, "Presiding Genius," p. 30; Robin Hallett, *The Penetration of Africa* (London, 1965), pp. 244–45.

33. Commager, *Empire,* p. 5. Hallett, *Records,* p. 275. Banks was a friend of Canadian explorer Alexander Henry the Elder. Henry and Jonathan Carver dedicated books to Banks.

34. R. C. Bridges, "Europeans and East Africans in the Age of Exploration," *Geographical Journal* 139 (June, 1973): 227; Bridges, "Sir John Speke and the Royal Geographical Society," *Uganda Journal* 26 (March, 1962): 25–26.

35. Dorothy Middleton, "The Search for the Nile Sources," *Geographical Journal* 138 (June, 1972): 211–12. Timothy Severin, *The*

African Adventure (New York, 1973), p. 219; Archibald Geikie, *Life of Sir Roderick I. Murchison* (2 vols., London, 1875) II, pp. 296, 298, 303.

36. See dedication in David Livingstone's *Missionary Travels and Researches in South Africa* (New York, 1857). Murchison was involved with John Palliser's exploration of Canada in the 1850s.

37. R. C. Bridges, "The Sponsorship and Financing of Livingstone's Last Journey," *African Historical Studies* I (1968): 90, 103. Livingstone had crossed the continent from west to east twenty years earlier.

38. Bridges, "Speke and the Royal Geographical Society," p. 32.

Chapter Six

1. Donald Jackson, ed., *Letters of the Lewis and Clark Expedition with Related Documents* (Urbana, 1962), p. 552.

2. Jonathan Bishop, "The Identities of Richard Burton; The Explorer as Actor," *Victorian Studies* 1 (December, 1957): 131.

3. Alexander von Humboldt, *Personal Narrative of Travels* (London, 1818), pp. 3–4.

4. Paul Russell Cutright, *A History of the Lewis and Clark Journals* (Norman, 1976), ch. 2. The French edition was the first translation of an account of the Lewis and Clark Expedition.

5. Ibid, pp. 33–34.

6. Ibid, p. 38; W. Eugene Hollon, *The Lost Pathfinder: Zebulon Montgomery Pike* (Norman, 1949), p. 177. First published in 1810 in Philadelphia, Pike's journal was republished the next year in London and later translated into Dutch, French, and German.

7. Cutright, *Lewis and Clark*, pp. 64–65.

8. Dale L. Morgan, *Jedediah Smith and the Opening of the West* (Lincoln, n.d.), p. 25.

9. William H. Goetzmann, *Exploration and Empire: The Explorer and the Scientist in the Winning of the American West* (New York, 1967), p. 159.

10. Allan Nevins, *Fremont, Pathmarker of the West* (New York, 1955), p. 117.

11. William H. Goetzmann, *Army Exploration in the American West, 1803–1863* (New Haven, 1965), p. 108.

12. Goetzmann, *Exploration and Empire*, p. 248.

13. Joseph Earl Arrington, "*Skirving's Moving Panorama*: Colonel Frémont's Western Expeditions Pictorialized," *Oregon Historical Quarterly* 65 (June, 1964): 148.

14. John Charles Frémont, *Narratives of Exploration and Adventure*, ed. Allan Nevins (New York, 1956) p. 20.

15. Ibid, p. 19.

16. Nevins, *Fremont*, pp. 606—07.

17. David B. Tyler, *The Wilkes Expedition: The First United States Exploring Expedition (1838–1842)* (Philadelphia, 1968), pp. 395–96; William Stanton, *The Great United States Exploring Expedition of 1838–1842* (Berkeley, 1975), p. 309.

18. Mark Twain, *Autobiography* (2 vols., New York 1924) II, pp. 120–21; Twain was also influenced by William L. Herndon's *Exploration of the Valley of the Amazon*; also see Joseph Conrad, "Geography and Some Explorers," in *Last Essays* (Freeport, N.Y., 1970), pp. 1–21.

19. Kenneth Lupton, *Mungo Park: The African Traveler* (Oxford, 1979), pp. 109–10. Helping the sales of Park's work was the fact that both abolitionists and proslavers seized upon his views.

20. H. Alan C. Cairns, *The Clash of Cultures: Early Race Relations in Central Africa* (New York, 1965), p. 3.

21. Richard D. Altick, *The English Common Reader: A Social History of the Mass Reading Public, 1800–1900* (Chicago, 1963), p. 388; one of Paul Du Chaillu's books on Africa sold ten thousand copies in two years.

22. David Livingstone, *Missionary Travels and Researches in South Africa* (New York, 1857), p. 8.

23. George Shepperson, "David Livingstone, 1813–1873, A Centenary Assessment," *Geographical Journal* 139 (June, 1973): 216.

24. Fawn M. Brodie, *The Devil Drives: A Life of Sir Richard Burton* (New York, 1969), pp. 278–79; Byron Farwell, *Burton: A Biography of Sir Richard Burton* (New York, 1965), p. 285.

25. Brodie, *Devil Drives*, pp. 333–36; Farwell, *Burton*, pp. 393–96.

26. *The Exploration of Africa in the Eighteenth and Nineteenth Centuries* (Edinburgh, 1971), p. 8; Byron Farwell, *The Man Who Presumed: A Biography of Henry M. Stanley* (New York, 1957), p. 93.

27. Richard Hall, *Stanley: An Adventurer Explored* (Boston, 1975), p. 234. A writer of African adventure stories, Charles Gibon, obtained many of his facts from Stanley's works. Joseph Conrad's Congo experience was influenced by Stanley. In the 1860s, Paul Du Chaillu wrote two children's books *A Journey to Ashango Land* and *Stories from the Gorilla Country*.

28. Robert I. Rotberg, *Joseph Thomson and the Exploration of Africa* (London, 1971), pp. 238–41. In *Allan Quartermain*, Haggard acknowledged his debt to Joseph Thomson.

29. Norman R. Bennett, ed., *Stanley's Dispatches to the New York Herald, 1871–1872, 1874–1877* (Boston, 1970), p. 241.

30. Rotberg, *Joseph Thomson*, p. 16; J. A. Hunter and Daniel P. Mannix, *Tales of the African Frontier* (New York, 1954), p. 60. Liv-

ingstone was instrumental in energizing John Palliser to explore Canada.

31. Arthur Friedman, ed., *Collected Works of Oliver Goldsmith* (5 vols., Oxford, 1966) IV, pp. 386–87.

32. John Livingston Lowes, *The Road to Xanadu, A Study in the Ways of the Imagination* (rev. ed.; Boston, 1964), p. 90. What Coleridge read was Cook's graphic description of the cannibalism of the New Zealand natives. For more on Cook's influence, see Hannah More's "The Slave Trade" in *The Works of Hannah More* (8 vols., London, 1801) I, pp. 97–115, especially p. 111; and William Cowper's "Charity" in H. S. Milford, ed. *The Poetical Works of William Cowper* (London, 1926), pp. 76–89.

33. Ibid, pp. 370–79, 365–67.

34. Lane Cooper, "A Glance at Wordsworth's Reading," *Modern Language Notes* 22 (April, 1907): II, p. 110.

35. Charles Norton Coe, *Wordsworth and the Literature of Travel* (New York, 1953), pp. 16, 56. George Crabbe's "Woman!" used both Ledyard's and Park's works.

36. Farwell, *Burton*, p. 311.

37. Roden Noel, *The Collected Poems* (London, 1902), p. 349.

38. R. W. B. Lewis, *The American Adam* (Chicago, 1959), p. 5.

39. John Greenleaf Whittier, "The Pass of the Sierra," from *Anti-Slavery Poems; Songs of Labor and Reform*, vol. 3, in *The Works* of John Greenleaf Whittier (7 vols., Boston, 1893–94), pp. 187–189.

40. John Greenleaf Whittier, "To John C. Fremont," in *In War Time* (Boston, 1864), pp. 19–20.

41. Newton Arvin, *Longfellow: His Life and Work* (Boston, 1963), pp. 106–07; Samuel Longfellow, ed., *Life of Henry Wadsworth Longfellow* (3 vols., Boston, 1891) II, pp. 65–66. Years later, Longfellow was moved by Ferdinand Hayden's discovery of the Mount of the Holy Cross to pen "The Cross of Snow."

42. Newton Arvin, *Herman Melville* (New York, 1957), pp. 79, 81.

43. Ibid, p. 93.

44. Stanton, *United States Exploring Expedition*, p. 310.

45. David Jaffé, "Some Origins of *Moby-Dick*: New Finds in an Old Source," *American Literature* 29 (November, 1957): 263–77.

46. W. B. Gates, "Cooper's *The Crater* and Two Explorers," *American Literature* 23 (May, 1951): 243–46.

47. W. B. Gates, "Cooper's *The Sea Lions* and Wilkes' Narrative," *PMLA* 65 (December, 1950): 1069–75.

48. E. Soteris Muszynska-Wallace, "The Sources of the *Prairie*," *American Literature* 21 (May, 1949): 191–200.

49. Ibid.

50. Polly Pearl Crawford, "Lewis and Clark's *Expedition* as a

Source for Poe's 'Journal of Julius Rodman,' " *Texas Studies in English* 12 (1932): 158–70; see John J. Teunissen and Evelyn J. Hinz, "Poe's *Journal of Julius Rodman* as Parody," *Nineteenth-Century Fiction* 27 (December, 1972): 317–38, for a different interpretation.

51. H. Arlin Turner, "A Note on Poe's 'Julius Rodman'," *Texas Studies in English* 10 (1930): 147–51; Wayne R. Kime, "Poe's Use of Irving's *Astoria* in 'The Journal of Julius Rodman'," *American Literature* 40 (May, 1968): 215–22.

52. Arlin Turner, "Another Source of Poe's 'Julius Rodman'," *American Literature* 8 (March, 1936): 69–70.

53. Henry David Thoreau, *Walden*, ed. Brooks Atkinson (New York, 1950), p. 286; for more on explorers and literature, see Edwin Fussell, *Frontier: American Literature and the American West* (Princeton, 1970), especially ch. 3, on Poe, and ch. 4, on Thoreau.

54. Thoreau, *Walden*, p. 287. Aldous Huxley in *Heaven and Hell* (New York, 1971), pp. 1–2, continued the metaphoric discussion of the human mind. "Like the earth of a hundred years ago, our mind still has its darkest Africas, its unmapped Borneos and Amazonian basins. In relation to the fauna of these regions we are not yet zoologists, we are mere naturalists and collectors of specimens." To Huxley, such metaphors expressed "very forcibly the essential otherness of the mind's far continents, the complete autonomy and self-sufficiency of their inhabitants."

55. T. D. MacLulich, "Canadian Exploration as Literature," *Canadian Literature* 81 (Summer, 1979): 72–85.

56. Christine Bolt, *Victorian Attitudes to Race* (London, 1971), p. 2.

57. R. W. Frantz, *The English Traveller and the Movement of Ideas 1660–1732* (Lincoln, 1967), p. 8; Alexander Murray, *The Life and Writings of James Bruce* (Edinburgh, 1808), p. 3, noted that travel books "enrich the mind with interesting truths, [and] they amuse it with the charm of novelty, and the attraction of personal adventure." A special course on the art of traveling (apodemics) was offered at the University of Göttingen.

58. P. T. Barnum, *Barnum's Own Story* (New York, 1961), pp. 248–50.

59. Ibid, 249–50. Besides Frémont, most explorers were at one time or another considered lost; for example, Lewis and Clark, Livingstone, and Stanley were all given up for dead.

60. Ibid, p. 250.

61. Allen Johnson and Dumas Malone, eds., *Dictionary of American Biography* (20 vols., New York, 1928–1936) VI, p. 339. Clarence King demonstrated that a western diamond mine discovery in 1872 was a hoax or more properly a swindle.

Chapter Seven

1. James Bruce, *Travels to Discover the Source of the Nile* (6 vols., Dublin, 1790–91) I, p. ii. For more on the traits of the revolutionary, see E. Victor Wolfenstein, *The Revolutionary Personality: Lenin, Trotsky, Gandhi* (Princeton, 1967), pp. 22–23.

2. Sigmund Freud, *Moses and Monotheism* (New York, 1967), p. 140; Ernest Jones, *The Life and Work of Sigmund Freud* (New York, 1961), p. xi; for more on the traits of the leader, see Freud, *Group Psychology and the Analysis of the Ego* (New York, 1959), p. 33.

3. Carl G. Jung, "In Memory of Sigmund Freud," *Collected Works of C. G. Jung,* (20 vols., London, 1966) XIII, p. 48.

4. Joseph Campbell, *The Hero with a Thousand Faces* (New York, 1949), pp. 30, 35–37.

5. For more on the stranger and strangers in Africa, see Georg Simmel, "The Strange," in *The Sociology of Georg Simmel* (New York, 1950), pp. 402–408; William A. Shack and Elliott P. Skinner, eds. *Strangers in African Societies* (Berkeley, 1979), especially ch. 11. In America, the example could be the difference in the behavior of the explorers when meeting with the Sioux and the Diggers.

6. K. David Patterson, "Paul B. Du Chaillu and the Exploration of Gabon, 1855–1865," *International Journal of African Historical Studies* 7 (1974): p. 657. These expeditions could be considered the first ego trips.

7. James A. Casada, "The Motivational Underpinnings of the British Exploration of East Africa," South Carolina Historical Association *Proceedings* 1973, pp. 68, 67; Herman Melville, *Moby Dick or The White Whale* (New York, 1961), p. 21.

8. Melville, *Moby Dick,* p. 26; Dante, *The Divine Comedy* Book I, *Hell* (Harmondsworth, 1976), Canto XXVI, lines 97–99.

9. J. H. L. Compston, *The Inland Sea and the Great River: The Story of Australia Exploration* (Sydney, 1964), preface.

10. J. R. L. Anderson, *The Ulysses Factor: The Exploring Instinct in Man* (London, 1970), p. 37.

11. James Cook, *The Journals of Captain James Cook* (4 vols., Cambridge, 1955–74) I, p. 380; Marcel Proust understood this feeling when he wrote, "And the most terrible reality brings us, with our suffering, the joy of a great discovery", *Remembrance of Things Past: Cities of the Plain* (New York, 1932), p. 367.

12. Daniel Conner, "Captain James Cook and the Pacific Frontier," *The American West* 16 (January-February, 1979): 58; Cook, *Journals* I, p. 380.

13. Anderson, *Ulysses Factor,* pp. 17, 20; John K. Wright, *Human*

Nature in Geography: Fourteen Papers, 1925–1965 (Cambridge, Mass., 1966), p. 76.

14. Rudyard Kipling, *Rudyard Kipling's Verse Inclusive Edition 1885–1918* (Garden City, 1921), p. 120.

15. Selma Fraiberg, "Tales of the Discovery of the Secret Treasure," *The Psychoanalytic Study of the Child* (New York, 1963) IX, p. 241.

16. Casada, "Motivational Underpinnings," p. 62; Richard F. Burton, *Zanzibar; City, Island, and Coast* (2 vols., London, 1872) I, pp. 16–17.

17. Fawn M. Brodie, *The Devil Drives: A Life of Sir Richard Burton* (New York, 1969), p. 1.

18. Ibid., 25. For a similar rejection of society in favor of nature, see John Charles Frémont, *Memoirs of My Life* (Chicago, 1887), p. 602.

19. Brodie, *Devil Drives*, p. 4. When Isabel Burton asked the dean of Westminster Abbey if her husband could be buried there, he said there was no space left.

20. Horace Waller, ed., *The Last Journals of David Livingstone* (London, 1880), p. 26.

21. James B. Thomson, *Joseph Thomson—African Explorer*, (2nd ed., London, 1897), p. 199; J. A. Hunter and Daniel P. Mannix, *Tales of the African Frontier* (New York, 1954), p. 61. O. Mannoni believed that the attraction of primitive areas to Europeans is to be discerned in the Prospero complex, the need to inhabit a society where individualism is enhanced; see his *Prospero and Caliban, The Psychology of Colonization* (London, 1956).

22. Casada, "Motivational Underpinnings," p. 62.

23. Frederick Bradnum, *The Long Walks: Journeys to the Sources of the White Nile* (London, 1970), p. 266; Richard Lander, *Records of Captain Clapperton's Last Expedition to Africa* (2 vols., London, 1967) I, p. 11.

24. Casada, "Motivational Underpinnings," p. 62.; E. A. Ayandele, *African Exploration and Human Understanding* (Edinburgh, 1971), p. 3.

25. James A. Casada, "James A. Grant and the Royal Geographical Society," *Geographical Journal* 140 (June, 1974): 246; see John Hanning Speke, *Journal of the Discovery of the Source of the Nile* (London, 1969), p. 102, on the "interests of Old England" and exploration.

26. Casada, "James A. Grant," p. 245.

27. Allan Nevins, *Fremont: Pathmarker of the West* (New York, 1955), p. 45.

28. Ibid, 40; Maurice G. Fulton, ed., *Diary and Letters of Josiah Gregg: Southwestern Enterprises: 1840–1847* (2 vols., Norman, 1942) I, pp. 20–21.

29. Cook, *Journals* I, 380; Robert I. Rotberg, *A Political History of Tropical Africa* (New York, 1965), p. 203.

30. Rotberg, *Political History*, p. 206; David Freeman Hawke, *Those Tremendous Mountains: The Story of the Lewis and Clark Expedition* (New York, 1980), p. 135. See John Smith, *Captain John Smith's America*, ed. John Lankford (New York, 1967), p. 138, who wrote "what so truly suits with honor and honesty, as the discovering things unknown"; Roland Young, ed., *Through Masailand with Joseph Thomson* (Evanston, 1962), p. 185, on being the first in the field.

31. Robert I. Rotberg, *Africa and Its Explorers: Motives, Methods, and Impact* (Cambridge, 1973), p. 4.

32. Ibid.

33. Casada, "Motivational Underpinnings," pp. 61, 63; Speke, *Journal of Discovery*, p. 18, on death.

34. Casada, "Motivational Underpinnings," p. 63.

35. Alexander von Humboldt, *Personal Narrative of Travels to the Equinoctial Regions* (2 vols., London, 1818–29) I, p. 3.

36. Hawke, *Those Tremendous Mountains*, p. 95.

37. I. Schapera, ed., *David Livingstone, Family Letters 1841–1856* (2 vols., London, 1959) II, p. 74; John P. R. Wallis, ed., *The Zambezi Expedition of David Livingstone 1858–1863* (2 vols., London, 1956) I, p. 108.

38. Dale L. Morgan, *Jedediah Smith and the Opening of the West* (Lincoln, n.d.), pp. 353–54; T. S. Eliot, "East Coker," in *The Complete Poems and Plays 1909–1950* (New York, 1952), p. 129. Eliot's lines on self-exploration come to mind:

> We must be still and still moving
> Into another intensity
> For a further union, a deeper communion
> Through the dark cold and the empty desolation,
> The wave cry, the wind cry, the vast waters
> Of the petrel and the porpoise.

39. Waller, *The Last Journals,* p. 211; see Everett V. Stonequist, *The Marginal Man: A Study in Personality and Culture Conflict* (New York, 1937), pp. 146–47. By the difficult and dangerous tasks that they performed, explorers separated themselves from their home and family. As a person who through exploration leaves his own milieu and finds himself in a completely different situation, the explorer sometimes found that he became a member of neither world. He became to some extent a modified marginal man, defined by Everett Stonequist as "one who is poised in psychological uncertainty between two (or more) social worlds; reflecting in his soul the discords

and harmonies, repulsions and attractions of these worlds, one of which is often 'dominant' over the other." One of the strongest characteristics of the marginal man was this ambivalent attitude. The two worlds that he has lived in become grand and glorious yet at times are oppressive and terrible. These changing positions are common in a marginal person and can be occasionally glimpsed in the writings of the explorers. Certainly the explorer's prime loyalty was to his homeland.

40. Margery Perham and J. Simmons, *African Discovery: An Anthology of Exploration* (London, 1957), p. 106.

41. Casada, "Motivational Underpinnings," pp. 63–64, 68.

42. Donald Jackson, ed., *Letters of the Lewis and Clark Expedition with Related Documents, 1783–1854* (Urbana, 1962), pp. 589–90; see *Proceedings* of the Association for Promoting the Discovery of the Interior Parts of Africa (2 vols., London, 1967) II, p. 2, on Mungo Park's qualifications as an explorer.

43. Anderson, *Ulysses Factor*, p. 31. These attributes were greatly admired by the British people. At the burial of Livingstone in Westminister Abbey, a Scottish newspaper praised him for his "virtues . . . which our country has always been ready to acknowledge, which our religion has taught us to revere, and seek to cultivate and conserve." The following lines appeared in *Punch* on the burial of Livingstone, April 18, 1874:

> He needs no epitaph to guard a name
> Which men shall prize while worthy work is known;
> He lived and died for good—be that his fame;
> Let marble crumble: this is Living-Stone.

44. Bernard De Voto, *The Course of Empire* (Boston, 1962), p. 437.

45. Perham and Simmons, *African Discovery*, p. 14; Casada, "James A. Grant," p. 245.

46. Christine Bolt, *Victorian Attitudes to Race* (London, 1971), p. 143.

47. Waller, *The Last Journals*, p. 267; Casada, "Motivational Underpinnings," p. 59.

48. Casada, "Motivational Underpinnings," p. 60. I will leave it to a psychiatrist to deal with the birth-delivery image that appears in much of exploration literature.

49. Ibid., p. 62.

50. Burton, *Zanzibar* I, p. 5.

51. John Bigelow, *Memoir of the Life and Public Services of John Charles Frémont* (New York, 1856), p. 391; LeRoy R. Hafen, ed., *Frémont's Fourth Expedition* (Glendale, 1960); William Brandon, *The Men and the Mountain: Frémont's Fourth Expedition* (New York, 1955).

Livingstone's inability to respond to the suffering of others can be clearly seen in the disasters that befell the Anglican Mission in the Shire Highlands in the 1860s.

52. Perham and Simmons, *African Discovery,* p. 14.

53. Mungo Park, *Travels in Africa* (New York, 1969), p. 364.

54. Ibid., p. 365.

55. E. W. Bovill, "The Death of Mungo Park," *The Geographical Journal* 133 (March, 1967): 1–9. Kenneth Lupton, *Mungo Park, The African Traveler* (New York, 1979), ch. 30 and appendix 3.

56. The median birthdate for African and American explorers was 1800. The median birthdate for African explorers was 1799, and for American explorers it was 1801.

57. See Gordon Donaldson, *The Scots Overseas* (London, 1966), ch. 12. George Shepperson, "Mungo Park and the Scottish Contribution to Africa," *African Affairs* 70 (July, 1971): 277–81; Joseph Thomson, *To the Central African Lakes and Back* (2 vols., London, 1881) I, p. 150.

58. John Kenneth Galbraith, *The Scotch* (New York, 1970), ch. 9. The history of Canadian exploration is filled with Scottish names.

59. David Livingstone, *Missionary Travels and Researches in South Africa* (Freeport, N.Y., 1972), p. 6; Tim Jeal, *Livingstone* (New York, 1979), p. 25.

60. Shepperson, "Mungo Park," p. 280.

61. Nevins, *Fremont,* p. 1; Frémont, *Memories of My Life,* p. 22. Andrew Rolle, in "Exploring an Explorer: Psychohistory and John Charles Frémont," *Pacific Historical Review* 51 (May, 1982): 151, wrote, "He lived as though he could, through repeated adventures, prove himself—as though his exploits would make him a legitimate child."

62. Richard Hall, *Stanley: An Adventurer Explored* (Boston, 1975), p. 103; Henry M. Stanley, *How I Found Livingstone* (London, n.d.), p. 262.

63. Jerome Hamilton Buckely, *The Victorian Temper: A Study in Literary Culture* (New York,1964), p. 13.

64. Rotberg, *Africa and Its Explorers,* p. 4. See James K. Tuckey, *Narrative of an Expedition* (London, 1818), p. xlvii.

65. Arthur O. Lovejoy, "Optimism and Romanticism," *Publications of the Moderan Language Association* 42 (December, 1927): 945.

66. Edward Lurie, *Louis Agassiz, A Life in Science* (Chicago, 1966), pp. 51–52.

67. Perry Miller, "Thoreau in the Context of International Romanticism," *Nature's Nation* (Cambridge, 1967), p. 175. The Comte de Buffon maintained that "sensible people will always recognize that the only and true science is the knowledge of facts", see Peter Gay, *The Enlightenment: The Science of Freedom* (New York, 1977), p. 153.

68. Henry Nash Smith, *Virgin Land: The American West as Symbol*

and Myth (Cambridge, 1971), ch. 5; Arthur K. Moore, *The Frontier Mind* (New York, 1963), ch. 7; see James Fenimore Cooper, *The Leatherstocking Tales.*

69. Perry Miller, "The Romantic Dilemma in American Nationalism and the Concept of Nature," in *Nature's Nation*, p. 202.

Chapter Eight

1. Francis Galton, *The Art of Travel; Or, Shifts and Contrivances Available in Wild Countries* (London, 1855), pp. 55–57.

2. Ibid.

3. David and Charles Livingstone, *Narrative of an Expedition to the Zambezi* (London, 1866), p. 80; Horace Waller, ed., *The Last Journals of David Livingstone* (London, 1880), pp. 159–60.

4. Bernard De Voto, *The Journals of Lewis and Clark* (Boston, 1963), pp. 194–95; John Bakeless, *Lewis and Clark: Partners in Discovery* (New York, 1947), p. 250; Walter Prescott Webb, *The Great Plains* (New York, 1931), pp. 68–84; Mary H. Kingsley, *West African Studies*, (3rd ed., London, 1964), p. 35, n. 48.

5. Byron Farwell, *Burton* (New York, 1965), pp. 249, 222.

6. Richard Hall, *Stanley: An Adventurer Explored* (Boston, 1975), p. 213.

7. David Freeman Hawke, *Those Tremendous Moutains: The Story of the Lewis and Clark Expedition* (New York, 1980), pp. 241–42.

8. T. C. Elliott, ed., "The Peter Skene Ogden Journals," *Oregon Historical Quarterly* 10 (December, 1909): 341, 344.

9. Warburton Pike, *The Barren Ground of Northern Canada* (London, 1892), p. vii.

10. Dale L. Morgan, *Jedediah Smith and the Opening of the West* (Lincoln, n.d.), chs. 12, 13; also see Meriwether Lewis and William Clark, *The History of the Lewis and Clark Expedition*, ed. Elliott Coues (3 vols., New York, n.d.) I, p. 134; also see Edwin James, *Account of an Expedition from Pittsburgh to the Rocky Mountains* (2 vols., Ann Arbor, 1966) I, pp. 132–33; Washington Irving, *Astoria, Or Anecdotes of an Enterprise Beyond the Rocky Mountains* (Norman, 1964), pp. 146–50, on John Colter's experiences.

11. De Voto, *Journals*, pp. xlvii–xlviii. For favorable comments by explorers about the Indians, see Lewis and Clark, *Expedition* I, pp. 12, 163; James, *Account* I, pp. 157, 161.

12. See Donald Simpson, *Dark Companions, The African Contribution to the European Exploration of East Africa* (London, 1975) on this subject, p. 161, for quote of Stanley; Robert I. Rotberg, *Joseph Thomson and the Exploration of Africa* (London, 1971), p. 102, for Thomson quote.

13. Galton, *Art of Travel*, pp. 58–59.

14. Richard F. Burton, *The Lake Regions of Central Africa* (New York, 1972), pp. 240–41.

15. Basil Davidson, *A History of East and Central Africa: To the Late Nineteenth Century* (Garden City, 1969), pp. 55, 197–98; the Nyamwezi strength in trade was based upon their important location, which made the trail to Ujiji their special area of interest. African chiefs (*ntemi*) were often selected because of their skill in organizing caravans. Difficulties with the natives in the caravan were largely based upon how close to or far from their home they were. Burton, *Lake Regions*, pp. 247, 53, believed that "the true principle of exploration" was to move out rapidly and return at a more leisurely pace.

16. Richard Burton, *Zanzibar; City, Island, and Coast* (2 vols., London, 1872) II, pp. 224, 292.

17. James A. Casada, "Sir George Grey and the Speke-Grant Nile Expedition," South African Library Quarterly *Bulletin* 25 (1971), p. 143.

18. Rotberg, *Thomson*, appendix 2.

19. William Gray, *Travels in Western Africa* (London, 1825), p. 369; see also pp. 369–82 for lists of presents to Africans.

20. Lewis and Clark, *Expedition* I, p. 3.

21. Burton, in *Zanzibar* I, p. 488, and in *Lake Regions*, p. 53, discussed the different kinds of starts.

22. Kinglsey, *Studies*, pp. 53–56, on the sounds of Africa; also see Ray Allen Billington, *The Far Western Frontier 1830–1860* (New York, 1956), p. 29, on the excitement on leaving for Santa Fe.

23. Robin Hallett, ed., *The Niger Journal of Richard and John Lander* (New York, 1965), p. 79.

24. Rotberg, *Thomson*, p. 43.

25. Burton, *Lake Regions*, p. 238.

26. Rotberg, *Thomson*, p. 43; Joseph Thomson, "Up the Niger to the Central Sudan," *Good Words* 27(1886), pp. 252, 114; see Burton, *Lake Regions*, pp. 132–133, on rebellion in Burton's caravan in 1857; H. H. Johnston, *The Kilima-njaro Expedition* (London, 1886), p. 49.

27. Galton, *Art of Travel*, p. 69; Joseph Thomson, *Through Masai Land* (2nd ed., London, 1885), pp. 104–105.

28. Frederick Bradnum, *The Long Walks: Journeys to the Sources of the White Nile* (London, 1970), pp. 243–44, 242.

29. Burton, *Lake Regions*, pp. xiv, 250; see Waller, *The Last Journals*, p. 194, on lack of system in Arab marches. American expeditions traveled faster, averaging 15 to 20 miles a day.

30. Burton, *Lake Regions*, p. 54; John H. Speke, *Journal of the Discovery of the Source of the Nile* (London, 1969), p. 77; Lewis and Clark, *Expedition* I, 167.

31. Burton, *Lake Regions,* pp. 514, 522, on slavery.

32. Waller, *The Last Journals,* pp. 5, 185, 95.

33. Mungo Park, *Travels in Africa* (London, 1969), p. 228. For a different view, see Kenneth Lupton, *Mungo Park, The African Traveler* (Oxford, 1979), ch. 18.

34. Burton, *Lake Regions,* pp. 243–244; Josiah Gregg, *Commerce of the Prairies* (2 vols., Philadelphia, 1962) I, p. 22.

35. Burton, *Lake Regions,* pp. 249–250.

36. Waller, *The Last Journals,* pp. 43, 48.

37. Hall, *Stanley,* 81, 48, 77–78. For a somewhat different quote see Henry Morton Stanley, *The Autobiography of Sir Henry Morton Stanley* (London, 1909), p. 327; Henry M. Stanley, *In Darkest Africa* (2 vols., N.Y., 1890) I, 300–301; Reginald Coupland, *The Exploitation of East Africa 1856–1890; The Slave Trade and the Scramble* (Evanston, 1968), pp. 324–326.

38. Coupland, *Exploitation,* p. 327.

39. Waller, *The Last Journals,* pp. 69, 142. Livingstone hoped that in the year 1861 he could be "more gentle and loving." Livingstone, like Joseph Thomson, never personally caused the death of a native. Burton in *Lake Regions,* p. 244, maintained that the natives were more pleasant to the outward bound expeditions than to those returning. Speed was often of the utmost importance and it did not allow time for friendly relations to develop between the explorers and the natives. For Thomson quote, see Robert I. Rotberg, *Africa and Its Explorers: Motives, Methods, and Impact* (Cambridge, 1973), p. 306.

40. Park, *Travels,* p. 244. For more on fear among blacks of being eaten by whites, see William D. Piersen, "White Cannibals, Black Martyrs: Fears, Depression, and Religious Faith as Causes of Suicide Among New Slaves," *Journal of Negro History* 62 (April, 1977): 147–59.

41. Waller, *The Last Journals,* pp. 148–49.

42. Speke, *Journal of Discovery,* pp. 35–36, 45–46; Simpson, *Dark Companions,* p. 19.

43. Park, *Travels,* pp. 95, 122.

44. Christine Bolt, *Victorian Attitudes to Race* (London, 1971), pp. 115–16.

45. Ibid., p. 113. Cameron felt that the Portuguese were wantonly cruel.

46. Henry Barth, *Travels and Discoveries in North and Central Africa* (3 vols., New York, 1857) I, p. vii.

47. Daniel Houghton may have been killed by natives, but probably died of fever.

48. Carl P. Russell, *Firearms, Traps and Tools of the Mountain Men* (Albuquerque, 1978), pp. 34–51.

49. J. A. Hunter and Daniel P. Mannix, *Tales of the African Frontier* (New York, 1954), pp. 52, 58; Bradnum, *The Long Walks*, pp. 167, 239; K. David Patterson, "Paul B. Du Chaillu and the Exploration of Gabon, 1855–1865," International Journal of African Historical *Studies* 4 (1974): 658; Samuel Baker, *Ismalia*, (2nd ed., London, 1879), pp. 285, 358, 468.

50. Bradnum, *The Long Walks*, p. 200.

51. Ibid, p. 174.

52. Henry M. Stanley, *My Early Travels and Adventures in America* (Lincoln, 1982), pp. xviii–xix.

53. Daniel R. Headrick, "The Tools of Imperialism: Technology and the Expansion of European Colonial Empires in the Nineteenth Century," *Journal of Modern History* 51 (June, 1979): 231–63; for more on American exploration and technology, see Richard G. Wood, "Exploration by Steamboat," *Journal of Transport History* 3 (November, 1955): 121–23.

54. Speke, *Journal of Discovery*, pp. 116, 123; Roland Young, ed., *Through Masailand with Joseph Thomson* (Evanston, 1962), p. 47.

55. Bradnum, *The Long Walks*, pp. 25–26.

56. Hawke, *Those Tremendous Mountains*, p. 147.

57. Henry Morton Stanley, *How I Found Livingstone* (New York, 1969), p. 61; Hall, *Stanley*, p. 185.

58. Burton, *Zanzibar* II, p. 289; H. Alan C. Cairns, *The Clash of Cultures: Early Race Relations in Central Africa* (New York, 1965), p. 3.

59. Burton, *Zanzibar* II, p. 399. On Lewis's suicide, see Howard I. Kushner, "The Suicide of Meriwether Lewis: A Psychoanalytic Study," *William and Mary Quarterly* 38 (July, 1981): 464–81.

60. See Gregg, *Commerce of the Prairies* I, p. 40, on deaths on the Sante Fe trail; also Richard J. Fehrman, "The Mountain Man: A Statistical View," in *The Mountain Men and the Fur Trade of the Far West*, ed. LeRoy R. Hafen (10 vols., Glendale, Calif., 1972) X, p. 14, on deaths caused by Indians.

61. Lewis and Clark, *Expedition* I, pp. 50, 82; II, p. 362; on the death of Floyd, I, p. 79; also see Charles G. Clarke, *The Men of the Lewis and Clark Expedition* (Glendale, 1970), under "Illnesses" in index; Eldon G. Chuinard, *Only One Man Died: The Medical Aspects of the Lewis and Clark Expedition* (Glendale, 1980).

62. James, *Account* I, p. 117; also see Zebulon M. Pike, *Journals*, ed. Donald Jackson (2 vols., Norman, 1966), under "Illness and injury" in the index. For the Great Surveys and diseases, see Richard A. Bartlett, *Great Surveys of the American West* (Norman, 1980), p. 12.

63. Waller, *The Last Journals*, p. 145.

64. Ibid., p. 153.

65. Ibid., p. 145.

66. De Voto, *Journals,* pp. 108–109, 139–40, 148; Bakeless, *Lewis and Clark,* ch. 13; Peter Matthiessen, *Wild Life in America* (Middlesex, 1978), p. 86. Raymond Darwin Burroughs, ed., *The National History of the Lewis and Clark Expedition* (East Lansing, 1961), pp. 57–68, on grizzly bears. Morgan, *Jedediah Smith,* pp. 84–85.

67. Morgan, *Jedediah Smith,* pp. 84–85.

68. De Voto, *Journals,* pp. 119–20.

69. Patterson, "Du Chaillu," p. 654.

70. Tim Jeal, *Livingstone* (New York, 1974), p. 82.

71. David Livingstone, *Missionary Travels and Researchers* (New York, 1857), pp. 12, 15; Jeal, *Livingstone,* pp. 82–83; Cairns, *Clash of Cultures,* p. 157.

72. Rotberg, *Thomson,* pp. 189–90; Young, *Through Masailand,* pp. 174–76.

73. Bradnum, *The Long Walks,* p. 262.

74. Bakeless, *Lewis and Clark,* p. 344; Erwin H. Ackerkneckt, *Malaria in the Upper Mississippi Valley 1760–1900* (Baltimore, 1945), p. 97.

75. Livingstone, *Missionary Travels,* p. 467; Gray, *Travels,* p. 9.

76. John H. Speke, *What Led to the Discovery of the Source of the Nile* (Edinburgh, 1864), pp. 224–25; Burton, *Lake Regions,* pp. 336–37, note.

Chapter Nine

1. Paul R. Cutright, "Meriwether Lewis: Botanist," *Oregon Historical Quarterly* 69 (June, 1968): 161. For more on this, see Cutright's *Lewis and Clark: Pioneer Naturalists* (Urbana, 1969).

2. Richard R. Burton, *Zanzibar; City, Island, and Coast* (2 vols., London, 1872) II, p. 393; K. Ingham, "John Hanning Speke: A Victorian and His Inspiration," *Tanganyika Notes and Records* (December, 1957): 307.

3. David Freeman Hawke, *Those Tremendous Mountains: The Story of the Lewis and Clark Expedition* (New York, 1980) pp. 91–92.

4. James D. Richardson, ed., *A Compilation of the Messages and Papers of the Presidents* (20 vols., Washington, D.C., 1897–1917) II, p. 878.

5. William H. Goetzmann, *Army Exploration in the American West, 1803–1863* (New Haven, 1965), ch. 1.

6. Roger L. Nichols, "Stephen Long and Scientific Exploration of the Plains," *Nebraska History* 52 (Fall, 1971): 61.

7. William H. Goetzmann, "The Wheeler Surveys and the Decline of Army Exploration in the West," in *The American West: An Appraisal,* ed. Robert G. Ferris (Santa Fe, 1963), p. 232, n. 48; also

see Earl Pomeroy, *In Search of the Golden West: The Tourist in Western America* (New York, 1957), pp. 91–92. King said of civilization that "It's a nervous disease!"

8. W. Turrentine Jackson, "The Creation of Yellowstone National Park," *Mississippi Valley Historical Review* 29 (September, 1942): 187–206.

9. William H. Goetzmann, *Exploration and Empire: The Explorer and the Scientist in the Winning of the American West* (New York, 1967), p. 232.

10. John P. Harrison, "Science and Politics: Origins and Objectives of Mid-Nineteenth Century Government Expeditions to Latin America," *Hispanic American Historical Review* 25 (May, 1955): 177–78.

11. William Stanton, *The Great United States Exploring Expedition of 1838–1842* (Berkeley, 1975), p. 314, note; David B. Tyler, *The Wilkes Expedition: The First United States Exploring Expedition (1838–1842)* (Philadelphia, 1968), p. 403.

12. Norman A. Graebner, ed., *Manifest Destiny* (Indianapolis, 1968), p. 31.

13. Ibid, p. 32.

14. Ibid, p. 36.

15. Ibid, p. 146.

16. Ibid, p. 37.

17. Norman Graebner, *Empire on the Pacific: A Study in American Continental Expansion* (New York, 1955), p. 28; Goetzmann, *Exploration and Empire*, pp. 238–39; Frederick Merk, *The Oregon Question: Essays in Anglo-American Diplomacy and Politics* (Cambridge, Mass., 1967), pp. 211–12.

18. Goetzmann, *Exploration and Empire*, p. 240.

19. Allan Nevins, *Fremont, Pathmarker of the West* (New York, 1955), p. 36.

20. Goetzmann, *Exploration and Empire*, pp. 243–44.

21. John Charles Frémont, *Report of the Exploring Expedition to the Rocky Mountains* (Washington, 1845), p. 105.

22. Ibid, p. 151.

23. Ibid, pp. 244, 249.

24. Graebner, *Empire on the Pacific*, pp. 27–28.

25. Nevins, *Fremont*, p. 142; Sarah Royce, *A Frontier Lady*, ed. Ralph Henry Gabriel (Lincoln, 1977), p. 3.

26. Donald Jackson and Mary Lee Spence, eds., *The Expeditions of John Charles Frémont* (3 vols., Urbana, 1970–) I, pp. 253–54; for more on Frémont, see Ferol Egan, *Frémont, Explorer for a Restless Nation* (Garden City, 1977).

27. William H. Emory, *Lieutenant Emory Reports*, ed., Ross Calvin (Albuquerque, 1951), p. 9.

28. Ibid, p. 16.

29. Goetzmann, *Exploration and Empire*, p. 263.

30. John Hanning Speke, *What Led to the Discovery of the Source of the Nile* (Edinburgh, 1864), pp. 158, 330; R. C. Bridges, "Europeans and East Africans in the Age of Exploration," *Geographical Journal* 139 (June, 1973): 229.

31. James A. Casada, "Verney Lovett Cameron: A Centenary Appreciation," *Geographical Journal* 141 (July, 1975): 212

32. Ibid, pp. 213–214.

33. Ibid, p. 213.

34. Robert I. Rotberg, ed., *Africa and Its Explorers: Natives, Methods, and Impact* (Cambridge, 1973), p. 300.

35. Ibid. Because warfare was endemic in both America and Africa, peacemaking was often part of the explorer's job. Meriwether Lewis and William Clark, *The History of the Lewis and Clark Expedition*, ed. Elliott Coues, (3 vols., New York, n.d.) I, p. 226, attempted to bring peace between the Mandan and the Snake Indians; John H. Speke, *Journal of the Discovery of the Source of the Nile* (London, 1969), pp. 79, 96, endeavored to placate some Arab merchants who were preparing to go to war with the Nyamwezi, and the Ngoni who were preparing to raid the Sukuma.

36. James A. Casada, "James A. Grant and the Royal Geographical Society," *Geographical Journal* 140 (June, 1974): 249–50; Casada, "James A. Grant: Victorian Africanist," *Historian* 39 (November, 1976): 93–94.

37. Robert O. Collins, "Samuel White Baker: Prospero in Purgatory," in Rotberg, *Africa and Its Explorers*, pp. 168–73.

38. Margery Perham and J. Simmons, *African Discovery: An Anthology of Exploration* (London, 1957), p. 33.

39. Rotberg, *Africa and Its Explorers*, p. 251. For more on the connection between exploration and imperialism see Raymond F. Betts, *The False Dawn: European Imperialism in the Nineteenth Century* (Minneapolis, 1975), ch. 1.

40. Roland Oliver, *The Missionary Factor in East Africa* (London, 1952), pp. 34–35; Norman R. Bennett, *A History of the Arab State of Zanzibar* (Cambridge, England, 1978), pp. 112–13.

41. Bridges, "Europeans and East Africans," pp. 229, 227; Rotberg, *Africa and Its Explorers*, p. 11. For more on Livingstone's links with imperialism, see H. Alan C. Cairns, *The Clash of Cultures: Early Race Relations in Central Africa* (New York, 1965), pp. 192–99. See Judith Listowel, *The Other Livingstone* (New York, 1974) for a less favorable view of Livingstone's accomplishments.

42. Ronald Rainger, "Race, Politics, and Science: The Anthropo-

logical Society of London in the 1860s," *Victorian Studies* 22 (Autumn, 1978); 57, 61.

43. Cairns, *Clash of Cultures*, pp. 246, 248.

Chapter Ten

1. Horatio Alger, *Ragged Dick* (New York, 1868), p. 116; Walter Rauschenbusch, *Christianity and the Social Crisis* (New York, 1907), pp. 251–52.

2. William Booth, *In Darkest England and the Way Out* (New York, 1890), pp. 13, 156. Emin Pasha is the name given the governor of Equatoria, Edouard Schnitzer. Cut off by the Mahdist revolt in 1885, he was "rescued" by Stanley in 1888.

3. Joseph Conrad, *Heart of Darkness* (New York, 1957), p. 61; Norman Sherry in *Conrad's Western World* (Cambridge, England 1971), writes on page 119, "This explorer [Henry M. Stanley] and coloniser was never far from the sidelines of Conrad's Congo experience both in terms of his exploits and of his ideals"; also see chs. 12 and 13. For another negative view of discovery and exploration, see Salvador De Madariaga, *The Fall of the Spanish American Empire*, (rev. ed., New York, 1963), pp. 210–11.

Index